AF658229

The Dynamics of Folk Religion in Society

Pericentralisation as Deconstruction of Sanskritisation

K. James Ponniah

SERIALS PUBLICATIONS
NEW DELHI (INDIA)

© K. James Ponniah

First Published -2011

ISBN: 978-81-8387-422-9

All rights reserved with the Publisher, including the right to translate or reproduce this book or parts thereof except for brief quotations in critical articles or reviews.

Published by

SERIALS PUBLICATIONS
4830/24, Prahlad Street, Ansari Road
Darya Ganj, New Delhi-110002 (India)
Phone: 23245225 Fax : 91-11-23272135
E-mail: serials@sify.com

Dedication

This book is dedicated in grateful remembrance to

My late mother

Irudhaya Mary

(1934–2006)

In memory

Everything has to do with everything else

Along with my dad and the family,
I lament the demise of my loving mother Irudhaya Mary.
Born and brought up in a devout religious family,
she had the grace of touching and
transforming the lives of all those
who came into her life by self-sacrifice.
We miss her loving presence in our midst.

CONTENTS

Foreword

Indian society is going through many conflicts and experiencing unprecedented contradictions. The issue of Dalits needs to be placed in this complex situation. While, on the one hand, their oppression continues unabated, we see, on the other hand, new breakthroughs in their struggles against a caste-ridden society and its hierarchy. The folk religions of Dalits seem to be a great resource and a new avenue for liberation.

Religious rituals, especially of the marginalized people, are often dismissed as superstition and as a stumbling block for their advancement. But a deeper study into folk rituals could show that they do not simply reproduce the social order but serve as an identity marker of an oppressed community, and a source of strength in their struggle against the domination of the upper castes. In this way, folk religious rituals are a symbolic capital. The present work goes into the analysis and study of the ritual power of a particular Dalit folk religion known as Cuṭalaimāṭaṉ Cult. *Koṭai,* ritual hunting, *cāmiyāṭṭam,* divination etc., are not to be viewed simply as religious functions; they have a performative role in the society. In the case of Cuṭalaimāṭaṉ Cult, the rituals connected with it go to the extent of subverting the hierarchical social order. The Brahmins and higher castes show great deference to the ritual person of *cāmiyāṭi* and his fearsome divine powers. The author calls this process of reversal of power as "peri-centralization".

This research by highlighting the process of peri-centralization challenges also the classical theory of Sanskritization propounded by M. N. Srinivas and others. This work is a substantial contribution to the field of Dalit and subaltern studies, folk religion and religious rituals, and to the study of social change in contemporary India. It is a well researched work with a clear focus and based on a rigorous field study and collection of data. The interpretation of the author is original; his language and style, clear and flowing. This research should interest all those who are involved in sociology and anthropology of religion, in theology and religious studies.

I am happy that my student James Ponniah has made such a significant contribution through his doctorial dissertation, which is now being published. Highly motivated, he was an exemplary doctoral student and researcher. His earnestness and labour of love has produced rich fruits from which, I am sure, the readers will benefit.

Chennai, **_Felix Wilfred_**
9 May, 2009

ACKNOWLEDGEMENT

With ineffable gratitude and immense joy, I gratefully acknowledge the valuable role of many people and institutions that facilitated my research and enabled the completion of this book.

First, I express my sincere thanks to the people of Naduvakurichi, Vijayanarayanam, Kayatar and Valliyoor. Without their openness, welcoming attitude and hospitality, it would not have been possible for me to record the ritual performances of the Cuṭalaimāṭaṉ cult. Being with them during the events of *koṭai* has been a moment of great learning in my life. My special thanks goes to all those village leaders, elders, folk artists Mrs. Thangavelu, Murugan, and Ms. Muthulaksmi, the ritual specialists, Ayyadurari, Muthumsamy, Balasubramaniayan, and other elders, Mr. Thirugnanasampandam and Muthuarumugam, and ordinary village folk who contributed to my research by giving me access to their ritual world either by accommodating me within the select few for the exclusive rituals or by cooperating with me as interviewees.

I thank immensely Prof. Dr. Felix Wilfred, the supervisor of this study and the Head of the Department of Christian Studies. His contribution to this study is immeasurable. Acclaimed as a seminal thinker, he has played a vital role in the shaping of this book by his creative insights, pertinent comments, and appropriate suggestions. His concern for the subaltern people, which is manifest in his writings and in his personal sharings, has been a tremendous source of inspiration to me. Moreover, his words of encouragement have kept my research alive and engaging till the very end.

I am very deeply indebted to Prof. Dr. Thomas George, founder member and former Head of the Department of Christian Studies, for all that he has been to me till today. Though I was not a student of the Department–completing my M.A. in Vaishnavism–he wholeheartedly welcomed me to use the library of the Department and to interact with scholars at seminars of the Department. His gesture of generosity towards me, an 'outsider', would later make me an 'insider' of the Department of Christian Studies. Furthermore, he generously provided me with comfortable boarding and lodging at his residence, Emmaus, for the last four years. But for his generosity, encouragement, concern, guidance and companionship, and for the serene ambience of Emmaus, the hard work that went into the completion of this work would not have been possible. I will always treasure remembrances of the loving family-ambience of Emmaus provided by its inmates—Tom , Francis Gonsalves, Andrews, G. Patrick, Joe Francis, Michael, Sonimon, James Thomas, Snehadas, and Saleth and Anthony, the kitchen staff. All of them have always been an inexhaustible source of moral support, concern and happiness.

I owe special thanks to my friend--Francis Gonsalves, Augustine, Lionel and Cyril for proof-reading and helping me improve the text, and Dr. Francis Clooney for his translation of one of the related texts for my research from French to English. Big thanks are due to my another friend Dr. Gnana Patrick, a lecturer of the Department for his keen interest, constructive remarks and intelligent critique throughout my research work. I am also grateful to other faculty-members of the Department–Dr. Joe Mannath, A.L. Sebastian, Dr. Roy Lazar and Dr. Pushpa Joseph, and office staff Ms. Rexy Joseph & Mr. Murthy. for their cordiality, resourceful interactions and services. I fondly remember the study circle meets of Prof. Dr. Felix Wilfred and valuable contributions of each of its participants: Maria Arul Raja, G. Patrick, George Thadathil, Jose Maliekel, L. Michael, Pushpa Joseph, A. Sebastian, Shalini, Lawrence Fernandes, Xavier Arul Raj, Joe Francis, Kulandaisamy, Mary John, Francis Gonsalves,

Metti and Jerome. These study circle meetings have been occasions to share the progress of my work and to receive critiques and ideas that consolidated, as well as challenged my views.

I immensely thank Fr. Jeyapathy, the then Director of the Folklore Resources and Research Centre (FRRC) at Palayamkottai for giving initial impetus to the study by his suggestion of the topic of 'power and folk religion', and for facilitating my field visits. Thanks to Fr. John Brittto, Dr. D. Lourdu, Dr. Dhananjeyan, Dr. Chellaperumal, Dr. Ramachandran, Dr. Dharmarajan of the centre, and other scholars elsewhere–Dr.Anantakumar Giri, Sivasubramaniyam, Dr. Thopa Paramasivam, Dr. Ponneelan and Dr. Tulasiramasamy for their valuable suggestions. I gratefully remember all the non-teaching staff of the FRRC centre, and all those who helped me during my field visits.

It is in place to recall with a sense of gratitude the help I received from the centres and libraries that provided me with valuable material to carry out my research. My sincere thanks to the FRRC library at Palayamkottai, Tamilnadu Archives at Chennai Directorate of Census of India at Chennai, the Madras Institute of Developmental Studies, Adyar Library at Chennai, Libraries of JDV and Ishwani Kendra, Pune, the library of the Tata Institute of Social Sciences, Mumbai, The Goethals Indian Library and the library of Anthropological Survey of India, Calcutta.

I fondly remember my father, Prof. Kulandai Raj and my brothers (Sahaya Raj, Paul, Manuel), sister (Amal Jothi), their spouses, all my sweet nieces and nephews and all my relatives for all the moral and spiritual support they gave me during this period. My special tribute goes to my late mother, Irudhya Mary who was a rock of our family and a tremendous source of strength all through my life. The completion of my research would not have been possible without the well-balanced emotional proximity and distance that they maintained all through this period of study.

My priest friends Frs. Kurien, Kuruvilla, Lawrence Raj, Puneet, Dossan, Paul, Arul Stephen, Jeyard, my cousins

Frs.Rajkumar and Rex, and other friends, Arul, Charlotte, Santosh and Chinnu, Jessy, Alphonsa, Rosaline, Rashmi, Gigi, Anju, Ananth, Selvi and Sini, had been a tremendous source of psychological strength to me during this journey of research and study

I owe a special debt of gratitude to the Presidents, Rectors and all the staff-members of my *alma maters*, Papal Seminary and JDV (*Jnana Deepa Vidyapeeth*), Pune, and especially to the then faculty members of its Department of Indian Studies, Dr. Noel Sheth and Dr. Subhash Anand for identifying my intellectual skills and recruiting me to serve as a teaching staff. On their prompting I was assigned to undertake doctoral research at the University of Madras, Chennai. Subsequently, the then Jesuit Provincial of India, Dr. Lisbert D'Souza, SJ, and the present Provincial of South Asia, Dr. Hector D'Souza, SJ, provided both, moral support and financial resources to pursue my studies. I wish to record my immense gratitude to them, and to the Society of Jesus. I also extend my gratitude to the then Bishop of the Sivagangai Diocese, Rt. Rev. Edward Francis and the newly appointed Bishop, Rt. Rev. Susaimanikam, for granting me permission to serve at JDV and for their wholehearted cooperation and fraternal concern.

The priceless contributions of all those mentioned above, and of several others whose helps I am unable to recall now, but whose efforts-visible and invisible-have gone into this study from its inception to its completion. I remain immensely indebted to each and every one of them.

Glossary

Āratti	–	a ritual waving of camphor flame.
Aruḷvākku collutal	–	an act of divination.
Cāmiyāṭi	–	literally, god-dancer (*cāmi*-god, *āṭi*-dancer).
Cuṭalai māṭaṉ	–	god of cremation ground.
Cāmiyāṭṭam	–	a possession dance.
Kāppu	–	a thread that strings together betel, a piece of turmeric and a steel ring.
Kāppuaṟuttal	–	breaking of *kāppu by the* Kaṇiyāṉs.
Kāppukaṭṭutal	–	tying of special kinds of amulets on the hands of *cāmiyāṭi's* by Kaṇiyāṉs.
Kaṇiyāṉ(s)	–	a social group that acts as catalyst for the performance of *Cāmiyāṭi's* many functions.
Koṭai	–	a festival in honour of a folk deity.
Kutiaḻaippu	–	a ritual of inviting (*aḻaippu*) deity from its oringinal abode.
Kuṟvai	–	making of a peculiar noise with the twist of the tongue.
Kumpam	–	a pot (silver or clay) with coconut surrounded by mango leaves on its top and water inside
Maiyāṉam pōtal	–	going to the cremation ground for a special ritual

Nañcai	-	wet land.
Palaiyakaran	-	a military chief or commander of a fortress, popularly known as Palaiyam
Pālkuṭam	-	a silver pot with milk with which the people wash the deities.
Paṭaippu	-	an offering of cook food often with non-vegeterian items.
Poṅkal	-	boiled rice, often cooked with sugar and spices.
Pramatēyam(s)	-	villages granted to Brahmins as royal gifts and inhabited by them, often exempted from taxation.
Puṉcai	-	arid land
Pūṭam	-	altar of the folk gods
Villupāṭṭu	-	singing of folk songs to the tone and rhythm of a bow-like instrument
Vēṭṭai	-	ritual hunting

Note on Transliteration

Method of transliteration followed in this study is taken from the Tamil Lexicon, published by University of Madras in the year 1982. Cf. *Tamil Lexicon,* Vol. 1,1982, ixviii.

All Tamil words, except the names of persons, places, hills, mountains and rivers that are in present usage, are transliterated and italicized. Names of gods and goddesses are transliterated but not italicized.

The common Sanskrit words such as *bhakti, darsan, dharma, moksa, varna, varnashrama dharma* etc... are not transliterated, but italicized. As a rule, the non-English words found in quotes or titles of works are given in their original form and not transliterated.

The Transliteration Table

அ	ஆ	இ	ஈ	உ	ஊ	எ	ஏ	ஐ	ஒ	ஓ	ஔ	ஃ
a	ā	i	ī	u	ū	e	ē	ai	o	ō	au	ḵ
க்	ங்	ச்	ஞ்	ட்	ண்	த்	ந்	ப்	ம்	ய்	ர்	ல்
k	ṅ	c	ñ	ṭ	ṇ	t	n	p	m	y	r	l
வ்	ழ்	ள்	ற்	ன்	ஜ	ஷ	ஸ	ஹ				
v	ḻ	ḷ	ṟ	ṉ	j	ṣ	s	h				

Chapter 1

Introduction and Tools of the Study

Situating the Study

'Cultural Studies' have gained centre-stage in the grooves of academe for the last three decades. Academics, worldwide, are entering into, and researching, new vistas in the realm of culture, as never before. This shows a shift of focus from economic analyses–which was the preoccupation of social studies from the beginning of the twentieth century till the late seventies–to cultural analyses.

One of the factors that gave an impetus to the study of cultures in colonized countries is the 'Postcolonial Studies' project. The specific contribution of Postcolonial Studies in former colonies like India is the emergence of 'situated' cultural discourses that have highlighted the cultural diversities and the social dynamics of various subsystems of a given society such as the caste system, the economic and religious systems. They have highlighted the vibrant existence of multifaceted socio-cultural universes whose dynamism revolved around various key factors such as caste hierarchy, temple honours and ritual complexes. The works of Susan Bayly, Nicholas Dirks, Arjun Appadurai, Saurabh Dube and Steven M. Parish are outcomes of such initiatives. This approach dovetails with the overarching intellectual ambience of postmodernism with its theoretical predilection for scientific inquiry of 'fragments' in place of eulogizing meta-narratives. These 'little narratives' have unravelled the emergence of micro-social processes and hitherto latent forces with their distinguishing characteristics. The present study, which is a 'situated' cultural discourse on the phenomenon of a folk religious cult in the district of Tirunelveli in south India, is a modest attempt for further contribution in this area.

Another commendable intellectual current is the 'Subaltern Studies' project, which is specific to the Indian context. One of the hallmarks of Subaltern Studies in India is its focus on the question of subaltern agency of the oppressed sections of the society vis-à-vis the caste hierarchy. Such initiatives have explored the innovative forms of marginal groups' struggle for liberation from the oppressive systems of caste hierarchy. Some studies have shown how the subalterns have made use of local cultural resources such as religion as an agency for negotiation of power and for identity assertion. It is in this context of subaltern studies that the present work concerns itself about how power operates through cultural schemes such as religion. This study resonates with the studies of Steven M. Parish and Saurabh Dube. The former has shown how religion can become a site of contestation to resolve the contradictions of caste hierarchy, while the latter has demonstrated how religion can become an active instrument for the emergence of subaltern agency in the process of identity assertion of a particular subordinated group. It is within this context, the present study on the ritual power of a folk religious phenomenon has to be situated, since this phenomenon exemplifies the empowerment of subalterns in their life and their struggles against subhuman conditions.

Another field where this study has to be situated is that of folkloristic studies in the context of Tamilnadu. The development of folkloristic studies in Tamilnadu shows that, in their own way, authors like Vanamamalai, Sanmugasundaram, Tulasiramaswamy, Lourdu, Sivasubhramainyam and others, have contributed to the knowledge of micro socio-cultural universes in the cultural landscape of south India. Through such attempts, they have brought to the fore 'the diversities, differences and discontinuities in the production of the many meanings of Hinduism."[1] However, their works are more ethnographically oriented than sociologically informed. The concerns of the oppressed sections of the society find a place in most of these writings, though the academic discussion on the notion of subalternity does not feature there, and they do not treat of religion as "a negotiated and contested resource, particularly by groups and communities who stood on the margins of religious categories."[2]

The present study aims to take this thrust forward by studying the social processes that underscored the growth of a particular folk religious phenomenon called Cuṭalai Māṭaṉ (henceforth, CM) Cult. It does this by inquiring into the question of ritual power, as ritual is "a window on the cultural dynamics by which people make and remake their world,"[3] and "rituals are recognised to have a type of efficacy or special power, not only to shape social organisation and thereby the dispositions of individuals (i.e., the shaping of social ethos), but also in the articulation, redefinition, and legitimation of cultural realities,"[4] as Catherine Bell observes.

The Topic of the Study

Folk religiosity and ritual power are the major topics of inquiry for the present study. Since religious meaning systems are socially embedded, to locate the religious universe of the CM cult in its social setting, the study will deal with the following questions: Which are the different social groups (castes) that worship CM? What are the prevalent myths about CM and about the particular village temples both in oral traditions and in written traditions? What are the life stories of the village *cāmiyāṭi*[5] and of the devotees? What do the myths tell us about: (i) the folk's operative notion on the power of CM and (ii) the relationship between the deity and the *cāmiyāṭi*, deity and the devotees, *cāmiyāṭi* and the devotees? What are the different rituals performed for the deity? For what purposes? How does religion help folk to deal with the forces of power (good as well as evil) in the society and in the cosmos? Having these as background questions, the study inquires into the ordering of meaning systems, and schemes of conceptualisation about the power of CM as manifest in the myths and rituals centred on the cult of CM. Along the same line, the study will more pointedly explore if and how religion and ritual can be perceived to be a source of power to tackle the exigencies of human life such as sickness, misfortune and fear of impending evil. In other words, the study articulates the concerns and voices of common folk found in their struggles and anxieties, and captures the mechanisms and strategies by which they obtain, tap, maintain, distribute 'channels of power' to deal with such basic issues of human living.

Objectives of the Study

The overall objective of the study is to explore if and how ritual, as a powerful arena, can exercise, through its symbolic schemes, a persuasive effect on the participants' sense of identity and their power of negotiation on social reality.[6] In order to do so, the study aims to map the phenomena of rituals, beliefs and myths of CM cult onto the agrarian village setting and on its socio-economic and historical background. Further, it attempts to evolve a cultural hermeneutic of the cult by exploring the underlying patterns which interrelate the various components and coalesce them into a single whole, called CM cult. The study also aims to investigate into the strategies and mechanisms innovated and employed by the folk to generate, to distribute, and to appropriate ritual power both in its function and performance. Subsequently, it seeks to explore if, and how, religion can become an agency not only for the negotiation of power but also for the 'display of power,' resulting in the generation of new typologies of discourses on the newly gained socio-economic identities. Besides, the study attempts to find out how the fear of the deity (CM) can impel different social actors (high and low castes) to generate, sustain, maintain and continue symbolic systems that can reverse the grammar of social equations within the caste hierarchy, and can draft a new but ambivalent portrait of micro socio-cultural worlds.

Clarification of Terms

A good study has to first clarify the working understanding of the key terms employed by it. Hence we propose to explain the meaning of words such as folk region, ritual power, in-society, and CM cult. While expounding the meaning of these terms as employed in the study, we will also dwell on the specific theoretical approaches undertaken by the study.

Folk Religion

Following the views of Tamil folklorists like Vanamamalai, Kesavan, Sivathampy and Kailasapathy,[7] the study understands 'folk' as referring to the socially and culturally marginalized. It is important to note that this study is not premised on the distinction between 'folk' and 'subaltern,' as the latter term is more associated with the question of contradictory consciousness–with which the study does not deal. However, it uses the term 'subaltern' to refer to the people who are in the position of subordination within caste hierarchy and their appropriation of religion as agency. Since this understanding of 'subaltern' comes very close to that of 'folk' mentioned above, both these terms are used interchangeably to refer to the voices of the subalterns and the assertion of their identity–that remain submerged (rather than manifest) in the performances of their rituals. Hence, both the concepts of 'folk' and 'subaltern' overlap in the present study as both have a certain common ground.

As regards 'folk religion' the study understands it as the religion of the peasants, the illiterate and the culturally marginal people. Folk religions have distinctive features, characteristics, ritual practices, belief-systems that demarcate them from non-folk, i.e., the classical or the dominant religions.[8] The definition of folk religion as belonging to the socially and culturally marginalised does not exclude the possibility of non-marginal groups adopting it and appropriating its ritual power. Even in such instances, this definition of folk religion is applicable for the following reasons: (1) Those non-marginals, in spite of their appropriation and use, still consider these ritual practices as belonging to the common, illiterate and oppressed group.[9] (2) The marginalized also look at such practices of the higher castes as imitation of their religious behaviour. (3) The so-called high castes have maintained, not altered, according to their worldview, the basic structures of folk rituals.

As regards the modern studies of folk religion in the context of Tamilnadu, the following works are available: *The Village Gods of South India* by Henry Whitehead, *Dravidian Gods in Modern Hinduism* by W.T. Elmore, *Nellaimāvaṭṭa Nāṭṭupura Teyvankaḷ* by Thulasi Ramasamy, *Nāṭṭārcamayam* by Gnanasekaran,[10] and seminar papers on "Folk Religion" held at the Folklore Department of St. Xavier's College, Palayamkottai (1999). It may be pointed out here that the book by Thulasi Ramasamy is a pioneering work on folk deities in the district of Tirunelveli, the area of the present study. The above studies are more descriptive in nature than explorative, and they have recorded the ethnographic data without much analysis. In general, they have not attempted to relate the social processes to the folk religious phenomenon as undertaken by the present study. Further, no work has looked into the question of *ritual power* of folk religious phenomenon in the South Tamilnadu context.

Ritual Power

Before taking up the meaning of ritual power, it is in place to mention the way ritual itself is understood in the present study. The study looks at rituals from the viewpoint of the role they could play in different realms of human life. For this purpose, the study draws on the distinction made by Peter Beyer between *function* and *performance* with regard to the role of religion as a whole[11] and applies that to one of its elements, namely, ritual.

According to Peter Beyer, 'function' refers to 'pure' religious communication, variously called the aspect of devotion and worship, etc. "Function is the pure, 'sacred' communication involving the transcendent and the aspect that religious institutions claim for themselves."[12] Performance, by contrast, occurs when religion is 'applied' to problems generated in other systems or sub-systems in society.[13] While function has to do with "the holism of religion, its effort to determine the whole of existence through the possibility of communication with the posited transcendence,"[14] performance deals with how religion relates to other subsystems such as economy, polity, law, etc. To put it differently, while 'function' refers to religion's ability to deal with the matters of its own domain, 'performance' refers to religion's ability to deal with the matters of other domains.

Based on this understanding of religion, the study dwells on both 'function' and 'performance' of ritual and its power. It focuses on the *function of ritual* (and its power) in that it deals with the efforts of the ritual to determine the whole of existence through the possibility of communication with the posited transcendence. To put it differently, the function of the ritual deals with those concerns which are perceived to be 'religious' in a given society, and in the context of folk religions, it refers to how the folk organize systems of meanings around a belief in a higher power and express it through the rituals. In fact, chapter four and parts of chapter five of the present work inquire into how the folk organize systems of meanings around a belief in a higher power, so as to tackle the exigencies of human existence. The study also focuses *on the performance of ritual* in that it deals with how ritual power can treat the problems generated in other subsystems such as economy and caste-system but not solved there. This is done in chapter six and in the later part of chapter five, by exploring the symbolic cultural schemes, generated by the rituals, can have wider implications for other subsystems.

In carrying forward the understanding of the role of ritual as performance, the study borrows the insights of Catherine Bell in following Bourdieu, Foucault and Comaroff, and treats ritual primarily as a kind of social practice,[15] which is structured and structuring, to use Bourdieu's expression. It structures the social body and therein constructs "social beings" via the internalisation of basic schemes and values. The socialised body in turn gives rise to dispositions that generate similarly, although not identically, structured and structuring practices. Social practice as such addresses a particular situation (a historical moment).

Social practice does not so much propose a solution to the situation as effect a complete change in the very definition of the situation itself. In other words, it produces the definition of a new situation instead of providing an answer to the old one. Proceeding from this understanding of social practice as proposed by Bourdieu, Foucault and Comaroff, and their ideal of ritual as a form of social practice, Bell proposes her idea of ritual as a *distinct* social practice which the aforementioned authors do not elaborate.

According to Bell, ritual is not a set of distinct acts, but '*a way of acting*' that deliberately establishes a '*privileged contrast*' to distinguish itself from other forms of social practice and thus acquires a special status of dominance.[16] "The strategy of ritual can alter the socio-cultural taxonomy so that certain symbolic schemes dominate others,"[17] and it is done through the 'work of ritualisation.' Bell holds that work of ritualisation results in the production of a ritualised body. It is this ritualised body which is capable of internalising and embodying these schemes. "Invested with a sense of privileged contrast with respect to other bodies, the ritualised body or agent possesses a 'practical mastery' of the schemes for ritualisation and can employ them to dominate others."[18] In other words, the deployment of such schemes can shift a variety of socio-cultural situations into ones that the ritualised body can dominate, without bringing any of the operations to the level of explicit discourse. Thus ritualised body becomes capable of promoting the restructuring of the larger cultural milieu. According to Foucault, what comes to exist as a result by the shaping of the social body through ritualisation is what he calls "economies of power." It is to be noted that ritual practices, as localization of economy of power, produce their historical milieu each moment. "The social or cultural context of ritual does not exist separately from the act; the context is created in the act.... Riutalisation is historical practice–historically structured, historically effective, and history-producing."[19] It is from this idea of ritual and ritualisation that the study moves on to define ritual power in the realm of religious performance, as we shall see shortly.

The present work tries to understand *ritual power* both in its function and performance. In the realm of function, the power of ritual refers to its effectiveness to tackle the exigencies of human existence either in the life of an individual or a community. People seek to solve their problems by turning to a higher power of a folk deity and tap the deity's power through rituals. The study–which begins its interrogation of ritual power of folk religiosity based on the ethnographic study of the CM cult–inquires in the fourth chapter and in the first part of the fifth chapter, into this aspect of power of *koṭai* rituals by dealing with those problems and offering of solutions, which are regarded as 'religious' in a given community.

In the realm of performance, ritual power stands for the capacity of rituals to empower agents especially the subjugated ones like the subalterns, in limited and highly negotiated ways, who, "have instinctive knowledge of these (cultural) schemes embedded in their bodies, in their sense of reality, and in their understanding of how to act in ways that both maintain and qualify the complex micro-relations of power."[20] In other words, it enables persons to deploy, play and manipulate basic schemes in ways that appropriate and condition experience effectively, that can manipulate the social order on some level and appropriate its categories for a semi-coherent vision of identity and action both at the individual level and at the collective levels.[21] It may be pertinent to note that the function and the performance of ritual power are closely and directly related. The more the perception of 'function of riiual power', the more the possibility for the 'performance of ritual power'. Thus people's perception of function of ritual power might result in new possibilities for its performance in other systems such social structure and political structure.

As regards the treatment of ritual power in ritual studies, the early rationalist approach was one of considering it as a non-utilitarian magical activity of the primitive people. For functionalists, rituals have a type of efficacy or power to shape social organisation and thereby the dispositions of individuals.

With the emergence of cultural/social anthropology, the latest trend has been to explore the power of ritual not only in the moulding of social ethos, but also in the articulation, redefinition, and legitimation of cultural realities. This new approach, contrary to those of the early rationalists, suspects ritual of greater power than before. While adopting the last mentioned approach, the study attempts to look at rituals of the CM cult from the viewpoint of ritual power. This study closely resembles Bell's view on ritual and power. Yet, the study has a methodological difference from that of Bell's work in that, while the latter is a pure theoretical treatise on ritual and power having no particular socio-historical and religious context as its referent, our study has, as its point of reference, the religious phenomenon of the CM cult embedded in the particular historico-social context of Tirunelveli district, and inquires into the applicability of ritual power as manifest in the context of social process that took place there. Moreover, the study differs from Bell's work on *Ritual Theory, Ritual Practice* also in that it has incorporated *the indigenous categories of understanding of power* (Indian view of power) along with that of theoreticians like Victor Turner, Bourdieu, Foucault and others, while Bell's work heavily relies only on theoreticians, as the author herself has acknowledged.[22]

As noted above, the study tries to apply these theoretical underpinnings of ritual power to the study of folk cult called the CM cult. To the researcher's knowledge, no such study has been undertaken on the phenomenon of folk cult and ritual power in the Tamilnadu context. On the Indian cultural landscape, a few studies have been undertaken. Susan Wadley's work, *Shakti: Power in the Conceptual Structure of Karimpur Religion,* is a monograph on power, not on ritual power proper. Though it refers also to the practice of rituals there, it looks at it from the viewpoint of conceptual scheme about relations of powerful beings, as the author herself admits.[23] Therefore, it does not sufficiently nuance the dynamics of ritual power. Further, the folk religious phenomenon is not the main focus of the study. It studies also the folk religious behaviours of the village, but more in relation to the dominant Sanskritic Hindu worldview. Besides, Wadely treats religion as a symbolic system, and heavily draws on the structuralist paradigm to interpret the data. Hence, the significance of socially embedded meanings of ritual performances does not become an object of concern for the work. The present research pays attention not only to the cultural meanings attributed by the people, but it also deals with the social implications of ritual performances. For this purpose, its theoretical frameworks are constructed in a way that both, the cultural meaning schemes (through Indian view of power), and the socially embedded meanings (Foucault's view of power and Bourdieu's symbolic power), are given due attention.

Another monograph deserving mention here is Saurabh Dube's *Untouchable Pasts: Religion, Identity, and Power among a Central Indian Community, 1780-1950*. It is a study on a particular caste, the Chamars of Chattisgarh, a community that has combined the features of a caste and sect. Our research is on a cult, not on a sect and it deals with the account of religious behaviours, not of one particular social group, but of different groups. While Dube's work deals with the appropriation of religious symbols, metaphors, myths of higher castes by a subordinated caste, our study deals also with the reverse process, namely, the appropriation of the symbols and rituals of the subalterns by those in the upper echelons of the caste hierarchy. Subsequently, the subject matter of study for Dube was the fund of symbols, customs, rituals, etc., of high castes, and its appropriation by the subalterns: their infusion of new meanings into it, and their negotiation of new power relations through such strategies. But our study has as its subject matter the corpus of rituals, myths, and symbols of the people of the lower strata of caste hierarch; it shows how their cultural resources are appropriated by different social actors in caste hierarchy and infused with different layers of meanings. In other words, as the very title suggests, Dube's work is all about the construction of a new identity through the agency of religion. The present study does not so much deal with the *construction* of new identity of a social group, as with the *display* of newly obtained identities of different social groups gained by economic and developmental schemes. Thus, in the present study, religion is shown to be a site of display of new identities through strategies of ritual power.

In-society

This expression in the title refers to study of religion, not from the philosophical/moral consideration of religion as a divine revelation/primitive superstition,[24] but from the viewpoint of understanding religion "as a socially produced, oriented and structured phenomenon, like any other aspect of culture."[25] The treatment of folk religion and its ritual power in the present study takes into account the historico-social dimension of the religious beliefs and practices in the context of the CM cult as found in the district of Tirunelveli.

The CM Cult

The point of departure for research in this study is the CM Cult. CM is the most popular male folk deity in the southern part of Tamilnadu (Tirunelveli, Thoothukudi and Kanyakumari districts). Almost all the villages in this area worship him in one form or another. His cult is also found also in quite a few places in the districts of Madurai, Trichy, Ooty and Pondicherry. He is worshipped by all castes, but mostly by the backward castes and the Dalits. In most of the cases, among Dalits and the backward castes, he is a carnivorous god (meat-eating deity); goat, cock, pig, chicken, even liquor are all offered to him. Quite a few high-castes including Brahmins worship him, and he remains an ambivalent god in their midst. The word Cuṭalai means 'cremation ground' and Māṭaṉ means 'one who has bull's head as his own head or a bull as his vehicle.' Therefore, as Sanmugasundaram notes,[26] the literal meaning of 'Cuṭalaimāṭaṉ' could be rendered as 'God of cremation ground having either bull's head as his head or bull as his vehicle.' However, it is not a defining statement, because many of his images have neither bull's head as his head nor a bull as his vehicle. Besides, his images and temples are equally found outside the cremation ground. He is also considered as the god of the dead, and, subsequently, also regarded as the god of devils. Cuṭalaimāṭaṉ could be either the principle deity of the temple, or one of the secondary deities of the temple or a guardian deity at the entrance of the temple, or outside the temple. As a folk deity, he has no fixed image, nor a fixed place of worship. He can be worshipped either in a tree, or a stone, a clay-statue. There is no one fixed structure for Cuṭalaimāṭaṉ temple. The temple may or may not have roofs. His temple could be located right at the centre of the village or outside the village near the cremation ground. Ordinary village folk, both male and female, like to be named after him to show their allegiance to him. He is worshipped for various purposes: for successful crops, to beget children, to ward off evil spirits, to be healed of sickness affecting both humans and cattle (cows and other animals). One of the most popular forms of worship in this area is called *koṭai* (literarily, 'gift'), an eventful celebration of nine days/three days festival held in honour of the folk deity. The present work which studies ritual power focuses on *koṭai* rituals of the CM cult, and explores how rituals can become effective means of tapping and appropriating the power of CM.

As regards studies on the CM cult, there are books in which scanty references to the CM cult are present; for e.g., books by Thulasi Ramasamy, Henry Whitehead, W.T. Elmore, Gnanasekaran.[27] Though these books provide some references and details about the CM cult, they are inadequate for a comprehensive study of it. The book *Cuṭalaimāṭaṉ Vaḻipāṭu* (Cuṭalaimāṭaṉ Cult) by Sanmugasundaram is the only book which specifically and extensively deals with the CM cult. This book traces the origin of CM to ancient Tamil literature, deals with the different dimensions of the cult and gives various references of the cult in the folk songs and local myths. However, as the author himself acknowledges, this book has its own limitations and shortcomings. First of all, the work is incomplete because the facts are based on the general knowledge of the author (he hails from this district) and based on limited sources of data, collected not through systematic fieldwork.[28] Secondly, it does not deal with the different aspects of cult in depth, though it brings out the different aspects and dimensions of the CM cult which other books have not focused upon. Thirdly, it is mostly descriptive. It does not discuss the problematic of social relations centred on the CM cult.

Another work that has reference to the CM cult is the monograph in French titled *Les Dieux et les hommes: etude des cultes d'un village du Tirunelveli, Inde du sud* by M.L. Reiniche.[29] This work, anthropological in nature, describes the cult of CM in meticulous details, while dealing with different local cults. But, like the work of Susan Wadley, it does not sufficiently distinguish between the major religious phenomenon and folk religious phenomenon in its description of the symbolic cultural framework. Besides, since it does not make a sociological inquiry into the cult, which is not the concern of the work, it fails to capture the specificity of the cult as a distinct socio-cultural entity.

Methodological Framework

Mixed Methodology

This study has adopted a mixed methodology, heavily drawn on the concepts, insights and techniques of both the qualitative research methods and the quantitative methods. For instance, it avails itself of the survey method and census data of quantitative paradigms, and the methods of participant observation, in–depth unstructured interviewing, folk theatre, proxemics and kinesis of qualitative research methodology.

Methods[30] of Data Collection: A Bricolage Approach

Bricolage approach means 'engaging in' diverse tasks of data collection ranging from interviewing to observing, to interpreting personal and historical documents, to intensive self-reflection and introspection, etc. These diverse methods of data-collection emerge from the fact of eclectic approach that draws ideas and inspiration from different interpretative paradigms.[31]

Fieldwork

Fieldwork refers to all those activities that I, the researcher, have undertaken while in the field, including watching, listening, conversing, recording and so on. It is an intensely personal and social process requiring physical stamina, intellectual openness and moral sensitivity.[32] Keeping these concerns in mind, fieldwork for the present study was done over a period of eighteen months from January 2001 to August 2002. Besides this period, periodic visits to the field were also undertaken. The range of fieldwork could be grouped under three categories: (1) Pilot survey during which the researcher went to different villages over a period of ten days (2) Fieldwork done during the peak season of koṭai rituals that involved staying in the villages during the festival of *koṭai* and partaking the koṭai rituals and collecting data through participant observation. During this time social survey in some of the villages was also undertaken (3) Periodic visits to the villages before and after *koṭai*, to witness the rituals during off-peak season, to conduct in-depth unstructured interviews with *cāmiyāṭi(s)*, village elders, *pūcāri(s)* and others.

Participant Observation

Participant observation is a commitment to enter into the world of those studied by sharing in their day-to-day experiences. Through participant observation, one can describe what goes on, who or what is involved, when and where things happen, how they occur, and why things happen as they do in particular situations.[33]

The present study, which focuses on the folk religion and ritual power, relies heavily on participant observation method to collect the data about the rituals of CM. It is the only method that I, the researcher, used to record the data about koæai rituals in all the four villages. I observed all the episodes of the rituals of koæai by partaking in it, and recorded them in chronological order. In my field – notes, I had documented all that he observed; the words uttered by the *cāmiyāṭi*, the articles used by the ritual specialists like Kaṇiyāṉ(s), the non-verbal communications that took place during the ritual performances, and the rituals performed by the devotees. Later on, they were arranged in order, edited and made into a readable text—which is presented in the third chapter. Some of the observations I had made, and the questions that arose during the participant observation of kotai rituals, had lead to further inquiries, insights and analysis for the study.

In-Depth Unstructured Interviewing

Unstructured interviewing is the most widely used method of data collection in ethnography. The researcher interviews people in any of their natural settings in their places of work like the fields so as to facilitate them to open up and express themselves in their own terms, and at their own pace.[34]

The interviews conducted with the *cāmiyāṭi(s)*, some village elders, and the folk artists such as Kaṉiyāṉs and *villupāṭṭu* performers *such as* Mr. Thirumalaisami, Mr. Thankalvelu, Mr. Murugan and Mrs. Muthulaksmi are of this kind. Besides the interviews in the field, interviews were held outside the field with another set of people. These interviewees include eminent thinkers, scholars and professors in area of folkloristics in Tamilnadu namely, Jeyapathy, the then director of FRRC (Folklore Resources and Research Centre, St. Xavier's College, Palyamkottai), Professor Dananjeyan, Dr. Ramanchandran, Dr. Lourdu, Dr. Sivasivasubramianyam, Tho. Pramasivam and Ponneelan. These interviews helped the researcher to know more about the folk cult in the district and to explore new areas of research in the study.

The Social Survey Method

The survey may be defined as a methodological technique that requires the systematic collection of data from populations or samples through the use of the interview or the self-administered questionnaire. The investigator approaches a sample of persons who have been exposed to a set of events or experiences and interviews them with respect to these experiences with a fixed set of questions.[35] In the present study, the researcher used this quantitative method technique to gather information about the socio-economic-cultural resources of all the people: the Paḻḻar(s) , Maṟavar(s), Illatu Pillaimār(s) and Brahmins. Further, three sets of questionnaires were devised to elicit data from the *cāmiyāṭi(s)*, from the villagers, and from the common devotees about their beliefs and ritual practices with regard to CM in a particular temple.

Proxemics and Kinesics[36]

Proxemics is the study of how the socially defined physical distance between people varies under differing social circumstances. Location of houses in the Indian villages, physical accessibility to the deity in the temple, etc.–all have social meaning. One's place in the caste hierarchy will determine one's place in all the above. Kinesics is the study of body language. A Dalit *cāmiyāṭis* physical movements in a *cāmiyāṭiām* , his glance, a devotee's prostration in front of the deity, his/her gestures in front of the folk god and before the *cāmiyāṭi*, etc., and many other physical movements are in fact symbolic statements. The interpretation of explicit and symbolic meaning of rituals of CM and of the folk's religious and social behaviour is derived from these methods in the present study.

Archival Research

Archival research is the study of the recorded past involving archival materials: government reports, census records, newspapers archives, personal diaries or photo collections, industrial data, medical records, school records, wills, deeds, records of court cases, tax rolls, and land-holding records. Archival resources can be particularly useful in studying cultural processes through time.[37]

In the present study, apart from land-holding records and travel diaries of foreign travellers, the Gazetteers and administrative report of the Tamilnadu Government have been used. The quantitative data from Census records have been largely used to bring out the current socio-economic situation of Dalits and Pallars in the district of Tirunelveli. Archival studies were undertaken after fieldwork in four places: Anthropological Survey of India, Calcutta; Goethal's Library at St. Xavier's College in Calcutta; Tamilnadu Archives in Chennai and Directorate of Census of India in Chennai. The records of the past were elaborately searched to construct the past of Tirunelveli district and to trace the past behaviours of the people of study.

Folk Tales, Folk Songs and Folk Theatres

The data on the myths about CM and origin of the CM temple and about the *cāmiyāṭi* is obtained through folk tales. Since folk songs such as *Villupāṭṭu* and Kaṇiyāṉ*pāṭṭu* are very much part of *koṭai* festival, they were heavily relied on for eliciting information about the CM cult. Similarly, folk theatres and performing arts such as Kaṇ iyāṉ kūttu, *Mēḷam,* and *Villupāṭṭu* have contributed to the gathering of data on the CM cult, as some of them accompany ritual enactments of CM's myth.

Theoretical Frameworks: An Eclectic Approach

No research can be done in isolation, nor can any ideas be framed into valid theory without the frames of references drawn from the established theories of the past. It must take into account the views and theories of the scholarly world that it aims to address. With this in mind, the researcher has used various theoretical ideas to study the folk religious phenomena of the CM cult. Our approach is 'eclectic' in the sense that our basic theoretical assumptions will not owe allegiance to one particular theoretical framework, and will not interpret the phenomenon solely from that perspective. Rather, the study will draw inspirations and insights from various standpoints to analyse the phenomenon. It is to be noted that various theoretical concepts and underpinnings that are delineated here are the basic building blocks with which the structure of the study is constructed. These conceptual bricks of the study are used at various times, and are not always visible as in the case of a constructed building. They are plastered and painted with other ideas, concepts and analyses.

Network Analysis

The study, which basically treats ritual as a network, avails of the basic concepts and theoretical underpinnings of network analysis, one of the most promising currents in sociological research.[38] "Network theory builds its explanations from patterns of relations and it captures causal factors in the social structural bedrock of society, by passing the spuriously significant attributes of people temporarily occupying particular positions in social structure."[39] Network analysis does not look at social behaviour as the result of individuals' common possession of attributes and norms, but rather as the result of their involvement in structured social relations. It gives primacy to the Durkheimian view that the organic solidarity of a social system rests not on the cognition of human beings, but rather on the interlock and interaction of objectively definable social relationships. The theorists in this school regard social facts as ecologically embedded within specific contexts of time and space, i.e., within particular interactional fields composed of concrete historical circumstances. Social facts are seen here as located in particular physical places and in particular social processes. They are also located within the temporal logic of one or more processes of succession, assimilation, conflict and so on. The structure of relations among actors and location of individual actors in the network have important behavioural, conceptual, and attitudinal consequences both for the individual units and for the system as a whole. The hallmark of network analysis, as Edmand Laumann notes, is to explain, at least in part, the behaviour of network elements (i.e., the nodes) and of the system as a whole by appeal to specific features of the interconnections among the elements.[40] More significantly, the network approach investigates the constraining and enabling dimensions of patterned relationships among social actors within a system.[41]

Narrative Research

Narrative research refers to any study that uses or analyses narrative materials. The data can be collected as a story from a literary work or from an interview or from the field-notes of the anthropologist. It can be the object of the research, or a means for the study of another question. It may be used to make a comparison among groups, to learn about a social phenomenon or historical period. It is to be noted that narrative research differs significantly from the positivist methods in its underlying assumption that it does not subscribe either to a single, absolute truth in human reality or to one correct reading and interpretation of a text.

The study, dealing as it does with the folk material (stories) about the CM cult, employs *the narrative analysis method*[42] to interpret the various components of the CM cult. To be more specific as regards the method, the study depends on the *holistic structural-content analysis of narrative method.* This structural-content perspective is a variation within Holistic Analysis of Form proposed by Amia Lieblich et al.[43] in the sense that in this model the researcher is interested both in the structure as well as in the content.[44] He is interested in the contents of the story in as much as it can provide the basic material for the structure. Similarly, he is interested in the structure in as much as it can unfold the development of themes and the plot of the content, around which the structure is organised.

While traversing the narrative trajectories of the folk stories, narrative research organizes its contents into different structural units that point to and focus on the different themes of the folk-tale. The social actor or cultural members arrive at the thematic foci of the narrative by exploring the meanings subscribed to 'in the structural units' in relation to the whole story. The meaning-direction is provided and supported by the narrative materials with which the method works. The worldview of the social actor and the perspective of the researcher intersect at the point of exploration of meaning and meaning-direction. Thus, as Lieblich notes, the analysis attempts to identify the dynamics of the plot.[45]

Theoretical Frameworks of Power

Since the study focuses on the question of ritual power, it summarises, in this section, important ideas on power drawing insights from different fields, from philosophy, sociology and from the viewpoint of Indian religion. It finally locates these ideas within the framework of phenomenology of power proposed by the Santa Barbara Conference on Ritual and Power.[46]

Indian View of Power

In order to evolve a discourse of folk semantics of 'ritual power', the study heavily draws on the Indian view of power from folk perspective. In this section we will take a brief look at some of their views that will be applicable to our study.

Primacy of Persons, Places and Objects in 'Power'

Though, according to the Indian view of power, all things and places are filled with omnipresent *cakti* or power,[47] some places, beings, things and some hours are endowed with more powers than others. For instance, many regard a king as the incarnate of the *cakti* of guardian deities, while the *cāmiyāṭi* or medium is said to be specially chosen by a particular deity to act on his/her behalf, which makes the *cāmiyāṭi* more powerful than others. Likewise, some days are more powerful than other days for a particular purpose or action. For instance, Thursdays and Fridays are more powerful than other days for the performance of magic and witchcraft, as these days are under the influence of *cakti*. Tuesdays are very bad days for such activities, because anything done or said on that day leads to nothing. On Tuesdays, spirits are very active and unmanageable, and cannot be exorcised.

Religions in general, and folk religions in particular, have devised mechanisms and strategies to identify, infuse, rekindle, tap, appropriate and distribute these effective sources of 'power' to the common folk through rituals. This ritual power, thus tapped and appropriated, is believed to be essential for the nourishment of life and society[48] by ensuring the growth of crops and the socio-physical and psychological well being of individuals and of the society through its control of evil powers.

Power Expressed as 'Heat'

A person or object with 'power' is described as 'very hot' (*uṣṇ am*) or 'burning' Many religious rituals and practices are meant to make the hot and dangerous power of god, cool. The *linga* of Siva, for that matter any idol of the deity, in particular folk deity, is supposed to be always in a condition of heat and requires to be cooled with showers of waters or milk. Sprinkling of water and milk or drinking of milk and applying of sandal paste and rose water on the body of ritual specialists is meant to cool their hot *cakti*, which they derive from god. The offering of *naivediya* or food to a deity has its object of cooling of the *cakti* of the deity. Further, *tapas* means heat. To perform *tapas*, thus, is to become heated up, to store one's inner heat. Understanding of *cāmiyāṭi*'s performance of *tapas* before *koṭai* from this perspective is in place here for the present study.

Power as 'Wind': A Symbol of Movement

Power or *cakti* in Tamil culture is symbolised by the element of wind. The movement of wind is creative and protective.[49] The 'powerful' beings such as lower gods or demons are often described as being made of wind, always wandering and swirling about. Such creatures never hold still and are regarded as restless, always moving, and never at peace. They manifest their behaviour in the bodies of their 'medium(s)'. That is one of the reasons why during '*cāmiyāṭiam,*' the *cāmiyāṭi(s)* become uncontrollable and get into frenzied bodily movements. It is for the same reasons that some of the village folk hesitate to erect a roof for the temples of folk deities or to erect a compound wall, lest the god's power be controlled. Movement is seen as expression of power. That is why the more one undertakes daring risky bodily movements as a *cāmiyāṭi*, the more is one identified as powerful.[50]

Cakti: A Power of Unification

The '*cakti*' possessed by the oracles is pre-eminently a moral and creative, not an immoral and destructive, power. Its moral creation takes the form of unification, especially, the unification of human beings. Through divination the *cāmiyāṭi(s)* try to cure the folk of the alienating physical ailments and bring about union and harmony (*amaiti*) within oneself. He or she is not only a healer of physical diseases but also a healer of interfamily squabbles, reuniting husband and wife, mother-in-law or between brothers or relatives.[51] Through the mechanism of *sattiyam* (promise), the *cakti* of god/goddess is seen as a power of 'settlement' and 'union' that put to rest all apprehensions and suspicions. When the folk take recourse to the deity in the event of 'robbery or stealing', the god/goddess is seen as a power of union with the lost things or stolen articles. They also help to find marriage partners, and bring about life-long union between a man and woman.

Mediation of Divine Power for Healing through Involuntary Non-institutional Human Medium(s)

According to the folk worldview–unlike orthodox priests of major Hindu temples or *pūcāri(s)* of the folk temples who obtain their religious role by institutional means such as inheritance through the male line–the *cāmiyāṭi(s)* often experience their calling through dreams *(kaṉavu)* or "more often through what was usually called *taricaṉam* (from the Sanskrit *darsan*: "seeing"), meaning an "appearance," "vision," or "revelation" of the goddess"[52] or gods. As Nabokov notes, the *cāmiyāṭi(s)* do not have much choice in their recruitment. They often claim that they do not choose to be possessed by god, rather they are involuntarily and randomly chosen by god.[53]

It is to be noted that their calling or first time experience of god/goddess 'coming on' (i.e., god or goddess possessing someone) takes place during moments of personal crisis or severe illness, but through their calling and dramatic acquisition of healing 'divine' power, repeatedly over a period of time, they are believed to bring to an end the crisis in other's lives by interpreting signs *(kuṟi collutal)*, i.e., by forecasting people's fortune, diagnosing their sickness, identifying causes of personal affliction and misfortune, and by exorcising the evil spirits that caught them.

Power as Embodiment

Unlike the major religions which lay more emphasis on 'abstract' spiritual power, the folk religious worldview focuses on the 'embodied' dimension of 'divine power'. The folk religious rituals set out to tap, create, capture and incarnate the 'divine power' into objects of sense perception, make it available to the folk and deal with it. The culminating point of such embodiment is the manifestation of deity in the person of '*cāmiyāṭi*', who acts and talks on behalf of god himself or goddess herself, as we have seen. The 'divine power' that 'comes on' is lived out, and manifested from within. Here, 'power' is actively appropriated and embodied. In the '*bhakti*' tradition of major religious traditions, one becomes a '*passive*' object of divine power. One would be appreciated, if one exhibits bliss and tranquillity as a result of one's encounter with the divine. Any outburst of ecstasy is generally neither appreciated nor encouraged. But the folk tradition makes the *cāmiyāṭi* an active agent of 'divine power.' Here, the more one is active and violent, the more is one recognised and appreciated. The embodiment of power, expressed through the dramatic possession performances, stresses the passionate and 'violent' nature of supernatural energy. Sarah Caldwell notes that, because it inhered in the physical landscape as well as in the bodies of human beings, this power is essential for the nourishment of life and society.[54] Power is revealed here as most dynamic, encountered by the folk as most productive and experienced as very protective. As one of the Brahmin respondents expressed that, it is these mechanics and technologies of 'power' that make the folk and subaltern temples more popular than the Sanskritic temples.

Power as Governing Relationships between God- God, God-Man and Man-Man

Conceptions of power operate not only in god-man and man-man relationships, but also in god-god relationships. Wadley maintains that, according to Indian conceptions, all beings are filled with some degree of power or the other. Gods also differ in their possession of power. Some embody more powers than others. Thus, there is a hierarchy of deities in terms of power. A deity of small and limited powers is, in many senses, as much under the control of higher, more powerful beings as men believe they themselves are. If a given deity can cause conditions of distress and another can remove them, then the latter can undo the actions of the latter of the former and can therefore be regarded as more powerful.

Similarly gods of varying degrees of power can enrich or control the different aspects of human life. As gods are understood as embodied powers, i.e., substance as well as power, human's interaction with them involves transaction of substances. Many transactions in the Hindu world involve substance-receiving substance, giving substance, "exchanging" substance. Because giving is valued over receiving, men must not only give to the gods (in services and food), but also receive from them. This explains the logic of '*prasātam*', the leftover of offerings made to the gods and returned to the worshipper after the gods have taken their share.[55] While the consumption of these leftovers reiterates the worshiper's lesser status, it also provides a means to appropriate the power of gods.

Conceptions of power operate also between man and man relations in Indian society. Men are also powerful beings in one way or another. They too are born with their share of powers of the universe. They too can alter their substance and thereby their powers through various means. Within the caste hierarchy, as intermediaries between men and god, Brahmins are more powerful than others, while Dalits are the least powerful. In general, Brahmins obtain more power than others *by birth* (action in their previous lives), although they must continue to maintain and increase these powers by correct actions in this life. In contrast, the village *cāmiyāṭi(s)* obtain their powers through their actions in this life, by manifesting the deity to others through 'possession'. Through his mediating role of intervention through divination, which helps the devotees to overcome crises in life, he becomes more powerful than others.

Direct Relationship between Power and Purity

Basing her study on 'Karimpur village', Wadley maintains that "purity and power" are two inseparable factors of any ideas of "being" or action in Hindu thought. One's quantum of power in this life and one's quantum of purity are both based on one's actions (*karma*) in previous lives. Thus Brahmins are both the most powerful beings and the most pure beings. The *avarnas* are the least powerful and the most impure. In this life, when one's bodily substance is believed to undergo transformations through ritual or non-ritual transactions, one's power and purity likewise change. After the sacred ceremony the male twice-born obtains an increase in both power and purity. On account of marriage, the woman receives power and purity of her husband's family.[56] The food consumed can likewise increase or decrease one's purity and hence one's power. Even the power of gods is connected to their purity- those with the most influence tend to be the most pure. Both power and purity jointly determine the hierarchical relationships.[57] The present research considers this view as something belonging to the classical Hindu tradition, and makes an attempt to show how the case is a different with folk religions and their ritual power.

Foucault's Framework of Power

Another analytical device that the study has employed to analyse the ritual power is that of Foucault's insights into the dynamics of power. Some of the dominant ideas that are used here are as follows.

Power as a Productive Multifunctional Network

For Foucault, the relations of power in its true nature are, above all, productive. It is a productive network that runs through the whole social body. Power cannot be reduced to an apparatus of control. It traverses and produces things; it induces 'pleasure', forms knowledge and creates discourses. In fact, power is multifunctional; it 'excludes', it 'represses', it 'censors', it 'abstracts', it 'masks' and it 'controls'. It produces domains of truth and rituals of truth.[58] The study will show how the ritual power of CM has generated different multifunctional networks of power that extend its domain of influence beyond the religious realm.

Capillary Form of Power

For power to exist from above to below, there has to be a capillarity 'from below to above' at the same time. It means that power from above must have as its "condition of possibility a rooting in forms of behaviours, bodies and local relations of power which should not be seen as a simple projection of central power."[59] The capillary forms of power are conspicuously manifest in the very structure and organisation of the cult of CM, in its ritual network and in the celebration of *koṭai* wherein almost all castes (the dominant as well as the subordinate) have one role or the other to play, to a greater or lesser extent, in constituting, maintaining and continuing the cult of CM.

The Plebeian Aspect of Power

The plebeian aspect resides in the social body. It operates as a counterstroke to power. Plebian quality is "everywhere in a diversity of forms and extensions, of energies and irreducibilities. This measure of *plebs* is not so much what stands outside relations of power as their limit, their underside, their counterstroke that which responds to every advance of power by a movement of disengagement. Hence it forms the motivation for every new development of networks of power."[60] Folk religions such as CM can be considered as an instance of a plebeian aspect to the networks of power of Brahminism and its Sanskritic Hinduism. They provide the subalterns with the alternative keys of divine power, not only for tackling by themselves the contingencies of human living directly and overtly, but also for countering the hegemony of caste hierarchy indirectly and overtly, in subtle and symbolic ways.

Power as Relations

From the Foucaultian perspective, 'power' means relations, open, a more or less orgainsed, hierarchical and co-ordinated cluster of relations. Power is co-extensive with the social body. Relations of power are interwoven with other kinds of relations.[61] In Indian village contexts, the structure of power manifests and exercises itself in the hierarchical caste relations. Besides, power is exercised through economic and religious relations. At the social level, the relations of power are not at all, all that hidden as in the Foucaultian framework, but this does not totally rule out the possibility of hidden relations of power that come to the fore in the ritual context.

Power: Both a Matter of Domination and of Capacity

Foucault considers power as a matter of domination, not of capacity.[62] But the caste-based power network of Indian villages demands that power be considered not only as a matter of domination but of capacity too. It is because power as domination derives itself from power as capacity vested with the hierarchy of immutable caste structure. High castes have more wealth, more land, more freedom, etc., as compared to the lower caste people. Accordingly, power is not only exercised over others but also over things. To put it more accurately, power in caste hierarchy means more possibility of domination over others, or greater capacity to convert this power into things like wealth, land, other assets, etc. Thus, we understand that power refers to both, the domination over other people, as well as the control over things.

Rituals as Locale for Power

"The techniques, technologies or strategies of power" exist in no other place but as fixed in "rituals". Rituals generate the body as the "space" where minute and local social practices are linked, or put in relation, to the larger-scale organisation of power.[63] For Foucault it is the "meticulous rituals of power" that produce a body that internalises and reproduces the schemes that localise power. The body is not only invested with and defined by power relations, but the body itself is transformed by the changes in the way power relations are ritually constructed in it. Power is neither a matter for coercion nor a thing to be possessed, but deployed by particular institutions. It resides only in practices themselves, that is, in the strategic acts of the social body. [64]

Bourdieu's View of Symbolic Power

Bourdieu explains 'symbolic power' not so much as a specific type of power, but rather as an aspect of most forms of power, as they are routinely deployed in social life.[65] For, in the routine flow of day-to-day life, power is seldom exercised as an overt physical force; it is transmuted into a symbolic form, and thereby endowed with a kind of legitimacy that it would not otherwise have. Symbolic power is an 'invisible' power which is 'misrecognition' as such and thereby 'recognised' as legitimate. The expressions 'recognition' and 'misrecognition' play a significant role. They underscore the fact that the exercise of power through symbolic exchange always rests on a foundation of shared belief. That is, the efficacy of symbolic power pre-supposes certain forms of cognition or belief, in such a way that even those who benefit least from the exercise of power participate, to some extent, in their own subjection.[66] They recognise or tacitly acknowledge the legitimacy of power, or of the hierarchical relations of power in which they are embedded; and hence they fail to see that the hierarchy is, after all, an arbitrary social construction that serves the interests of some groups more than others. To understand the nature of symbolic power, it is therefore crucial to see that it presupposes a kind of active complexity on the part of those subjected to it. Dominated individuals are not passive bodies to which symbolic power is applied. Rather, symbolic power requires, as a condition of its success that, those subjected to it believe in the legitimacy of power and the legitimacy of those who wield it.[67]

An Interpretative Framework on Ritual Power

In this section we locate 'ritual power' in the phenomenology of power as proposed by Holdrege at the Santa Barbara Conference on Ritual and Power, as mentioned earlier. Distancing herself from most theorists who work on two-fold axes of sacred power (vertical axis) and socio-political power (horizontal axis),[68] she proposes a phenomenology of power that distinguishes among four different dimensions of power: ontological, existential, material and socio-political. It is to be noted that the term 'dimension' is preferred to 'types', as these various dimensions "do not constitute fixed, strictly bound categories, but rather are fluid, permeable and overlapping."[69] The different characteristics of power which we have described fall into one of these dimensions, while some of the other characteristics have to do with more than one dimension.

Ontological Dimensions of Power

The ontological dimensions of power are constituted of those aspects of power that are conceptualised by a religious tradition as inherent in the very nature of 'sacred' reality. The sacred reality can be considered as transcendent and/or immanent. Accordingly, as Holdrege observes, this power can be characterised as the absolute ground of all power beyond the relative world (Omnipotent Allah or Yahweh), cosmic power of creation, maintenance, and destruction (Hindu concept of *cakti*), an all-pervading cosmic ordering principle (Taoist conception of *Tao)*. In different religious traditions rituals are believed to have power that can serve a variety of functions. In some instances, rituals are utilised for the appropriation of this ontological power internally to catalyse existential transformations of consciousness, while in other occasions rituals are appropriated for the harnessing of its potential externally to attain specific material and socio-political ends.[70] In this perspective, ontological power is viewed as the encompassing category of which the existential, material, and socio-political dimensions of power represent different expressions. Needless to mention that ontological dimensions of power are the basis for any ritual power in any religion.[71]

Existential Dimensions of Power

When ontological power is appropriated at the level of individual human existence, it brings about a variety of existential dimensions of power, in which an individual or community embodies and radiates what is termed as 'charisma' by Max Weber. The Hindu *yogin,* the Taoist sage, and the *shaman* of folk religions, etc., manifest in varying ways the personal acquisition of ontological power. These individuals who embody such existential power represent the convergence of sacred and socio-political power. Rituals of different kinds in different religious traditions constitute one of the primary means to appropriate ontological power in order to attain various kinds of existential transformations in varying degrees.[72]

In our study, the aspects of power such as '*power as governing relationships between god-god, god-man and man-man,*' '*Cakti: A power of unification*', which are described in our theoretical framework, have to do more with the existential dimension of power.

Material Dimensions of Power

The material dimensions of power encompass any manifestation of power that is embedded in concrete structures of the relative, material world and objects, whether natural or man-made. This category contests the two-axes model, and overcomes the bifurcation of the vertical and horizontal axes of power. It includes the ontological power invested in particular objects, whether natural or manmade, as well as the socio-economic power.

Rituals that aim at garnering the material dimensions of power comprise "any type of ritual practice that involves the maintenance, manipulation or control of the material realm, including rituals that seek to perpetuate the natural order or to attain some specific material end such as wealth, fertility or good health."[73]

Many of our descriptions on different understandings of the Indian view of power refer to the material dimensions of ritual power. They are 'primacy of places and objects in power,' 'power as wind: a symbol of movement,' 'power as embodiment' and 'power as heat.' They all belong to the *material dimension of power* related to that of the human body or of inanimate things.

Socio-Political Dimensions of Power

The socio-political dimensions of power envelope the social structures, institutions, and practices, together with their ideological representations, that control and sustain power relations both within and among different groups in the social hierarchy. The conceptualisation of this type of power implicitly challenges the autonomy of the vertical axis of sacred power by giving precedence to the socio-political foundations of power. Looked at from this perspective, the ritual practices can be shown to legitimate and sustain the hegemony of dominant classes in religious or social hierarchy, as well as to reaffirm or raise the status of other "upwardly mobile" groups.[74] Some ritual practices "may involve strategies of domination whereby asymmetrical relations of power within a society are inscribed in the 'social body' of its constituent members (Bell) or legitimated through ideological discourse (Pollock)."[75] In contrast, there are also other rituals that are employed to resist, and to empower otherwise powerless, marginalised groups within the larger social order. The plebeian aspects of ritual power of the CM cult, which we have discussed earlier, refer to such kind of rituals.

Besides, there are other characteristics of our theoretical frameworks of power that belong to this dimension: the aspect of 'direct relationship between power and purity' (Indian view of power), 'power as relations' (Foucault's view of power), symbolic power (Bourdieu's view of power) are some of them. As regards the aspect of 'direct relationship between power and purity', no doubt, it has its foundations in socio-political dimensions of power. Hence any ritual that aims at promoting and maintaining purity is expected to have more ritual power in the social realm than other rituals. But this will be contested in our study. *Koṭai* rituals indicate that even those rituals which have to do with the impure realm can also be regarded as powerful, and as such can be employed not only by the marginalized as described above but also the dominant castes (Brahmins). Thus our data on *koṭai* ritual reveal different hidden scripts of social economic foundations of ritual power.

Further, it has to be mentioned that some characteristics of power in our theoretical frameworks of power overlap between different dimensions described here. Rituals have 'ritual power' because they function as mediating categories between ontological dimension and existential dimensions- and this existential dimension of ritual power makes it a productive multifunctional network of power (to employ Foucault's expression) operative at socio-political level, and thus ritual power obtains a socio-political dimension of power too.

Further, our description of 'power both as a matter of domination and of capacity' (Foucault's view) belongs both to the material dimension as well as to the socio-political dimension mentioned here. This type of power has its roots in the material dimensions and has its influence and repercussions on the socio-political dimensions of power. The appropriation of the ritual power of the CM cult by different social actors such as Maṟavar(s) Brahmins and Paḷḷar(s), as we will see, have their origin as a matter of domination and capacity *in the material dimension* (such as lands, robbery, etc.), but eventually produce new truths of rituals in some cases (Brahmins) and, in other cases (Dalits), re-inscribes old ritual of truth *in the socio-political dimension of power.*

Socio-Phobics: A Theoretical Framework on Fear

As fear is one of the key concepts that informs the dynamics of CM, for that matter any folk religious phenomenon, 'understanding of fear' can play a vital role not only in understanding the various ritual dimensions of the cult, but the systems of meaning the folk subscribe to it and the surplus of meaning it can generate in the social realm.

'Socio-phobics' as proposed by Scruton et al. attempts to articulate a socio-cultural model for understanding fear. It works on a logic that fear, as an emotional and individual human behaviour, "no matter how personal and internal it may appear, can be effectively related to that fact that we are a social animal and are found to live only in a cultural milieu".[76] Socio-phobics refers to:

> [T]he study of human fears as these occur and are experienced in the context of the socio-cultural systems humans have created, lived in, been shaped by, reacted to for numberless millennia. We propose that human

> fears are most efficiently understood as social phenomena. Fearing is an event that takes place in a social setting. It is performed by social animals whose lives and experiences are dominated by culture, that complex set of patterns of learned behaviour that sets us apart from the rest of the beasts.[77]

In other words, fear is a social act which occurs within a cultural matrix. 'To fear' and 'to be afraid' are social events which have social consequences. Fearing, as a cultural mode, can serve important social functions of conformation and adherence to compelling values and norms. It raises questions not only like 'what is the part that fear plays in one's life', but more importantly 'what is the function of fear in the community's ongoing existence'.

Socio-phobics fundamentally reveals 'fear' as an act of intra-personal and often interpersonal communication that conveys significant cultural meanings.[78] "The techniques through which this is accomplished are of cultural origin, and are powerfully influenced by cultural habits and expectations."[79]

Cultures produce, communicate and manage fear. "Cultures can create institutions, supported by fear and situations defined by fear, actions to be feared, persons to be feared, and events to be feared."[80] Fears deal with basic but great issues of human life arising from the necessity one faces of adjusting to oneself, to other humans, and to the natural world. Fear alerts one to immediate life hazards. When one is born into a culture, one automatically imbibes the boundaries of symbolic geography of a particular culture. In this symbolic universe one discovers its systems of cues and meanings that feature areas of threat, places of dangers and times of terror. When one fears an object, one commits oneself to the cultural conclusion and responds to it through the culturally designed idioms of behaviour which announce the society's belief systems and show that, by experiencing and expressing this feeling, one shares the socially constructed principles of fear.

Thus fears are created by society for its own purposes. Some consider fear as an instrument and adjunct of social life.[81]

Scruton regards fearing as an art, and "learning this social skill is a vital part of an individual's preparation for life. It is part of learning to perceive the nature of reality,"[82] as given in a particular society. Fear belongs to the cultural lexicon of emotions, which is peculiar to a society. For Scruton, like language and others emotions, fear serves collective ends. Fear is largely a social product, and such socially constructed fears are not aspects of anxiety.[83] Fear can be viewed as "having the natural proclivity either to transmute into or coalesce with something more socially functional."[84]

Human fears are situational, occurring when culturally defined situations appropriate to fear present themselves. Though fear of evil powers of various kinds is the most toxic of all emotions, it is regarded as inescapable in an agrarian context of the area of our study. Understanding of fear may provide an added measure of control over this toxic situation. Various rituals of the folk religions are not only the common folk's way of analysis of causes of fear but aim to deal with it firmly and eliminate them. While the folk do not articulate the fact that 'fearing is a technique'-"which enables an individual to avoid danger-some threat to his well-being, perhaps to his very life,"[85] yet they attempt to overcome its causes and transcend it through rituals.

Nevertheless, fear in a particular culture is perceived and believed to have "direct objective referents in real relationships, situations, and environmental hazards."[86] No doubt a culture can impose as irrational "a set of fears on their members as ones having bases in objective reality."[87] Since verification of such claims largely depends on 'whose perspective one employs', we focus more on the social implications of such fear rather than on the truth claims of such fears. In other words, we focus on the sociology of fear, not the ontology of fear.

Conclusion

Having introduced the topic, objectives, methodology, and frameworks of reference in this chapter, we are now all set to study the CM cult. But before that, the study will analyse, in the next chapter, the socio-economic profile of the district of Tirunelveli, with a view to explore later on, if any change that took place in the agrarian economy of the district and within the caste hierarchy would have bearing on the dynamics of folk cult such as the CM cult.

Notes

1. Saurabh Dube, *Untouchable Pasts: Religion, Identity and Power among a Central Indian Community 1780-1950*, State University of New York Press, Albany, 1998, 5.
2. *Ibid.*
3. Catherine Bell, *Ritual Theory, Ritual Practice*, Oxford University Press, New York, 1992, 3.
4. Catherine Bell, "The Ritual Body and the Dynamics of Ritual Power," *Journal of Ritual Studies* 4/2 (1990), 299.
5. Cāmiyāṭi literally means 'god-dancer' (cāmi-god, āṭi-dancer). He/she is the one on whom the deity descends. From then on, he/she is said to act on behalf of the deity. He/she is also known as kōmarattāṭi.
6. Cf. Catherine Bell, *ibid.*, 299-314.
7. As mentioned by G Patrick in *Religion and Subaltern Agency*, Department of Christian Studies, University of Madras, Chennai, 2003. 9.
8. Cf., *ibid.*, 9-14.
9. At first consideration, it might seem that Allan Dundes's non-exclusive definition of folk can be applicable to the CM cult that is practised by all caste people. According to him, folk refers to a group which has at least one common factor and that the group "will have some traditions which it calls its own" (as cited by G. Patrick, ibid.). This points to a felt-sense of solidarity among the folk on a common factor. But the problem for the worshippers of CM is that high castes like Brahmins would not acknowledge explicitly that their worship of CM establishes certain solidarity with other lower castes that worship CM elsewhere in the vicinities.
10. Cf. Henry Whitehead, *The Village Gods of South India*, Summit Publications, Delhi, 1976 (1921); W.T. Elmore, *Dravidian Gods in Modern Hinduism*, Asian Educational Services, Delhi, 1984 (1913);

Gnanasekaran, *Nāṭṭārcamayam*, Queri Publications, Coimbatore, 1992, and Thulasi Ramasamy, *Nellaimāvaṭṭa Nāṭṭupura Teyvaṅkaḷ*, World Tamil Research Centre, Chennai, 1985.

11. Cf. Peter Beyer, *Religion and Globalisation*, Sage Publications, London, 1997, 79-81. Peter Beyer uses Luhmann's terms.
12. *Ibid.*, 80.
13. Cf., *ibid.*
14. *Ibid.*, 81.
15. Cf. Bell, "The Ritual Body," 301.
16. *Ibid.*, 302.
17. Barbara A. Holdrege, "Introduction: Towards a Phenomenology of Power," *Journal of Ritual Studies*, 4/2 (1990), 24.
18. *Ibid.*
19. Bell, "The Ritual Body," 310.
20. Bell, *Ritual Theory*, 221.
21. Cf., *ibid.*, 216-21.
22. Let me quote Bell herself "My discussion remains focused on an explicitly theoretical level of reflection about ritual rather than one more linked to ethnographic data." (Bell, *Ritual Theory*, 4.)
23. Susan S. Wadley, *Shakti: Power in the Conceptual Structure of Karimpur Religion*, Munshiram Manoharlal Publishers, New Delhi, 1985, 10.
24. Cf. G. Aloysius, *Religion as Emancipatory Identity*, New Age International Publishers, New Delhi, 1998, 3.
25. *Ibid.*, 4.
26. Cf. Sanmugasundaram, *Cuṭalaimāṭan Vaḻipāṭu*, Kavya, Bangalore, 1997.
27. Cf. Elmore, *Dravidian Gods* ; Thulasi Ramasamy, *Nellaimāvaṭṭa Nāṭṭupura Teyvaṅkaḷ*, Whitehead, *The Village Gods*; also Gnanasekaran, *Nāṭṭārcamayam*.
28. Dr. Thulasi Ramasamy, who wrote the first book on the folk cults of the district of Tirunelveli, also supported this view of mine in a personal discussion.
29. Marie-Louise Reiniche, *Les dieux et les hommes: étude des cultes d'un village du Tirunelveli, Inde du sud*, Mouton, Paris, 1979.

30. Besides these methods of direct data collection, the researcher has made use of various other methods by which he has sifted, analysed and reported the data in the study. Some of such methods are iteration and triangulation. Iteration involves a succession of interactions and question-and-answer cycles between two worlds, models and orientations (Cf. Norman K. Denzin and Yvonna S. Lincoln eds., *Collecting and Interpreting Qualitative Material,* Sage Publications, Thousand Oaks, 1998, 186.). In the current research it involves iterations between three different worlds: the world of the researched (the field of study), the world of the researcher and the world of ideas. Triangulation involves the use of multiple data sources, multiple investigators, multiple theoretical perspectives, multiple methods or all of these (Cf. Thomas A. Schwandt, *Qualitative Inquiry,* Sage Publications, Thousand Oaks, 1997, 163).
31. *Ibid.,* 10.
32. Cf. W.B. Shaffir and R.A. Stebbins, eds., *Experiencing Fieldwork: An Inside View of Qualitative Research,* Sage, Thousand Oaks, CA, 1991.
33. Cf. Bernard Russell, *Research Methods in Anthropology,* Altamira Press, New Delhi, 1995.
34. Cf., Ibid.
35. Cf. Norman K. Denzin, *The Research Act,* McGraw-Hill, New York, 58.
36. D. Fetterman, *Ethnography Step by Step,* Sage Publications, California, 1989.
37. *Ibid.,* 336.
38. Mustafa Embirbayer and Jeff Goodwin, "Network Analysis, Culture and the Problem of Agency," *American Journal of Sociology* 99/6 (1994), 1411-1454.
39. *Ibid.,* 1411.
40. Cf., *Ibid.,* 1411-1412.
41. Cf., *Ibid.,* 1418.
42. Narrative research has become a significant part of the repertoire of the social sciences. It has earned a place in various disciples such as psychology, psychotherapy, education, sociology, anthropology, and history and gender studies. For example, on women's issues Cf. Gluck & Patai , *Women's Words: The Feminst*

Process of Oral Hisotory; Josselen, *Finding Herself: Pathways to Identity of Women*; on psychology and education Cf. Capps & Ochs, *Constructing Panic: The Discourse of Agoraphobia*; for sociology read Nelson, *Narratives from the Crib*.

43. Amia Lieblich *et. al*, *Narrative Research*, Sage Publications, New Delhi, 1998.

44. This process of combination of both the structural and content perspective is already noted by Amia Lieblich in the book *Narrative Research* in the final chapter, Cf., 168-172.

45. Cf. ibid. and W.M.C. Runyan, *Life Histories and Psychobiography: Explorations in Theory and Method*, Oxford University Press, New York, 1984,

46. The Proceedings of the Santa Barbara Conference on 'Ritual and Power' held in 1988 are recorded in the *Journal of Ritual Studies* 4/2 (Summer 1990). Different essays from this issue have been cited in this chapter.

47. Abbot notes that creative, dynamic force or power is present in everything visible and invisible, in things animate and inanimate. "It pervades everything assuming a separate entity in individual things in which it becomes a transmissible personality" (J. Abbot, *The Keys of Power*, Methuen & co, London, 1932, 3).

48. Cf. Sarah Caldwell, *Oh Terrifying Mother*, Oxford University Press, New Delhi, 1999, 16.

49. The vātam or wind in the body is believed to be responsible for the nervous system and for the nervous diseases

50. Cf. Susan S. Wadley, ed., *Powers of Tamil Women*, Manohar, New Delhi, 1991, 23-4.

51. Cf. Isabelle Nabokov, *Religion Against Self: An Ethnography of Tamil Rituals*, Oxford University Press, New York, 2000, and Wadley, *ibid*.

52. Nabokov, *Religion Against Self*, 20.

53. Through this, they seek undisputed divine sanction for their role as cāmiyāṭis, and justify and consolidate their position as such.

54. Caldwell, *Oh Terrifying*, 16.

55. Wadley, Sakti, 152-153.

56. *Ibid*., 186-7.

57. *Ibid*.

58. Michael Foucault, "Truth and Power," in *Power and Knowledge:Selected Interveiws and other Writings –1972-1977*, ed. C. Gordon, Pantheon Books, New York, 1980.

59. Foucault, "The Confession of Flesh", in *Power and Knowledge*, 201.

60. Foucault, "Power and Strategies", in *Power and Knowledge*, 138.

61. Kritzman, ed., *Michael Foucault*, Routledge, New York, 1990.

[62] J.G. Merquier, *Foucault*, Fontana Press, London, 1985, 109-10.

63. Cf. Hubert L. Dreyfus and Paul Rainbow, *Michael Foucault: Beyond Structuralism and Hermeneutics*, University of Chicago Press, Chicago, 1982, 111.

64. Cf. Michael Foucault, *Discipline and Punish: The Birth of the Prison*, trans. A. Sheridan, Vintage, New York, 1979 and Hubert L. Dreyfus and Paul Rainbow, 109-119.

65. Cf. Pierre Bourdieu, *Language and Symbolic Power*, Polity Press, Cambridge, 1991.

66. Cf., *ibid.*

67. Cf., *ibid.*

68. The problem with these theories is that, in conceptualizing power and its relation to ritual, scholars tend to give prominence to one axis or the other. For instance, Gerardus van der Leeuw and Mircea Eliade emphasise the sacred dimension of power with little focus on the socio-political implications, while Rene Girard, Jean Comaroff and others have interpreted the power dynamics of ritual primarily in socio-political terms.

69. Holdrege, 'Introduction,' 8.

70. *Ibid.*, 9.

71. The folk religious traditions lay more emphasis than the major religions on the immanent nature of this ontological dimension of the sacred power, which is blatantly manifest during the time of festivals like koæai. This is not to deny their belief in the transcendental nature of the deity, which is a basis for the efficacy for its ritual power. Only an ontological power, which is transcendent, can have the power of encompassment as we see in the case of CM. Only such a god can ensure the efficacy of rituals performed for him. Because he/she is transcendent and ontological, his power can be made available through rituals, which are immanent and material.

72. Holdrege, 'Introduction, 9-10.

73. *Ibid.*, 10.

74. *Ibid.*, 11.

75. *Ibid.*

76. David L. Scruton, *Sociophobics:An Anthropology of Fear*, Westview Press, Boulder & London, 1986, 1.

77. *Ibid.*, 9.

78. *Ibid.*, 33.

79. *Ibid.*

80. *Ibid.*, 101.

81. *Ibid.*, 43.

82. *Ibid.*

83. Fear is focused, anxiety is not. Fear is specific, anxiety generalized. Anxiety is a state of unidirectional arousal following the perception of threat, or as an unresolved fear, 63.

84. Scruton, *Sociophobics*, 69.

85. *Ibid.*, 33.

86. *Ibid.*, 117.

87. *Ibid.*

CHAPTER 2

BACKGROUND OF THE STUDY

Introduction

This chapter endeavours to set the background for the understanding of the field of research, i.e., the villages under study and their people, by locating them against the wider context of Tirunelveli district. The chapter consists of two parts: Part I, "Socio-economic Profile of Tirunelveli District: Past and Present" and Part II "A Profile of the Villages under Study."

The first part, "Socio-economic Profile of Tirunelveli District: Past and Present," is composed of two sub-sections. The first sub-section, "Tirunelveli District: The Past" attempts to reconstruct the historical past of the Tirunelveli region based on archival materials. It does this by focusing on "land and its ownership" and on the related issues of "property rights" (*paṅku* and *paṭṭam*). For this purpose, it employs David Ludden's classification of land in the district into "wet zone", "dry zone" and "mixed zone," as each zone gave an impetus to different patterns of landownership. This part further delves into how the new measures of rationalisation of the land revenue system by the British during the nineteenth century such as *ryotwari* system had to be altered to fit into the cultural mosaic of the political economy of the region, on the one hand, and how it triggered, among various social actors, different kinds of initiatives for acquisition of land in different zones, on the other. It also deals with some of the new measures, undertaken in the Post Independence era to bring about equal distribution of land by providing it to the weaker sections of society.

The second sub-section "Tirunelveli District: The Present", based on the findings of census data, discusses the changing dynamics of the present Tirunelveli district, and the villages and Dalits. In its analysis, it focuses on urbanisation and literacy, and moves on to discuss the growth of such variables as general population, cultivators, agricultural labourers, household activities and marginal labourers in order to identify the changes taking place in the rural life of these villages. It does so by placing the micro within the macro context, situating the villages within the district and the district within the state context.

The second part, "A Profile of the Villages under Study," is the firsthand data of the villages under study collected through social survey, personal interviews with the villagers, and through participant observation.

Part–I

Socio-economic Profile of Tirunelveli District: Past and Present

Tirunelveli District: The Past

Tirunelveli district, established as an administrative unit by the East India Company, was successively part of the erstwhile kingdoms of Te<u>n</u>pāṇtināṭu of the early Pāṇtiyas, Muṭikoṇṭa Cō<u>l</u>amaṇṭalam of the Imperial Cō<u>l</u>ā(s) and Tirunelveli Cīmai of the Nāyakās.[1] The name "Tirunelveli" derives from three Tamil words, i.e., "Tiru- Nel-Vēli" to mean "Sacred Paddy Hedge."[2] Of course, like many other names in the Tamil country, this name is also based on a popular myth.[3]

A Brief Historical Sketch

The writings of Megasthenes, the Greek ambassador, and later on, those of other foreign travellers, make mention of the rule of the Pāṇtiya kingdom in this area during the first half of the first millennium of the Christian era. The Pāṇtiya king Neṭu-ñe<u>l</u>iya<u>n</u> who ruled round 210 C.E. was a popular ruler. The

Pāṇtiya rule continued till the end of the 15th century, with intermittent short spells under the Cōēā and the Muslim regimes. In 1063 C.E., the Tirunelveli territory was conquered by Rācēntra Cōḻā, who governed for a short period, and after his rule, the area passed on to the Muslims of Delhi Sultanate of the Tuklaks. Under their rule it was part of Madurai Sultanate, whose rulers were Uluk Kāṉ, Asaṉ Sah and Utaiyi. They kept it under their regime till 1365 C.E. The Pāṇtiya ruler Tāvē was helped by the Vijayanagar kings to regain power by 1520 C.E. But the Pāṇtiya dynasty was ousted by the Nāyakās of Vijayanagar. The Nāyakās ruled Tirunelveli areas from Madurai as their capital during the 16th-17th and the early part of the 18th centuries. The irrigation system found in the district owes its origin to the Nāyakā rulers. Nākamā Nāyak and his son Viāwanātā Nāyak were important rulers. Rāṇi Maṅkammāḷ ruled this area from 1689 to 1704 C.E. as representative of the Vijayanagar kings. The last ruler of the Nāyakās died in 1731 C.E and after that the area fell into the hands of the Muslims, whose power lasted till 1805 C.E. During the Nāyakā rule, Poligars or feudal chiefs were well established and had a firm foundation for their power. With the fall of the Nāyakās, the territory passed on to the hands of Carnatic Nawāps in 1736 C.E. Mohamat Ali and Cantā Sākip were the claimants to the throne of Carnatic, in which were included the territories of Madurai and Tirunelveli. The British supported Mohamat Ali while the French allied with Cantā Sākip, giving rise to a series of conflicts in this part of the country. During the latter half of the 18th century, the East India Company was frequently at war with the Poligars on behalf of the Carnatic Nawāps in Tirunelveli and Madurai. With the fall of Tippu in 1799, the British intensified their forces in the south and suppressed the Poligars. By that time the Nawāps, who became powerless passed on the management of the territory to the British under a treaty in 1801. Thus started the British rule which lasted till 1947. [4]

Geographical Description

The Census Handbook 1991 mentions that this is the only district having all types of lands described by Tamil poets in ancient Tamil Literature. The scholars have classified the land surface of the district into five kinds:[5]

1. Kuṟiñci - Hills-Some parts of Tenkasi and Ambasamudram Taluks
2. Mullai - Forest - Shengottai Taluk
3. Marutam - Field-Tirunelveli and Ambasamudram Taluk
4. Neytal - Seashore-Radhapuram Taluk.
5. Pālai - Desert-Some parts of Radapuram Taluk

The river Tamiraparani that flows over the land makes it very fertile. The main crop of this district is paddy. In some of the areas, sugarcane and plantain are cultivated. The general appearance of Tirunelveli is said to have changed greatly in the eighteenth century "owing to destruction of jungles and of trees of all kinds to make room for a rapidly extending cultivation under British encouragement."[6]

Land and its Ownership

As "owning of land" is of great significance for one's individual identity or a community's collective identity in the rural agrarian economy, an inquiry has to be made not only into how different social/caste groups acquired ownership of land in the history of the district, but also how different types of lands gave rise to different types of ownership among various social/caste groups.

Different Types of Lands

Tamils divide agricultural lands into two main categories, *naṉcai and puṉcai. Naṉcai* refers to the irrigated, wetland; and, the unirrigated, dry land is named *puṉcai*. Each of these categories of cultivation supports its own staple grain, rice or millet. In the Tamil tradition, *naṉcai* stands for the good and prosperous life, and *puṉcai* for meagre subsistence.[7] For this study on Tirunelveli district, we have adopted three categories of land, following David Ludden: The Wet Zone, The Dry Zone and the Mixed Zone,[8] so as to explore how human habitats shaped up in this area over a period of time.

The Wet Zone

As expected, the first and core agricultural settlements took place in the wet zone, clustered along the length of the Tamiraparani and the Chittar rivers. During the Pāṇtiya period of rule, i.e., before 1300 C.E., seasonal dams, short channels, and tanks were made, and *Pramatēyam*(s)[9] were created in the wet zone of Tamiraparani River valley. The major caste groups at that time were the landowning Veḷḷāḷar(s) and Brahmins; and the Paḷḷar(s), Paṟaiyar(s), Vaṉṉiyar – the agricultural labourers.[10] In the wet zone, the irrigated agriculture developed under the Veḷḷāḷar-Brahmin alliance, through which high-caste landowners brought under their control land, labour, and water.

The irrigating peasant farmers pooled their resources within the *ūr* assemblies[11] from early times, and the village was owned by a group of shareholders, each endowed with a portion of (*pākam*) of the village's collective assets expressed as a fixed number of shares (*pankus*). Owning land within a community of farmers on irrigated land (wet zone) was analogous to membership within an extended family. Families who possessed shares in the village were *Kāṇiyāṭcikkāraṉ* (Tamil; literally "controlled"); in the Anglo-Indian official lexicon they became known as *mirāsitār(s)*.[12] The expanding paddy culture attracted a few outside castes and groups such as non-Tamil Brahmins, Vaṭugā(s) and a few Cānār(s) who, by making use of the institutional means of ritual honour, could obtain rights to village resources. Court records show that by the nineteenth century, it was possible for high castes other than Veḷḷāḷa(s) and Brahmans to own shares.[13]

From Pāṇtiya to British times, village *mirāsitār(s)* in wetland areas were powerful people in and through whom the state worked. *Mirāsitār(s)* became official revenue contractors and merchants; indeed, *mirāsitār(s)* were "the government in the wet zone, not only at village level; they and their caste stratum peers comprised the sub regional ruling class."[14] As this group prospered, they became more and more detached from agricultural labour, and to own a land in the villages of wet zones meant overseeing its productive use, foreseeing its productive potential, and seeing that the irrigation works were built, repaired and managed properly. Thus it came to be that one of the words used for land and land right in Tamil was "kāṇi" meaning to oversee, suggestive of features of landowning among medieval paddy farmers.[15]

As the Vijayanagar Empire collapsed, Nāyakā armies reunited the Tirunelveli region through victories in wars that spanned the sixteenth century. Combined with military might and ceremonial splendour, they ruled from Madurai, while Tirunelveli town became the southern provincial capital, with a fort at Palayamkottai wherein a governor, a *talavāy*[16] (literally 'commander') was enthroned to take care of the region. Under the *talavāy* were two distinct political realms, one the irrigated zone of old Pāṇtiya territories controlled by *mirāsitār(s)*, and the other, the sub-regions commanded by Telugu and Maṟavar chiefs, known as Pāḷaiyakāraṉ(s), or in Anglo-Indian usage, Poligar.[17] The lands of the irrigated zone were to be called *circār*[18] lands, which came directly under the king. Since the sub-regions were under the control of lesser royal authorities, Pāḷaiyakāraṉ, the king, had very little control over the lands in those regions.[19]

The Poligar domains were later known in 19th century as '*zamindaries*'. In his "Geographical and Statistical Memoirs of Tinnelveli and its Zamindaries," Thomas Turnbull mentions about the existence of 28 Zamindaries in the year 1823,[20] among which twelve were under Maîavar chiefs, twelve Telugu chiefs, two Vaṉṉiyaṉ(s), one Ampalam and one Brahmin. The Poligars were more prominent outside the wet-zone political core than they were within it.[21] "Immigrant Telugu and Maṟavar bands carved out domains in the mixed and dry zones, outside core Pāṇtiya territory."[22] The territories of Poligar were considered as tightly organised, militant caste domains. Poligar domains, in general, "were defined by territorial segments linked hierarchically by caste status and military rank.."[23] Overlapping with the caste domains they constituted a military and administrative apparatus that employed a number of castes, linking the Poligar to each village. Poligars divided their territory among their kinsmen and subsidiary chiefs belonging to other castes, called *cērvaikāraṉ*. They owed military allegiance and tribute to the Poligars and demanded the same from village headmen under their control. It is in place to mention that violence was considered as "a legitimate means to establish authority in Poligar territory and struggles by those below to resist demands from above were constant features of order itself."[24]

Dry Zone

In the parched terrain of the dry zones—the Poligar domain, situated north and south of the Tamiraparani, land was abundant and the population could spread thinly over it through the generations. Waves of warrior and peasant migrations[25] were undertaken by Maṟavar chiefs from Ramanathapuram, northeast of Tirunelveli, by Cāṉār(s) from Travancore state, and by Kannada and Telugu-speaking Vaṭugā(s) from the northern peninsula during and after the Vijayanagar empire. They subdued tribes that commanded stretches of dry land between medieval agricultural cores in the Tamil country.[26]

"A farming jati in the dry zone became self-sufficient by necessity. With open space all around, no single caste was in a position to control access to land in the dry zone."[27] Since land owning, work in the fields, and dominance were closely interrelated, "getting one's hands dirty in raising crops conferred relatively high status in the dry-zone cultural economy."[28] As a result, caste did not reify specific roles in the production process and did not play a very dominant role in determining access to the means of production.[29] Hence the biggest landowner and the landless labourers in a village could be of the same caste.[30] In these villages very low-caste families, such as untouchable Paḷḷar(s) and Paṟaiyar(s) could set themselves up as relatively independent peasant households, and their low social status had much less degraded social content here than in the wet zone.[31]

This is not to deny the inequalities in the dry zone in control over productive resources which seems to have risen due to various factors.[32] One of the sources of local superiority was the legacy of hereditary village officers such as headmen (*nāṭṭāmai*) and accountant and the watchman (*kāvalkāraṉ*), all of whom served as links between the local and the central political power. Headmen almost always came from the locally dominant peasant caste.[33] They, like accountants,[34] came from different castes, while *kāvalkāraṉ* were mostly Maṟavar(s) in the dry zone. Officers in the dry zone commanded sizable grants of tax-free (*inām*) land to support their position in the community.[35]

Mixed Zone

The mixed zone both in the north and in the south of Tamiraparani had the characteristics of both, the dry land and the wet land. It was a parched *red* terrain. The landscape over the crest of the Tamiraparani valley was everywhere dry, often blown with dust, and a harsh place to inhabit. There were pockets of bright green, more closely spaced to the Ghats, normally supporting one paddy crop each year. There were many wells and tanks that supported garden crops of all types. Besides, coarse millets such as *cāmai* and *varaku*, were the main food grains here.[36] The stature of *mirāsitār(s)* who occupied the land was less secure in the more isolated, less irrigated villages of the mixed zone. Since the value of the land as capital depended on its water supply, the prominence of the elite *mirāsitār(s)* depended on access to water-resourceful land and control of the best drainage for irrigation. Those Brahmin-Veḷḷāḷar elite *mirāsitār(s)* who did not have it were less secure and less powerful than their counterparts who had it in the wet-zone.

The revenue records show that the Veḷḷāḷar *mirāsitār(s)* preferred to work in the land with their own hands more often in the mixed than in the wet zone. There were many non-*mirāsitār(s)* Veḷḷāḷar(s) who worked as tenants on Brahman *mirāsitār* dry lands in the mixed zone. On this dry land of the mixed zone surrounding the irrigated villages, peasant households from various castes could set up dry crop production on this better soil but did not get any irrigation facility, which was under *mirāsitār* control. But the *mirāsitār(s),* supported by Pāṇtiya kings, staked a claim over these lands, and dry land farmers of the mixed zone paid a cash fee called "cvāmibōkam" ('gift for the lord'). This customary fee, that existed till the nineteenth century, indicates that the state authorities continued to patronize the Pāṇtiya elite, the *mirāsitār(s)*, in their dealings with the mixed zone. The *mirāsitār(s)* remained as state agents and revenue intermediaries in *circār* lands of this zone. The Maîavar chiefs who assumed strong positions in the mixed zone had no custom of "cvāmibōkam" payments to *mirāsitār(s)*.[37] Thus "the mixed zone *mirāsitār(s)* from the north to the south were more vulnerable to harsh political winds than their wet-zone counterparts." [38]

Property Right

Two Tamil terms, *paṅku* and *paṭṭam* express the principles of property right in Tamil culture. *Paṅku* means 'share' which refers to rights conferred on the members of a group as in the paradigmatic case of family property. *Paṭṭam* means 'title.' "Rights founded on the *paṭṭam* principle accrue to a person as the recipient of a title from higher authority, be it king or god or both."[39] People in Tirunelveli region applied these principles to build dominant caste domains. Property rights depended on the maintenance of group boundaries and relations of hierarchy among different castes. *Paṭṭam* principle made the high castes the owners of the land and the lower castes the labourers. It reproduced the maintenance of rituals of rank, kept low-caste families in their place and defined low-caste subordinate proprietary status. "Caste boundaries, rituals of ranking, and state grants of entitlement were cultural implements for the social reproduction of rights."[40]

In case of the wet-zone, in medieval times *paṅku* principle was extended to embrace whole irrigated villages, where Brahmins and Veḷḷāḷar families shared village assets under the terms of grants from Pāṇtiya kings.[41] For everyone caste status marked clear social strata within which families shared assets under the authority of *mirāsitār* village shareholders.[42] The village labourers, the Paḷḷar(s) and Paṟaiyar(s) who worked for *mirāsitār* villages shared among themselves a portion of grains of the village harvest and in the provision of labour services. This shows that any failure of crop and any loss in cultivation due to drought or floods, etc., had to be primarily borne by the labour castes as it meant no grains for them to eat, which would have definitely led to aggravation of their poverty.

As regards the dry land, peasants traced their title to land to the Pāṇṭiya kings through the persons of warrior chiefs called "Poligars", who occupied the dry agricultural tracts with their military power along with their followers after 1300. Titles passed through the lineages and dominant sub-castes down to peasants who worked in their land primarily with their own family labour. Lineage and caste factions lined up to define the village power structure, but did not seem to have systematised shareholding in village agricultural production. There was no village grain heap to be divided among labourers, no village irrigation to maintain, nor gang labour[43] organised, the likes of which were found in the wet zone. Families maintained their rights to farmland by working on their own land and defending the territory dominated by their dominant caste alliance.

In the mixed zone, wet and dry traditions confronted each other. *Mirāsitār* sharehold villages saw themselves surrounded by warrior-peasants after 1300. At their border, *mirāsitār(s)* and peasants staked claims to the same land. The former cited entitlements conferred by Pāṇṭiya kings. Dry-farming peasants traced theirs to warrior chiefs and to generations of labour that made the land productive. In such situations of conflict, *mirāsitār(s)*, mostly Brahmins, whose claim rested on prior settlement, superior caste status and periodic support by regional rulers, enjoyed an advantage over the others. The open character of village boundaries enabled *mirāsitār(s)* to claim and hold rights to land throughout the mixed zone cultivated by independent peasant farmers,[44] including Paḷḷar, Maṟavar, and Shanar families who resided in hamlets at some distance from the core *mirāsitār* settlement.

Yet both for *mirāsitār(s)* and for dry-farming peasants alike, the question of right to land control derived from transactions and shared interests between themselves and the rulers. The principle of *paṭṭam* and *paṅku*, which remained in force till the nineteenth century, would cause considerable conflict between the landowners and state officials under the British rule when they wanted to revamp the old system.

Revenue Systems in the District

The revenue system in Tirunelveli district, which was primarily based on the income of agricultural lands, changed over a period and this, in turn, redefined the property rights of the people while exploring new ways of revenue systems to cover new economic realities. Such new initiatives of the revenue system will be dealt with in the following pages.

Pre-British period

During the Nāyakā period, financial transactions that provided state revenues became increasingly prominent in definitions of property right. The practice of payments in cash and in kind which had surely solidified claims to property according to the *paṭṭam* principle under medieval Pāṇṭiya kings were carried out during this period. The terms *naṉcai* (wet land) and *puṉcai* (dry land) in common parlance became one of the very important parameters of the revenue system of lands. Since the characteristic crop of *Naṉcai* was paddy, which had a higher market value, *naṉcai* also meant land assessed by state officials in kind so that the state might profit from sales of its share of the crop, the *mēlvaram*.[45] On the other hand, *puṉcai*, because of its dry crops of low market value, meant, in turn, land assessed at low rates, in cash collected directly by village leaders and paid to state officials. Since Poligar lands were mostly dry, they did not mean much to the Nāyakā revenue system in cash. However, instead of cash, they paid tributes in the form of ceremonial gifts, ritual homage, and, above all, military service. Dry lands and Poligar realms were for the Nāyakās a critical military base but not a lucrative source of revenue.[46]

British Period

When the British officials introduced the *ryotwari* system, the appointment of village officers, mostly from dominant castes, brought its own nuanced specificity into the issue of ownership of land.[47] While for Munro (who introduced the *ryotwari* system) the term '*ryot*' designated all peasants, its application to the peasantry could not be carried out uniformly and indiscriminately by the district collectors of Tirunelveli, as it called for distinguishing between farmers from the wet and the dry zones of Tirunelveli District.

In the village itself, to be a peasant meant much more than paying rent to the state. It entailed caste identity and customary relations of inequality that put each farmer in his place in the local society, which the *ryotwari* theory did not recognise. Similarly it did not take into account the zamindaries who remained little kings for their subjects; they retained the title of *raja* and held customary authority in ritual and caste structures that defined their territorial domains. Even the native officers appointed by the British did not see themselves as mere agents of the new British bureaucracy. Many of them had been "regional" officers much before the new system. They got new opportunities to increase their status in the society by expanding their family resource base, to accumulate wealth, dispense patronage and wield influence in their spheres of action.[48]

One of the important things that took place around this time was the acquisition or purchase of vast tracts of land by the native officers[49] of the Veḷḷāḷar-Brahmin group who had a free hand more in the dry and mixed zones than in the wet zone. About one-third of this land had been acquired after obtaining office.[50] Another important development that took place around this time in the 1860s was the survey of the land. By mapping everything of government interest on the land, it recorded a comprehensive set of rights including that of ownership of lands, both individual and communitarian. "Registration records, settlement records and *paṭṭā(s)* now became absolutely authoritative symbols of ownership."[51] Survey and settlement enabled the state and its officials to make more decisive moves into local affairs, and thus altered the course of conflicts and conflict resolution. This process brought more information, which gave a few low castes fringe benefits to make new claims to liberate themselves from the brunt of social depredations and economic enslavements–a new possibility that emerged as a collateral outcome of the new administrative system, absent in the previous structures.

The champions of change in the village property custom during the nineteenth century British period came from three camps: state officials, leading *mirāsitār(s)* and resourceful tenants. Since *mirāsitār(s)* played a vital role in securing for the new regime in the countryside 'revenue' through agreements between the district officials and the peasants, the powerful *mirāsitār's* were most advantaged both in dry and wet-zones where government showed its commitments to protect the *mirāsitār's* rights.[52]

But the revenue system also brought about new forms of conflict between the *mirāsitār(s)* and the tenants. Though early collectors did issue *paṭṭā(s)* to tenants in the mixed zone as prescribed by the *ryotwari* scheme, the contending *mirāsitār(s)* took the matter to the court, where judges, depending on documentary evidence favoured more often the *mirāsitār(s)* than others. "Resistance by tenants became one of the insecurities that *mirāsitār(s)* faced during the leases and in, fact, became one of the key issues."[53] Where the government officials favoured the *mirāsitār(s)*, the tenants went to the court. Doubtless all this led to a certain amount of conflicts between Revenue and Judicial departments. By the end of the nineteenth century, the leading *mirāsitār(s)*, being influential in government, skilled in the workings of state institutions and financially endowed, were well equipped to benefit from the settlement process. The worst battle between these two groups took place in the case of relatively weak *mirāsitār(s)* particularly from the mixed zone and the strong upstart tenants such as cāṉār(s) and others.[54] When such disputes over the ownership of lands led to social conflict, "[s]tate officers adjudicated disputes, many of which seem to have ended to the distress of poor tenants and poor *mirāsitār(s.)*"[55]

Social Transformations of Nineteenth Century

Commenting on the social changes that took place in the 19th century as a result of government land policies, development works, trade and commercial opportunities, and geographical conditions such as drought, flood, etc., Ludden singles out the dry zone: "[T]he dry-zone agrarian economy experienced most dramatic transformation of all during the nineteenth century."[56] The dry zone, once a barren land, became "the scene of an economic boom that would last through the end of the century and beyond, as its town continued to grow rapidly and to attract workers and investors in trade and small-scale industry."[57] The construction of roads and blooming of cotton trade and its prospects in market and export contributed to its development. This meant a good deal of cash income, which provided:

> [P]easant families with means to pay their own land revenue, and when opportunities for trade and work in town provided income independent of landowning, the social dominance of village officers, having been based for centuries on a segmented agrarian system, must have declined quite substantially from a high point during the eighteenth century.[58]

The formerly subordinate castes moved into new realms of opportunities in the countryside. The dry zone experienced decline of many zamindars who became impoverished compared to upstart agrarian capitalists, "The relative decline of military men–Maṟavar(s)–in the countryside would be but one of the subtle shifts in social relations that would trigger strife in village life,"[59] the significance of which will be important for the present study.

Already, at the end of the 19th century, the social impact of "change" effected by the British began to be felt in this area: aged *mirāsitār(s)* felt that they had lost inherited privilege; high caste patriarchs no longer received the deference enjoyed by their elders; new social upstarts defied and flaunted the ancient rites of respect; the elders of agricultural labour castes would have complained over their loss of rights to serve particular families and to have a share in the village harvest in customary proportions. Now the fate of their future was thrown open to the dynamics of a fickle job market, though in the final analysis it would prove to be more advantageous than the previous system of enslavement based on the rigid caste-system.

During the decades of growing state power of the British rule, the conception of rights introduced into the agrarian system enabled the villagers to change for themselves their assumptions about property rights, as the new system changed the rural distribution of rights to village land. After the mid-nineteenth century, as the urban population expanded, conflicts over rights to urban space and to the public domain reflected a redefinition of caste-relations to state authority. Subtle shifts in social power manifested themselves in conflicts between groups over rights. But in the process of conflict build up and conflict resolution, it did alter the peasant culture's perspective and descriptive ideas about who had what rights in society.[60]

Developments In the Twentieth Century

After the survey of lands in 1861 for the purpose of the *ryotwari* system, once again land was surveyed in 1904, and the settlement was done. The details of what type of social conflicts and societal re-configurations in terms of landownership it brought about, if any, are not available. The absence of such data could perhaps indicate the social *insignificance* of such surveys, though it may be too premature to make such statements without further investigation into the matter. However a significant development that took place in this century was the Nattam survey[61] work done in 1988, in which *paṭṭā(s)* were issued to cultivating farmers on the *puṉcai* land including one lakh SC farmers.[62]

Implementation of the Land Reform Act was another major step undertaken in eradicating inequitable distribution of wealth, as land was an important source of production. In the district of Tirunelveli, an extent of 14,385 acres of land was notified as surplus as of 30th November 1994. Out of this, 14,215 acres of land have been given to 7877 eligible persons,[63] i.e., agricultural labourers. The lands disposed thus far constitute 98.82% of the total lands available for this purpose as against 87% of the state average.[64] While the figures are encouraging on record, they may not always concur with the ground reality, given the role of vested interests in finding loopholes to circumvent the law. Yet, the subtle difference it could have made cannot be ruled out, as quite a few instances indicate, in allotting lands to landless labourers, mostly Dalits,[65] who demanded it in the wake of growing Dalit consciousness in the district.

Some of the benefits of the land-related acts, enacted in the Post-Independence era, impelled by political considerations, have reached the beneficiaries—scheduled castes and scheduled tribes (the primary constituents of the agricultural labourers and rural artisans) much more effectively in this district in the context of the overall picture of the state. For instance, in the implementation of Tamilnadu Agricultural Lands Record of Tenancy Right Act 1969 in Tirunelveli district, the total number of tenants registered for the land were 69,628, out of which 32,850 belonged to scheduled castes and 36,778 to scheduled tribes. They constitute 14% of total beneficiaries of the scheme in the state as of 31st October 1994.[66]

Another significant step in this regard was 'The Tamilnadu Occupants of *Kuṭiyiruppu* (conferment of ownership) Act 1971' which conferred, free of charge, ownership rights of *Kuṭiyiruppu* (home steads) on agricultural labourers and rural artisans. Government paid to the owners of the *Kuṭiyiruppu* a compensation amount on behalf of the agricultural labourers. Its implementation has yielded more encouraging results to the depressed classes in this district than their state-level counterparts. As per the figures available upto 1994, the scheduled caste and scheduled tribe beneficiaries of the scheme at the state level make 56 per cent of the total beneficiaries, and in *Tirunelveli* district they form 76.60 per cent.[67]

The People of Our Study

The Paḷḷar(s)

The Paḷḷar(s), demographically speaking, form 5.5 per cent of the total population of Tamilnadu.[68] This district had the highest number of Paḷḷar(s) in the old Madras Province according to the 1931 survey.[69] Of the total Dalit population in the district, 'Paḷḷar'(s) constitute 56.45 per cent. Since the term 'Paḷḷar' is derogatory, these people prefer the word Maḷḷar or Tēvēntra Kula Vēlāḷar. The word 'Maḷḷar(s)', by which they claim that they are the descendants of the god king Intirā,[70] is found in many of the Tamil literary works from the *Sangam* period, though the expression has become obsolete now.[71]

According to a myth collected by Richards,[72] the sweat of Tēvēntra, one of the chief gods, fell on a plant. On growing, it became the ancestor of 'Paḷḷar'(s) namely, Vadivel Kudumbar. The ancestor had two wives. By the first wife he had four sons who, in turn, were the ancestors of Devendran, Thattaya Nattan, Pandya Nattan and Kadaya Nattan. Through the second wife the minor 'Paḷḷar'(s) such as Kongu, Vettai, Ati, Kalkatti, Vanni, Thavalai Thinni were born. Another myth says that the Maṟavar(s) and 'Paḷḷar'(s) are brothers. Intiraṉ had two daughters. Both of them gave birth to two sons. One daughter delivered the son in a secluded place (*maṟaivilē petu eṭutā*) hence Maṟavar; another delivered the son in a pit (*paḷḷam* in Tamil) hence Paḷḷar.[73]

As regards Tirunelveli district, most of the agricultural labourers in this area are Paḷḷar(s) and Paṟaiyar(s). They settled down in places where Brahmins and Veḷḷāḷar(s) were the land owning castes, according to a 1881 survey, though Paḷḷar(s) approximate the pattern more closely than others.[74] Some consider that these tribal groups, after defeat in wars, became slaves and labourers. "Pandya's[*sic*] wars with tribal chiefs probably procured workers from the defeated populations, because both major landless labour castes–Pallas and Pariahs [*sic*]–boast even today of distant martial traditions, (though) some families from these castes maintained themselves as independent cultivators outside the wet zone."[75] Mackenzie's

Manuscripts takes note of an oral tradition that claims Paḷḷar(s)' as 'mountain people' but settled in the plain.[76]

As labour itself became lowly in the cultural economy of irrigated agriculture, the physical lowliness *(paḷḷam)* of fields and channels (*paḷḷakkāl*) "embodied the lowliness of fieldworkers, known as *paḷḷakkuṭi*-low people–Paḷḷar(s)."[77] Paḷḷar(s) performed a variety of the most gruelling works in paddy cultivation, in building and repairing irrigation works, and in building roads, temples and other structures. They worked under *mirāsitārs* either as families or as a community. Some worked for daily grain wage, paid seasonally or by the task performed. In some villages a Paḷḷar headman would be asked to raise work gangs when needed, for which he would receive special social status by his position.[78] In some villages, the Paḷḷar headman would take care of the entire production process on behalf of an absentee landowner or upon temple land, requiring considerable skills as seen in the seventeenth-century Tamil folk drama, Mukkuṭal paḷḷu.[79]

Besides, Paḷḷar(s), who constituted the vast majority of the poorer tenants, were dependent on *mirāsitār* capital and food advances, and without having capital or crops to repay debts, they would have to repay with family labour. In such situations, many Paḷḷar families became perpetually bonded to *mirāsitār* families or to whole *mirāsitār* villages.[80] "Rights to the labour of Paḷḷar(s) became an asset like any other for shareholders, one that could be bought and sold, given as dowry, and attached to plots of land, an integral part of the soil."[81] In undertaking common tank works and its repairs, the *mirāsitār(s)* paid the Paḷḷar(s), their bonded labourers, at whatever rate they pleased and they always contrived to appropriate a part of the money allowed to their own use. As a British collector remarked, "the execution of repairs has thus become a source of income for the Meerasidars [*sic*],"[82] but at the expense of physical labour of Paḷḷar(s) who were exploited by the *mirāsitārs*.[83]

The new regime of the ryotwari revenue system, by and large, was not favourable to the Paḷḷar(s), because they were not potential sources of revenue for the government. But the subsequent developments through judiciary had some positive but subtle effects on the Paḷḷar labour force. For instance, after 1820, judges denied Paḷḷar claims to security of income and employment in *mirāsitār* villages. But it was a blessing in disguise as "this decision would have had the effect of freeing worker movement and increasing worker competition in labour market."[84] Though the courts could not make labour, such as that of Paḷḷar(s), free to move and seek the market value of its service, yet "the principles of *ryotwari* encouraged judges to make decisions that pushed the legal terms of property transactions toward those of free market, where land and labour become commodities,"[85] the subtle impact of which would be gradually experienced by Paḷḷar(s) during the twentieth century.

The productivity of agricultural lands, even its negative effects, seems to have altered the prospects of Paḷḷar(s). As Jayarathnam and Ravindra K. Jain have observed in separate studies about the Indian migration to the neighbouring Asian countries, when the farmers faced diminishing returns in the district after 1910s and 1920s, many of the landless labouring PaÀÀar families were pushed into exploring labour potentials not only in town but overseas on plantations in Sri Lanka and Malaysia.[86]

Further, the schemes and polices such as 'education to all' (irrespective of caste) and social welfare programmes started by the British Raj and carried forward by the nation state have thrown open opportunities to many of the Paḷḷar(s), to become Government employees, doctors, lawyers, engineers, other professionals and holders of public offices. "The complex of events and intellectual practices inaugurated by colonialism and these transformations had contributed to the so-called '*Panchamas*'[87] acquiring a measure of dignity and self-worth."[88] 'Caste' consciousness enabled by social changes thereupon has uplifted them from tillers to land owners. Caste associations such as "Immanuel Devendarar Peravai" and "Devendra Kula vellalar Peravai" are working for social, educational and economic changes. All along the wet zone of the Tamiraparani basis, today, these people are cultivating the lands as owners and tenants. One of the studies done in this area shows a sharp decline in Brahmin and Veḷḷāḷar landlordism, as they migrated to towns and cities leaving the villages. The villages thus underwent a process of change due to transition from Brahmin and Veḷḷā landlordism to owner cultivation by agricultural castes, mostly the Paḷḷar(s) and Maṟavar(s) "In short the ones who tilled the soil as tenants turned the owners of the soil."[89]

In this what is significant for our present study is the fact that the new measures of the revenue system, the introduction of market economy, the process of industrialisation, etc., introduced by the British had brought about a drastic alteration in the socio-economic cultural mosaic of the district.[90] This process of modernisation threw open new avenues of economic growth for different social actors, though such growth was dependent on different local variables, starting from soil type (dry, wet, and mixed), rain fall, irrigation technology transportation routes, settlements patterns, and market structures. But though the appropriation of such growth processes by different social actors took place within the context of local dynamics of caste hierarchy, largely in favour of people on the top, what cannot be ruled out is the local diversity of social reality brought about by the people on the periphery, especially, the upstart constituency of the oppressed classes, i.e., Paḷḷar(s). What made that possible for these subalterns was the new range of economic options brought about by the schemes of modernisation, such as education and employment opportunities both within the state machinery and in the industries.

The Maṟavar(s)

This district had the highest number of Maṟavar(s) in the old Madras Province.[91] The Maṟavar(s) of Tirunelveli district are said to have moved to this district from the old Ramanathapuram District and they are mostly concentrated in the area from Kalakadu to Sivagiri at the foothills of the Western Ghats. There were a number of Maṟavar *Pāḷayam*(s) (Zamins) in this area. They were Singampatti, Urkkadu, Uththumalai, Vadadaṛai, Surandai, Naduvakurichi,

Chokkampatti, Kurukkalpatti, Alagapuri, Nerkattumseval, Thalaivankottai, Thenmalai (Sivagiri), Kollamkondam, and Sethur. Maṟavar zamindars proved troublesome for the governance. These powerful warrior feudal chieftains disputed with the British for the possession of Tirunelveli during the latter half of the eighteenth century and the beginning of the nineteenth century. These series of confrontations are known as "Poligar wars" in the history of South India.[92] They broke the laws of civil society, resisted efforts by the Court to manage their estates, and fought the government to have the control over hillside forests. Crime, criminal investigations and punishments remained very much a local affair in their hands. Burglary and cattle-lifting are some of crimes they are known for.

However, the general population paid private Maṟavar protection services to secure life and property for villagers and many folks alike in Tirunelveli District through the end of British rule.[93] They were paid for their service and it was estimated way back in 1861 that their emoluments amount to Rs. 1,26,888 partly in *inām* land,[94] partly in grain. They performed both Revenue and Police duties in the villages, besides watching the crops of the villages. Interestingly, it is the same Maîavar(s) who hold the first place amongst the criminal classes of the district. Probably, the reason why they were preferred for protection service was the principle: "Set a thief to catch a thief." One collector observes:

> The Cavilgars [*sic*] of one village never interfere with the watch of those of another. If at anytime, any robbery or theft is committed in one village, by the Maṟavar(s) of another, the watchers of the village....bring the robbers to punishment, because it is considered to be a discredit and disgrace to Cavilgars [*sic*], if a robbery is committed within the limits of their watch.[95]

As a rule, the institution of *kāval* system was willingly supported by the village folk who made annual contributions among themselves towards its maintenance.[96] In return Maîavar *Kāvalkar* secured the protection of sturdy fearless watchmen for his crops and cattle during the night:

> The strength of the system is that it stimulates a corporate life and a feeling of self-reliance and to a great extent prevents crimes; its obvious weakness is that it encourages the people to hush up offences when they occur and provokes retaliation against invading thieves.[97]

No offences to the property could occur without the connivance of the *kāvalkar*(s), but when they did take place, the policemen in search of a clue were often at the mercy of the Maîavar informer.[98] The Maṟavar(s) were so much part of the village system that one collector strongly pleaded for their inclusion in the new police force and recommended that the new police force should work in tandem with them.[99]

Incidental to the post of *Kāvalkar* was the important duty of offering of sacrificial animals on feast days to Cuæalaim□taì and his host of attendant deities not only in their own temples but also in those of other Sudra castes.[100] A regular ritual that often used to precede the "hunting expedition", i.e., burglary, were the offerings made by the Maṟavar(s), the thieves to Cuṭalaimāṭaṉ and Karuppaṉ the night before. Pate describes the ritual as follows:

> [A] crow-bar is placed before the image or *pudam[sic]*, and a promise is made that further offerings will be made in proportion to the fruits of the outing. Omens are looked for anxiously during the ceremony and afterwards; the chirp of a lizard on the left, the hoot of an owl, a cat running across the path from left to right—these things foretell disaster, and expedition must be postponed.[101]

He further notes, "existing as it does in almost every settlement of Maṟavar(s), the demon-temple (Cuṭalaimāṭaṉ temple) serves as a rallying-point for the community... [H]is yearly festivals are celebrated by the Maṟavar(s) on a scale which no other caste can emulate."[102] Each Maṟavar community, as a rule had a *nāṭṭāmai*,[103] whose office was hereditary; "the questions of divorce, of fines in cases of misconduct, and of the apportionment of the amount to be paid in restitution to the victims of thefts came before him for decision."[104] It is in place to note that the role of *cāmiyāṭi* (the shaman) in the CM cult in *aruḷvākku* (divination) emulates that of *nāṭṭāmai*, the semiotic meaning of which will be dealt with in the following chapters.

It must be noted that Poligar rule kept their agricultural labourers, the Paḷḷar(s), in subhuman conditions as the District collector, Lushington observes of the then situation in the beginning of the nineteenth century:

> The Poligars kept the chief part in their own hands and cultivated it with Pullers [*sic*] who received no share of the crops but were daily subsisting with a little dry grain given by the Poligar. As I know that the continuation of such a measure would be repugnant to those principles of general protection and justice.[105]

The Maṟavar population had steadily increased over the years in this district, more rapidly in this district than other districts in the beginning of the twentieth century. A Census of India 1921 report notes, "The Maravas of Tinnelvely [*sic*] have increased by 30% while in Ramanad their numbers have risen 9.2 per cent. ... and in Tinnevely [*sic*] there is a marked fall in the number of Vellalas and of Paraiyans [*sic*] but it is unnecessary if not impossible to regard their increase and these decreases as cause and effect."[106]

The Brahmins

According to the 1931 census data, this district had the second largest Brahmin population in the state.[107] By religious ideology, there are two types of Brahmins, the Saivites and the Vaishnavites. The former are found throughout the fertile part of the district especially in Ambasamudaram, Tirunelveli, Cheranmahadevi and in Sengottai taluks in large numbers. The latter are found in the surroundings of the Vishnu temples in Nanguneri, Thirukkurungudi and Palayamkottai. However, the Brahmins of this district are enamoured of the worship of minor gods and goddesses. As Pate already refers in 1916, some of the Brahmins worship the folk deities such as Cuṭalaimāṭaṉ and kāḷi[108] and others. "The dance in honour of Śāstā which the Brahman himself performs, is not of Vedic origin."[109]

Kjaerholm notes "In Pate's opinion, although the Brahmins are much revered in Tirunelveli, it is rather they who have accommodated local folk religion, than the other way around."[110] Pate himself put this more succinctly "In regard to its spiritual masters aboriginal Tinnevelly has undoubtedly 'led captivity captive'."[111] Gujaratis, Marathis, Telugu and Kanada speaking Brahmins migrated into the district as administrative agents in the expanding Vijayanagar imperial domain. The Brahmins in the district were mostly landowners and temple priests. The high social status they enjoyed in earlier days helped them become a wealthy community. Only a few Brahmins now eke out their living by priestly services. Due to the change in agrarian rural economy, most of the Brahmins have migrated to large towns in other parts of India and abroad. The majority of the Brahmins are engaged in white-collar jobs, as lawyers, doctors, teachers, bank officers and government servants. They have disposed of their lands and houses to non-Brahmin backward and forward communities.[112] However, quite a few still prefer to live in *agraharams* (the streets of the Brahmins so called) around the temples to maintain their identity

Temple in Society

Temples were always linked to usurpation and ascendancy of political power in the Tamil country.[113] As the kingdom expanded, the regalia of temples and their ceremonial repertoire too increased. For instance, when Tirunelveli became the Southern capital of Pāṇtiya kingdom, the Nellaiyappa temple became its ceremonial centrepiece in the south. "Here they recorded their conquests and announced their new Brahmadeyas... they and their followers patronised God, so that four of every five inscriptions in the temple date from the thirteenth and fourteenth century."[114] After the fall of the Pāṇtiya rule, the warriors (called Nāyakās) continued to patronise the temples along with the Veḷḷāḷar-Brahmin elite. "Inscriptions reveal a related rise in warrior initiative in temple management after 1400, and a parallel decrease in Brahmadeya transactions etched into temple walls. It seems then that the relative importance in temple affairs of non-local, non-landed elites rose dramatically under Vijayanagar."[115]

The Nāyakās's affinity with the temples is seen in the appointment of temple officers such as supervisory personnel, accountants and managers, who themselves seem to have become more influential in managing some of the large temples. Brahmadeyas and the precincts of temples, besides being centres of religious activities, were also related to agriculture, craft, trade and commerce. Big temples held annual fairs with large groups of merchants and petty traders. Many festivals associated with the temples too attracted immense trade and commercial activities.[116] Thomas Munro, a British official, reported to British Parliament in 1812 that "in India, religion and trade are sister arts: the one is seldom found in any large assembly without the society of the other."[117]

Temples were also centres of power. By patronising temples and offering gifts to temples people sought to maintain and enhance one's social status. Ludden notes that as late as the nineteenth century, some families claimed this status, and received in turn recognition special honours and favourable tax rates.[118]

> The ritualised exchange-relations that supported temple worship and Brahman communities..... effectively defined criteria for entitlement both wide enough to include all exchanges necessary to develop irrigation and narrow enough to keep paddy culture in the hands of a coherent caste alliance, the core Pāṇtiya elite, mostly made of Veḷḷāḷars. By patronising temples and Brahmans, Veḷḷāḷars established themselves as a status group identifiable by regional dominance and ritual stature, so that ritual became the vehicle for alliances across kinship and territorial divisions. [119]

This shows the fluidity of access to honours in Tamil society and the then ongoing social negotiations for power through claiming of honours by different caste members. As Sudras and lowest caste made attempts to the temple honours through gifts to temples as we see in the temple inscriptions,[120] the high castes including Brahmins began to appropriate the space of the folk religious realm to obtain honour and to establish their social status, as we will see soon.

During the time of rationalisation of the revenue system, when claims to rights came into conflict, to establish any person's position in the property system, the person had to be "located in a group whose collective set of rights could be located in relation to other groups and traced back to a ritual moment of entitlement".[121] As ritual in the major temples was used as a site of power to claim one's right for property and social status by the dominant castes, the same technique was also used by the subalterns in their terrain of folk religious rituals to have access to title and honour conferred upon them not by kings, not through the intermediaries of Brahmin priests, but by their folk gods and goddesses directly without any human mediation.

Tirunelveli District: The Present

In any study of this kind, both, the past and the present are important. While the knowledge of the past shows where the society *was*, the study of the present shows where the society *is* and where it has reached up to. It thus brings out the changing dynamism of the given society. This section attempts to capture that change in Tirunelveli district in the following pages.

Truths Emerging from the Census Data

One of the ways we can perceive the change of a society is to measure the progress of its people in areas like literacy, urbanisation, etc, and by comparing the corresponding figures over a period of time. Since such figures are available in the census data of India taken every ten years, the following pages attempt to analyse the change by comparing some of the figures from the records of 'Census of India.' The tables presented in this section are based on the figures collected, categorised and calculated specially for the purpose of the present study.

Urbanisation in Tirunelveli District

Table 41 of the 1991 census (*District Census Handbook, Tirunelveli, Villages and Town Directories*) shows that the urban population of the district of Tirunelveli for the period of 1991-2001 has gone up by almost 15% per cent, while Tamilnadu's average rate of increase in urban population has gone up by 9 %. It is to be noted that one of the indicators for urbanisation as mentioned in the 2001 census handbook is that at least 75% of the main workers are engaged in non-agricultural and allied activities.[122] The growth rate of urban population among Dalits with 96.80% between 1991 to 2001 in this district is much higher than that of the general population (64.94%) during this same period. The rapid growth rate of urbanisation among the Dalits compared to the general population in the district does indicate the growing impulse among Dalits for economic independence from the agrarian caste-ridden rural economy, as one Dalit informant told the researcher "now our men do not look forward to work in the fields of caste Hindus. Many of us are working in the factories nearby. During harvest, if the high castes offer us good remuneration, then we decide to go there on our own terms, not on their terms as our elders did."[123]

Urbanisation among the Paḷḷar(s)

First, it must be noted that, according to the 1991 census, the Paḷḷar(s) are the second largest Dalit group in the state. While Āti Tirāviṭar(s) make 48.9% of total Dalit population, the Paḷḷar(s) form 17.9 of the total SC/Dalit population. Though the Paḷḷar(s) in the district of Tirunelveli constitute 13.4% of the total Paḷḷar(s) of the state,[124] they are however the major Dalit group in the district of Tirunelveli constituting 56.5% of the total SC population as enumerated in 1991 census.

The above Table (1) shows that the total population growth rate of Paḷḷar(s) in the state between 1961-91 has been 107.46%, registering a difference of almost 40% over the 'All SC population' growth-rate in the state (76.56%). The numerical growth of the Paḷḷar(s) has taken place more proportionately both in the rural and in the urban setting than in the case of other scheduled castes. At the state level its rate of growth

Table 1
Growth of SC Population in Tamilnadu

Tamil Nadu		Total Population			Rural Population			Urban Population		
	Year	Person	Decadal Variation	Var. in %	Persons	Dec. Vari.	Var. in%	Persons	Dec. Vari.	Var. in %
All S/C	1961	6067327			5141487			925840		
	1971	7315595	1248268	20.57	6050302	908815	17.68	1265293	339453	36.66
	1981	8881295	1655700	21.4	7090664	1040362	17.19	1790631	525338	41.52
	1991	10712266	1830971	20.26	8428040	1337376	18.86	2284226	493595	27.56
	61-91			76.56			63.92			146.62
Pallar(s)	1961	950266			829979			120287		
	1971	1326745	376479	39.62	1170499	340520	41.02	156246	35959	
	1981	NA			NA			NA		
	1991	1971391	644646 (71-91)	48.59	1650701	480202 (71-91)		266696	110444 (71-91)	70.68
Paiaiyar(s)	*61-91*			107.46			98.88			121.71
	1961	1513627			1358480			155207		
	1971	1533482	19855	1.31	1343484	-14936	-1.1	189998	34791	22.4
	1981	NA			NA			NA		
	1991	1342281	-191201	-12.47	1114066	-229418 (71-91)	-17.07	228215	38217	20.11
	61-91			-91.32			-17.99			47.04

(98.88%) in the rural area has exceeded that of 'All SC population' during these years, while in the urban setting its growth of 121.71% is 25 % less than that of the SC population in the state. In the case of another important Dalit group in the state, i.e., Paṟaiyar(s), their overall growth has been negative (-91.32%) between 1961-91. They have increased by 47% in the urban areas, while their numbers in the rural settings has gone down by 17.99%. The more equitable distributive growth of Paḷḷar(s) in the state both in the rural and as well in the urban settings explains why they pride themselves as the more powerful Dalit group in the state as the ones who can face up to the onslaught of caste oppression in the rural areas. Perhaps it is their equitable numercical strength that has enabled them to assert their identity much more forcefully than others as we see in the caste clashes in the recent past for the last two decades.

The above Table 2 indicates that the situation of the SC population growth in Tirunelveli district is slightly different from that of Tamilnadu state. The district has experienced only a small growth of the total SC population (3.83 %) from 1961 to 1991. Its rural population has decreased by 1.41% in this period while the urban population has gone up by 29.58%. But in the case of Paḷḷar(s), the people of our study, the percentage rate of their growth (76.81 %) *vis-à-vis* total population (3.83%) is very high. Both the rural and the urban Paḷḷar folk have increased by 83.61 % and 53.61% respectively with a good growth rate. Here again we witness a considerable numerical growth of Paḷḷar(s), on the one hand, and their equal distributive growth both in rural and urban setting on the other, as we see at the state level.

Though the story of population growth is the same, both for the state and for the district as far as the Paḷḷar(s) are concerned, yet a low growth rate of all SC total population in the district between 1961-1991 makes the background different and considerably alters the hermeneutic of the data of Paḷḷar's growth in the district. It points to the fact that the Paḷḷar(s), as a Dalit entity, have grown against all odds in spite of unfavourable and negative living conditions, in whatever form

Table 2
Growth of SC Population in Tirunelveli

'Tamil Nadu		Total Population			Rural Population			Urban Population		
	Year	*Person*	*Decadal Variation*	*Var. in %*	*Persons*	*Dec. Vari.*	*Var. in%*	*Persons*	*Dec. Vari.*	*Var. in %*
All S/C	1961	431150			358144			73006		
	1971	504956	73806	17.19	407679	49535	13.83	97277	24271	33.25
	1981	589468	84512	16.74	476804	60125	14.75	121664	24387	25.07
	1991	447654	-141814	-24.06	353056	-11478	-2.41	94598	-27066	-22.25
	71-91		-57302	-11.35		-54623	-13.40		-2679	-2.75
	61-91			-3.83			-1.42			29.58
Pallar(s)	1961	142932			110495			32437		
	1971	262431	119499	83.61	219566	109071		42865	10427	32.15
	1981	NA			98.71			NA		
	1991	252717	-9714	-3.70	NA			49840	6975	16.25
		(71-91)			202877	-16689	-7.6			
	61-91		109785	76.81			83.61			53.65
Paiaiyar(s)	1961	61503			47046			14457		
	1971	101659	40156	65.29	78431	31385		23228	8771	22.4
	1981	NA			66.71			NA		
	1991	66793	-34866	-34.28	NA			15109	-8119	20.11
		(71-91)			51664	-26747	-34.1			
	61-91			8.6			9.86			47.04

they may be, experienced by an average Dalit in the district between 1961-1991. Further, a second look at the data reveals a deeper inner story that took place between the years 1971-1991. While the decline of all SC population during this period was 11.35%, the decrease of Paḷḷar's population has only been 3.70% as against that of Paṟaiyar(s), which stood at 34.28%. During that period Paḷḷar(s) are the only group who showed an increase in the urban area (+16.27 %) and least decrease in the rural area. This figure highlights the greater sense of 'struggle for survival' and a strong 'impulse for assertion' that prevails among the Paḷḷar(s) in this district (probably absent among other SC groups), which can perhaps explain, in a way, the repeated caste-clashes between them and the dominant BC caste Maṟavar(s) this particular area.

Further, Paḷḷar(s) of this district like their counterparts at the state level, have recorded both numerical[125] and geographical growth, as we see their growth both, in the rural and in the urban setting. They constitute 57.46 % of the total SC population in the rural areas and 52.68 % in the urban areas. They have made their presence felt both in the rural and in the urban area. In fact, as the above figures reveal, every other Dalit in the village and in the city of this district is a Paḷḷar.

Literacy

The urge for literacy is spread both in the urban and in the rural settings of the district. It is significantly different from the state level. As the above table indicates, the findings of 2001 census indicate that rural literacy rate in Tirunelveli district with 71.70 % as against the state average of 66.21 % has the sixth highest rural literates among different districts in the state of Tamilnadu, while in urban literacy the district of *Tirunelveli* with 80.79% is almost two per cent below the state average of 82.53 %. But the total literacy rate of the district with 76.09% is three per-cent more than the state average of 73.45%. The above data show that the gap between urban literacy and rural literacy in this district is much less than that of the state level. This indicates that consciousness of and the need for literacy is more prevalent among the people in this district than is the case at the state level, and that the "sense of literacy" in the rural area in this district is much higher than the state level. While the difference between rural literacy and urban literacy in the state is 23.4 %, in Tirunelveli district it remains at 14.11 %. This indicates a better overall growth rate of literacy across the rural and urban areas in the district than in the state.

As regards the literacy among the SCs, the ratio of the scheduled caste literates to total scheduled caste population in the state is 46.74 %, while that of Tirunelveli District is 48.91 % (Cf. Table 3). This district features among eight districts that have recorded higher literacy of the scheduled caste population as per 1991 census data. The literacy rate of total Dalits in the state is 46.7 %, while the Paḷḷar(s) have an average of 48.4 %. In the rural-urban divide of literacy among the total scheduled

Table 3
Literacy Rate in Tamilnadu and Tirunelveli including SC Population

	Percentage of literates in 1961	*Percentage of literates in 1971*	*Percentage of literates in 1981*	*Percentage of literates in 1991*	*Percentage of literates in 2001*
Tamil Nadu					
General Population		39.5	46.76	62.66	73.45
Total		32.13	38.56	54.59	66.21
		56.12	63.45	77.99	82.53
Rural					
Urban					
Tamil Nadu	17.20	21.82	29.67	46.74	
Total SC	14.72	19.24	25.92	35.83	
Population Rural	31.07	34.17	44.54	52.95	
Urban					
Tirunelvelli General					
Population		44.83	52.14	65.58	76.09
Total		40.12	47.17	61.06	71.70
Rural		54.76	61.53	75.17	80.79
Urban					
Tirunelvelli ...	20.31	25.99	34.13	48.91	
Total	19.26	25.00	32.96		
Rural	25.40	30.13	38.63		
Urban					

caste population in the state, the urban literacy (62.2%) is 20% higher than rural literacy (42.5%). But in the case of Paḷḷar(s) the rural literacy of 46.6 % is less by 11.5% than the urban literacy (59.9%). This means that the urge for literacy is felt more among the rural Paḷḷar(s) than among an average rural Dalit in the state. According to the 1971 census, the rural literacy rate (25.32%) of the Paḷḷar(s) in this district was less only by 2.97% than urban literacy (28.29%). In contrast, at the state level, the difference was 8.45% between the urban (31.68%) and rural areas (23.23). This also shows that the rural Paḷḷar(s) of Tirunelveli district excelled more in their literacy-consciousness *vis-à-vis* their counterparts at the state level. However, the rural Paḷḷar was ahead of an average rural Dalit in the state in literacy consciousness.[126]

Further, the rural-urban difference in the literacy rate of all SCs in the district in 1971 is 8.12 while that of Paḷḷar(s) is only 2.97. This shows that the literate SC persons in the rural area are found more among Paḷḷar community than among other SCs. However, literacy among rural Dalits was spread more in this district than in the state[127] according to 1971 data, which is the only available SC data for the district.

What emerges from the above analysis of the statistics on literacy may be summarised as follows: (1) An average rural Paḷḷar in this district was almost as literate as his counterpart in the urban settings in 1971. (2) Further the urge for literacy was present more among rural Pallar(s) than most of the other rural Dalits in the district as well as in the state. (3) Education was spread more among rural Paḷḷar(s) of this district than in the case of rural Paḷḷar(s) at the state level. Perhaps Paḷḷar(s) in this district look to "education as the only way to achieve economic independence and improvement of their material existence."[128]

Industrial Development[129]

The main occupation of the people is cultivation. However, during the last seven decades, the district has witnessed the establishment of such reputed large scale industries as India Cements of Talayuthu, co-operative spinning mills at Pettai

Table 4
Index of Literacy among SC Population

SC PopulationT = Total U = Urban; R = Rural (% to the caste population)			Literates		Primary and below		Above Primary elow graduation		Graduation and above	
			1971	1991	1971	1991	1971	1991	1791	1991
All S/C	Tamil Nadu	T		46.7						
		U	34.17	62.2	31.69	30.56	2.38	20.79	0.07	1.58
		R	19.24	42.5	18.51	25.44	0.69	9.84	0.02	0.53
	TirunelVeli	U	30.13		28.41		1.67		0.09	
		R	22.01		24.22		0.75		0.02	
Pallar(s)	Tamil Nadu	T		48.4						
		U	31.68	59.9	29.36	29.9	2.29	19.06	0.1	2.18
		R	23.23	46.6	22.32	28.13	0.89	10.62	0.2	0.71
	TirunelVeli	U	28.29		26.43		1.72		0.14	
		R	25.32		24.33		0.87		0.03	
Paraiyar(s)	Tamil Nadu	T		50.4						
		U	33.6	47.6	31.33		2.18		0.08	
		R	20.37	63.9	19.58		0.74		0.02	
	TirunelVeli	U	35.51		33.74		1.70		0.07	
		R	27.42		26.55		0.78		0.02	

near Tirunelveli and other spinning mills in Ambasamudram and Vikramasingapuram, the Sun Paper Mill at Cherahmahadevi, Tharani Sugars at Vasudevanallur and so on. The upcoming projects are the Skylark Naval Project, Liquid Propulsion Scheme Centre at Konalkinar and the Atomic Power Plant at Koodankulam.

A survey conducted way back in 1972 by the Indian Overseas Bank mentions twenty-six large scale industries and 1,388 registered small scale units besides numerous cottage and household enterprises: "[M]ore than 100% rise in the number of SSI units (small scale industries) has been recorded between 1967 and 1971 manufacturing commodities like matches, soap, chemicals, glass and ceramic products, etc." [130]

The latest Gazetteer of the district published in 2002 gives an extensive list of industries: old time industries (cotton and silk weaving, looms, lace thread, mat and basket-making, palm products, cottage industries), power industries, cement industry, chemical industry at Sankar Nagar, paper industries, textile mills, sugar industries, mineral industries, handloom industries, flour mills, etc. Besides these, there are various cooperative societies such as pottery cooperative society, carpentry and blacksmith industrial cooperative society, bricks industrial cooperative society, pulses and foodgrains cooperative society, mat and fibre products industrial cooperative society, palmyra industry cooperative society, tannery industries cooperative society, jaggery manufacturing cooperative society, palm leaf cooperative society, and the like. These village industries "aim to improve the standard of living of people who are living below the poverty line by providing employment opportunities and by tapping the local, natural and human resources."[131]

Part–II

A Profile of the Villages under Study

In this part, we take up for discussion, the four villages where the field work was done. It is to be noted that these villages are well known in their respective localities for the celebration of the CM *koṭai* by four different castes: Brahmins at Valliyoor, Maṟavar(s) at Vijayanarayanam, Illatu Piḷḷaimār(s) at Kayatar and Paḷḷar(s) at Naduvakurichi. They represent the whole range of various social groups—from top (the Brahmins) to bottom [the Paḷḷar(s)]—that form the spectrum of caste hierarchy. Besides, these villages were chosen because of their multi-caste settings wherein different castes, including the Brahmins, have different types of roles to play in the celebration of *koṭai* by a particular caste.

In the following pages we try to enter into the world of these people by inquiring into the socio-economic cultural profiles of their villages, thereby setting the stage for the understanding and analysis of their religious behaviour during *koṭai* festival in the later chapters.

Naduvakurchi

The Naduvakurichi village, which is in the northern dry zone (see Map 1), is situated near Tirunelveli at a distance of 15 kilometres in the northeast direction. It is in Palayamkottai Taluk of Tirunelveli district. It belongs to the Palayamkottai assembly constituency.[132]

The People of Naduvakurichi

According to the recent census data of 2001, the total population of the village is 2539. There are 1208 (47.58 %) men and 1331 women (52.42%). There are 499 Dalits in the village, making up 19.65% of the village population. The largest caste group in the village is the Tēvar community, while the second largest group is the Paḷḷar(s). This caste equation of co-existence can be very dangerous as evidenced by caste clashes in some villages in this district. However, this village is free from such incidents of social conflicts, the reasons of which could be explored in the dynamics of the CM cult Kaḷḷattiāṉ. The Paḷḷar(s) are all Hindus, while most Paṟaiyar(s) consider themselves Hindus although there are some among them who follow Christianity.

As regards education, the literacy rate of the people of Naduvakurichi is better than that of the rural population of

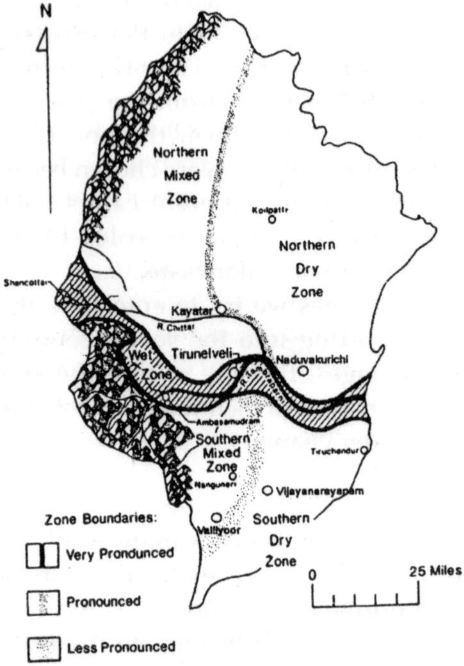

Location of the Villages under study on the Map of "Agricultural Zones of Tirunelveli" given by Ludden in *Peasant History in South India*.

Map 1

Tirunelveli district. 77.97% of the people of the village are literate as compared to the rural literacy rate of the district, which is only 71.70 %. The literacy rate of men in the village is 86.27 % while that of the rural men in the district is only 81.69%. As regards women in the village, 70.63% are literates as compared to a 62.63% average of education among rural women. The village has only one middle school.

The Economic Profile

Agriculture is the most basic economic activity of the villagers. Some of the local varieties of paddy that are cultivated in the *nañcai* fields are *poṉṉi, campā, Kottacampā, Āṭuttuṟai,* and *I.R. 20.* Groundnuts, plantains and different vegetables are cultivated in the *puṉcai* fields (dry land). Vegetables, cucumbers, and some grains are also cultivated in different seasons. Agricultural products are taken to the markets in Palyamkottai and Tirunelveli towns, while a portion of them is kept for the consumption of the villagers.

The village heavily banks on wells, canals and *kuḷams* (tanks), for its irrigation purposes. There are about twelve *kuḷam(s)* such as *vepaṅkuḷam, alaṅkuḷam, ciṟukuḷam,* from which water is taken through narrow canals for irrigation. There are other wells, tanks and pipes that provide drinking water to the villagers. There is one water tank for the Dalits, and two others for the other castes.

As we discussed in the first part, the overall economic situation of Dalits in this village of the dry zone is fairly good. There are a handful of upstart Dalit families. Some Dalit families do own sizeable area of lands in this village. Five Paḷḷar(s) and two Paîaiyar(s) own more than ten acres of agricultural *nañcai* land, while two Paḷḷar(s) and two Paṟaiyar(s) own more than ten acres of *puṉcai* land. One Paḷḷar owns five acres of *nañcai* land and three Paḷḷar(s) own five acres of *puṉcai* land. Twenty-five Paḷḷar(s) and three Paṟaiyars own less than five acres of *nañcai* land, while four Paḷḷar(s) own less than five acres of *puṉcai* land. The ownership of land by the Dalits in this village has to be understood in the context of the changing ground reality that we discussed earlier for the dry zone where more and more higher castes like Brahmins and others have become impoverished and sold their lands to the upstart low castes, in this village. In fact, during my fieldwork, I did meet here both the poor Brahmin priests as well the affluent Paḷḷar business men of this village who came to attend the *koṭai*. However, about 50 Paḷḷar families and 25 Paṟaiyar families do not own any land, and some of them work as agricultural labourers, and they are mostly paid in cash, not in kind, and others work in the industries nearby. A comparative analysis of the census data of this village, as discussed in appendix I, shows that more and more agricultural labourers are becoming marginal labourers in this village than is the case elsewhere, indicating their greater freedom of economic mobility.

Another prominent economic activity both in the PaÀÀar and Paîaiyar settlements in the village is the rolling of *beedies*, the basic raw materials of which are brought from outside the village. There are some families both from Paḷḷar(s) and Paîaiyars who are settled down in Tirunelveli. Among them a few have their own business while others work in different places. As one of the Paḷḷar(s) remarked, "now many of our families have shifted to the city. Even one of the *cāmiyāṭi(s)* is working in the factory. We go wherever we get paid. Our educated boys from St. Xavier's College (a famous college run by the Jesuits at Tirunelveli) are employed in many places in the state. Now we do not depend on these Maṟvar(s) and Reææiyār(s) to fill our bellies." This indicates that the Dalits in the village are increasingly becoming economically independent from the agrarian rural economy.

The Socio-Cultural Mosaic of the Dalits

The Paḷḷar(s) and the Paṟaiyar(s) are the two major Dalit groups in the village. While the Paḷḷar settlement is situated in the north of the village, the Paṟaiyar's is in the south. The Paḷḷar(s), who comprise the largest Dalit group in the village, are economically better off than Paîaiyar(s). One Paîaiyar family, known as 'president family', which held the post of panchayat president for two terms, seems to enjoy greater social status than the other Dalits. As regards the inter-community meal, the Paḷḷar(s) and Paṟaiyar(s) share food with one another. Tēvar(s), Veḷḷāḷar(s), Brahmins and Āsāri(s) (traditional goldsmith caste) do not eat with Dalits. Both Paḷḷar(s) and Paṟaiyar(s) say that they can walk through streets of other high castes. Paḷḷar(s) can enter the houses of Paṟaiyar(s), while Paṟaiyar(s) claim that they have access to the houses of Tēvar(s), Koṉar(s) and Piḷḷaimār(s). Though the Tēvar(s) and higher castes would not prefer to go into the streets of Dalits, yet they often do so whenever they seek the help of a Dalit shaman.

Among the Paḷḷar(s) there are two sub-castes, *ammā cāti* and *āttā cāti* and they are endogamous groups, i.e., they cannot marry outside the sub-caste. The Paṟaiyar(s) do not have sub-castes, therefore they are free to marry among themselves. Most of the male children among Paḷḷar(s) and Paṟaiyar(s) are named after 'Kaḷḷattiāì' (the name by which CM is called at Naduvakurichi) while the girls are named after 'Pēcciammaì' (a female folk deity). The society being patrilineal, the boys are considered to be natural inheritors of the family wealth. If a couple is issueless, the women is blamed and considered to be the cause. The family prays to all gods to get children. The wife observes a fast, a goat is sacrificed, and *poṅkal* is cooked and offered to different gods. Even before the child is conceived, the empty womb of the mother is named as Kaḷḷattiāṉ or Pēcciammaṉ. And when the child is born, he or she is given one of the names accordingly. There is a strong belief that the dead will be reborn as children in the family. The pregnant lady is referred to as *kuḷikāma irukkāḷ* (not taken bath). She is also known as *cūli*. She should not lift heavy things and should not eat papaya and mustard. The mother observes *tīṭṭu* (pollution rules) for forty-one days after delivery, i.e., she is confined to her home since society considers her to be contaminated by the flow of blood during childbirth. During this period she is not supposed to visit any temple including that of the Kaḷḷattiāṉ. After forty-one days, her house is whitewashed. The washerman who washes the clothes of the mother is given special remuneration. Unlike the Brahmin women, these women do not practice "confinement" during the period of their menstruation. They move about freely, take a bath, keep themselves clean, but they avoid going to any temple. Marriage among Paḷḷar(s) and Paṟaiyar(s) takes place in the groom's house. During the marriage ceremony the couple goes to the Kaḷḷattiāṉ temple, break coconuts and worship him. On one chosen day after the marriage, the couple cooks sweet *poṅkal* and offers it to the god as a thanksgiving. Like all others, the Paḷḷar(s) and Paṟaiyar(s) also employ the horoscope for matchmaking. The Tamil month of Āṭi is considered to be very inauspicious for marriage, therefore avoided. One of the reasons cited for this is that if marriage takes place during Āṭi, there is likelihood of the first child's birth occurring in the month of Cittirai, which is believed to portend disaster or doom for the family concerned.

The occurrence of death also involves the performance of certain rituals, as the following will indicate. A one-rupee coin is fixed on the forehead of the deceased. The house of the deceased is smeared with cow dung after the dead body is taken to the cremation ground where the dead body is buried. After the death, the people observe *tīṭṭu* (pollution) of sixteen days for the whole village. During this time no celebration takes place. During the burial ceremony, a barber shaves the heads of the relatives and washer-men blow the conch as a mark of bereavement. A special payment is made for rendering these services. For forty-one days, the family members of the dead are not expected to visit temples including that of Kaḷḷattiāṉ.

As mentioned earlier, in Naduvakurichi, CM is known as Kaḷḷattiāṉ, and this deity is considered the god of the Paḷḷar(s), because it is they who maintain its temple and arrange its festival every year. People perform *pūcai* (ritual of worship so called in India) to Kaḷḷattiāṉ on all important occasions such as when a new house is constructed, or inaugurated, or when a new bull or a cart is bought, etc. Paḷḷar(s) keep fasting on the last Friday of every month, and on the new moon days of the Tamil months of *Āṭi* and *Tai*. There are about five temples in the village: the PaÀÀar(s) have two temples, i.e., Ammaì temple and Kaḷḷattiāṉ temple. The Ammaṉ temple faces the north while Kaḷḷattiāṉ temple faces the east. The temple of a folk deity, known as *pēi kōvil* in common parlance, faces the east in sharp contrast to the common view that the deities of demonic nature face the west while the classical gods of benevolence face the east.[133] It is only Paḷḷar(s) who pay temple tax to these two temples to maintain them. All Paḷḷar(s) consider Kaḷḷattiāṉ as their *kula teyvam* (clan deity). Though the Kaḷḷattiāṉ temple is regarded as the temple of Paḷḷar(s), others have their role to play in the festival: the Tēvar(s) sacrifice goats, and washermen make the torches. There is a common belief among the villagers that if they celebrate *koṭai* every year there will be uninterrupted prosperity in the village all through the year. Thus, all people, irrespective of caste, have invariably named their children, vehicles and shops after Kaḷḷattiāṉ.

Kayatar

Locality and its People

This town, which is located on the Madurai-Tirunelveli road, was made part of the district of Thoothukudi only in the last two decades. As it is situated at a distance of fifteen kilometres from Tirunelveli city, the people consider themselves belonging to Tirunelveli rather than to Thotthukudi. This town belongs to Kovilpatti Taluk and is part of the Ottpeetaram constituency.

The census data of 2001 puts the total population of the town at 9214, of which 4555 are men (49.43%) and 4659 are women (50.56%). The largest groups in this town are Muslims, Tēvars and Christian Nāṭār(s), while the second biggest groups are Paḷḷar(s), Paîaiyars and Christian Piḷḷaimār(s). Hindu Nāṭār(s) and Kōṉār(s) are of sizeable number. The local population of Illattu Piḷḷaimār(s) who celebrate *koṭai* in this town is said to be only forty-two. The numerical strength of this most backward caste community which once had about 500 hundred people has drastically come down over the last four decades. Some of them are said to have converted to Christianity and consider themselves as Christian Piḷḷaimār(s), while most of them have moved over to different towns and cities.

Economic Profile

One of the basic economic activities of this place in this mixed zone is agriculture. Though forty-two per cent of the people depend on agriculture, only about 15% of the total population owns land. About 7000 people do not own any agricultural land. According to the figures given by the local people, about four thousand acres of land are being cultivated in this town. This consists of hundred and fifty acres of *nañcai* (wet land) and three thousand eight hundred and fifty acres of *puìcai* (dry land). Tēvar(s), Piḷḷaimār(s), Nāṭār(s) and Kōṉār(s) are the landowning castes in this town, while the Paḷḷar(s) and Paṟaiyar(s) work as agricultural labourers.

The land available for agriculture is made up of clay soil. The crops of *nañcai* are paddy and plantains. The rice varieties that were traditionally cultivated in this village were *Kuruvai kōvaṉ* and *Āṉaikōmbaṉ*. But those crops are rarely cultivated now. At present, the prominent varieties are *Ambaipatiṉāru, I.R. 20, Āṭuttuṟai,* etc. During agricultural activities such as ploughing, sowing, harvesting, etc., people perform *pūcai* to different gods in the field itself. One such custom is that before sowing, they place the seeds on a plate–which is currently used at home for eating–along with coins and a conch, and perform *pūcai* to the gods. After the harvest, they put a heap of new rice in a cloth and tie it onto a tree in the vicinity of temples. In the *puṉcai* land, they cultivate cotton, maize, chillies, etc. The crops of these fields are sold out in the market at Tirunelveli, Thoothukudi and Kovilpatti. For purposes of irrigation, the people depend on water resources such as wells and tanks. Some of the tanks that provide water to these fields are *Kuṭṭikuḷam,* Periakuḷam and *Kotaṇṭarāmapērikuḷam.* There are about seven hundred wells that supply water to the villages through pumps.

The Socio-Cultural Universe of Ilathu Piḷḷaimār(s)

The cultural world of *Ilathu Piḷḷaimār(s)* is described here, as they are the ones who conduct CM's *koṭai*. As mentioned earlier, many of them have moved out to different parts of the country in search of employment. Though traditionally they were farmers and weavers, some of them now work as teachers and government employees, as they are educated. They were originally called *Iḻuvar(s),* indicating their migration from *Ilaṅkai* (Sri Lanka), a neighbouring country. They have a tradition that holds that they were brought from Sri Lanka by a Cōḻā king, Karikalan, to construct the walls of the dam for the river *Kaveri*. They are also variously known as Paḷikar and Saḷiar in different places. Since it is a patrilineal caste, it is the men who are eligible as heirs. The 'temple-duty' assigned to a particular family is passed on to the eldest son of the family. The children take the surname of their fathers or grandfathers.

As regards their religious beliefs and practices, some information is in place here. They have a high regard for *neem* trees as the female deities, *Ammaṉs,* reside in them. When a particular couple remains issueless, it prays to CM, and women offer turmeric to CM, grind it and apply it to their body. Couples also consume fruits offered to CM. Besides, they tie miniature cradles to the trees in the vicinity of these temples with the belief that they will soon do the same for a new child in their homes. They also undertake a fast for this purpose. Women also consume the rice balls offered to the dead of the family since it is believed that the dead will be reborn again as children in their own homes. The people also have the custom of naming a child even before conception. A pregnant woman is not supposed to cross the flagpole of the temples generally after four months of pregnancy. However, she is allowed to go to CM temple till the eight month of pregnancy although women are not generally not expected to visit CM temple during menstruation. The worship of CM has a special place in the lives of this people as he is regarded as their clan deity (*kula teyvam*). They worship CM both at home and in the temple on all important occasions such as the laying of the foundation stone for a new house, inauguration of a new house, starting of a new business, purchase of a new bullock-cart or new motor vehicle, digging of new well, etc. During the time of marriages the families concerned sponsor *pūcai* to CM in his temple. After the marriage, the newlywed couple makes it a point to pay a visit to CM to get his blessings. Besides, they also perform *pūcai* for him on important Hindus festivals such as *Karttikai, Tīpāvaḷi, Āṭipiṟappu,* etc. The temple of CM is situated in the northwest direction, but his statue faces east like any other major deities such as Civā or Perumāḷ of Hinduism. Though CM of Kayatar is known as belonging to Illattu Piḷḷaimar(s), yet, the other castes also have their own role to play in the CM cult: for instance, the Tēvar(s) function as night guards of the temple, the Pāṇaì(s) make torches called *pantam,* and the barbers shave people's heads during *koṭai.*

Vijayanarayanam

The People

This big multi-caste village is situated in Tirunelveli District in Nanguneri Taluk, about 20 kilometres from Nanguneri. This village belongs to Nanguneri assembly constituency. According to the 2001 census, the total population of the village is 24023, out of which men make up 49.02% (11775) and women are 50.98% (12248). The Tēvar(s) are in a majority in the village while there are also a few Brahmins, Veḷḷāḷar(s), Washermen, Āsāri(s), and Dalits. These villagers are mostly Hindus, while twenty Tēvar families follow Christianity officially; while most of the Hindus also drop in at churches to worship Jesus and Mary, some Christians are also said to sacrifice goats to the CM's temple.

The Economic Profile

The basic economic activity of the village is agriculture. Three fourths of the village folk are engaged in agriculture and have their own lands. Mostly, the Dalits and a few Maṟavar(s) are landless agricultural labourers. Some of the villagers are settled in the big cities like Mumbai and Chennai where they do some business, or work in Government or private sectors. Every alternate year, when the Manimutharu dam is open for irrigation, there is a lot more agricultural activity in the village engaging almost all the villagers; however, in the intermittent year when the dam remains closed, about thirty per cent of the people have to earn their livelihood by working outside the village. Some go to work at the INS Navy centre about five kilometres away from this village. In the *nañcai* land, mostly paddy, cotton and plantains are cultivated. The rice varieties that were traditionally cultivated in this village were Ceôkaìi, *Campā, Kottacampā, Āṭuttuṟai, etc.* but these crops are rarely cultivated now. The prominent varieties at present are *I.R. 20,* Aipaci, P*oṉṉi,* etc. During agricultural activities such as sowing, reaping and ploughing people perform *pūcai* to different gods like Civā, Perumāḷ and CM.

As regards irrigation, the farmers were earlier dependent on the Numbi river water from the Thirukannakudi hill, but now the Manimuthuaru dam supplies water through three canals that irrigate about 2515 acres of *nañcai* land and 1500 acres of *puṉcai*. About 90 electric motor pumps in *nañcai* and about 50 diesel pumps in *puṉcai* are employed for irrigation. There are other tanks, taps, wells, etc., open to all for drinking water facilities and day-to-day usage. Agricultural products such as rice, plantains, and vegetables are taken to the markets in Kerala, Trichy and Tirunelveli.

The Cultural Universe of Tēvar(s)/Maṟavar(s)

Tēvar(s) consider themselves as soldiers belonging to the princely class. Tēvar(s) came to this village five hundred years ago from Ramnad district. Tēvar(s) have a unique sub caste system called *kiḻai* (branch). There are two types of *kiḻai*, *ammā kiḻai* or *appā kiḻai*. The children in *ammā kiḻai* get the roots of their caste identity from the mother and they cannot marry another person in the same *kiḻai*. Similarly the children in *appā kiḻai* get their lineage from the father. As the Tēvar(s) are a patrilineal group, the sons, not the daughters, are inheritors of the ancestral wealth.

There is a practice of ancestral worship among the Tēvar(s). On the day of the death anniversary of elders, the people light lamps, offer new clothes, cook rice, *vaṭa(s)*, etc., and offer them to the deceased members of their family, praying to them to fulfil their needs. The children are named after the father and mother of the husband. Many in the village are named after the god Perumāḷ, and some after Cuṭlai and Icaki Ammaṉ. They also strongly believe that the deceased elders will be reborn as children in the same family. In the event of a boy being born, there is a practice of *kuṟavai* (making of a peculiar noise with the twist of the tongue). The absence of such a practice for the birth of a female child indicates that a girl's entry into the family is regarded as inauspicious and unwanted, as common in other patriarchal societies. The mothers observe *tīṭṭu* (kind of social seclusion) for 10 to 12 days after delivery during which they do not go to any temple including that of

Cuṭalai. When girls come of age, they do not have any special ritual involving CM.

When a death occurs, the family of the deceased observes '*tīṭṭu*' for three days. Some bury their dead, others cremate them. The children are normally buried in a separate place. In the event of a death in a Tēvar family, the other castes have their fixed roles: barbers blow the conch and shave the heads of the sons, the dhobis bring the cloth to carry the dead body, and also spread *dhothi* along the way on which the dead body will be taken to the burial ground. They are paid in kind for this service, barbers are paid 24 *mākkā* rice and 5 litres of milk, while dhobis are paid 24 *mākkā* of rice, apart from some tips in cash.

There are four major temples in the village–one each for Civā, Perumāḷ, Ammaì and Cuṭalai. The Civā's temple's tax was traditionally paid by the eighty high caste Veḷḷāḷar families, but now it is taken over by the Government. Dalits cannot enter the temples of major religions such as a Civā temple and Perumāḷ temple. The only exceptional occasion is the event of carrying of *pālkuæam* to *CM* temple when all caste groups, including Dalits, enter the Civā temple. The CM's temple belongs to the Government and it is renovated recently. Many Tēvar(s) in the village have their own clan deities. People go to Chitoor, Thirukazhukudi and Poolaudaiyar. Some even have family deities such Murukaì, Piḷḷaiyār, Viṣṇu, etc. Close to the CM Government temple, there is another temple of CM generally known as *Mēlakōvil* which belongs to a family. People believe that worshipping gods and celebrating *koṭai* for gods like CM will bring prosperity to the village, save them from diseases and natural calamities such as drought and flood.

Valliyoor

Locality and its People

The Valliyoor town, which is located in the southern mixed zone (see Map 1), is one of the fast growing towns along the national highway. It is situated between two major cities, namely, Tirunelveli and Nagercoil. It is in Rathapuram Taluk of Tirunelveli district and in the assembly constituency of Nanguneri. The surrounding villages regard this town as the best marketing centre for agricultural products such as rice, chillies, tamarind and vegetables.

According to the 2001 census, there are about 5,632 households in this town. The total population of the village is 24,023 out of which 11,775 are men (49.02%) and 12,248 are women (50.98%). The people who live in this town are the Brahmins, Civāveḷḷāḷars, Mutaliyār(s), Yātavā(s), Āsāri(s), Mūppaṉār(s), Maṟavar(s), Nāṭār(s) and Dalits. They follow different faiths such as Hinduism, Islam and Christianity.

The Economic Profile

The people of Valliyoor have multiple sources of income from: cultivation, business, service sectors (schools, hospitals, banks, transport services, hotels) and factories. There is a declining interest in agricultural activity as more and more people find jobs in the Government or private sectors, or in factories. Paddy and plantains are the most suitable crops for the place. *I.R. 8* and *I.R. 16* are the most common varieties of paddy cultivated. Though there are big tanks such as Sivalaperi and Valliyoor tanks, of late, more people depend on well-water for irrigation. Further, the 2001 census indicates that a sizeable number of people are switching over to the category of marginal workers from main workers of a particular occupation. During the period of 1981-2001, the number of marginal labourers has gone up from 113 to 882 registering a variation of + 680%. This indicates that more and more people are depending on multiple sources of income. What deserves mention for this township is the significant growth of household activity in the period between 1981-2001, which registers a growth rate of 278%. One of the famous household activities of the town is the rolling of *beedies*.

The Socio-Cultural Profile of the Brahmins

The Brahmins who started coming to this village about two centuries ago from Thanjavur, Kerala, Andhra Pradesh, etc., to join the hierarchy of temple servants, are economically and educationally well placed. The earliest settlement of Brahmins in the town is said to have taken place during the period of *Aivarājākkaḷ*[134] who ruled a kingdom from Valliyoor as its capital. Apart from a few low-grade temple servants, all others are landlords and continue to maintain their lands. Some of the Brahmins who were landlords do their cultivation at present through tenancy. While most families keep one of their sons back at home to take care of ancestral assets , the rest of them have moved out of the district; some have even moved out of the state, and a sizable number have left the country. This is particularly true of the family of *cāmiyāṭi(s)* who maintain their hold over lands through arrangement in which one family takes care of the family property, while most of their children are settled either abroad or in India's mega cities.

As mentioned in the previous section, Brahmins would have acquired the vast majority of the lands either as a gift from the kings for maintaining the temples, or, most likely, by appropriating the loopholes of the revenue system introduced by the British. The latter is very true of the two big families in this village, known as VAO (village administrative officers) families who are also big landlords. As the surrounding villagers openly talk about it, both had the possibility of acquiring vast tracts of land in this *mixed zone* while in office, as we observed in the previous pages. Another biggest landlord in the place is a *mirāsitār(s)* family known Panagkudi Pannaiyar family who came to Valliyoor from a place called Panagkudi and 'purchased' vast tracts of land at Valliyoor during the period of introduction of the new revenue system. As mentioned earlier, it is the open character of village boundaries of the mixed zone which enabled the VAO's and *mirāsitār(s)* to acquire, and hold rights to land cultivated by independent peasant farmers, including Paḷḷa and other backward castes who resided in the neighbouring villages. Interestingly, all these three families are closely associated with the CM cult. The reason why these families came to worship and continue to worship the CM will have to be inquired into.

As regards education, almost all the Brahmins are well-educated and work in different government and private concerns all over the world. Among the Brahmins, the major divisions are *Aiyar(s)* (Saivites) and the *Aiyaṅkār(s)* (Vishnavites). Their settlements are mostly concentrated in the north, northeast and a few in the north-south side of the town. The Brahmins can walk freely through all the streets in the locality, while originally the Dalits were not allowed to enter the streets of the Brahmins, though such discrimination is no more in force now. At present, one does not perceive a great deal of social isolation of this community from the rest of the people. An old man, a barber by caste, vividly described to me the age-old sociability, not discrimination, between the VAO (village administrative officers) family and the other low castes. He almost broke into tears when he said, "One lady in VAO family, was so kind to all SC people. When we used to go to her house, she would not let us go unless we eat or drink something from her house. She was so kind, so generous. No marriage in our families used to take place without contribution from their family. Our children used to mingle with their children. Even now the Brahmin children who come down for koæai from London, Dubai etc., continue to interact with our boys and girls."[135]

The religious behaviour of the Brahmins here is in contrast with the rest of the Brahmins, as they themselves acknowledge. As a social group, the Brahmins of Valliyoor continue to take active part in the folk religious worldview of the area—which Pate had recorded in his book a hundred years ago.[136] The folk religious characteristics of Brahmins at Valliyoor are manifest in the worship of following class of deities

The Worship of Cāstā(s)

Like other Sudra castes and outcastes, they worship a Cāstā called Peruvēmpuṭaiyān, as narrated by a Brahmin informant Venkatasuppu, and Muthu Arumugam, a high caste Veḷḷāḷar. Pate also mentions the singular importance of this district as regards the folk religious behaviour of the Brahmins.[137] He also mentions about four Brahmins as *kōmarattāi(s)/cāmiyāṭi(s),* i.e, god-dancers . What characterizes this worship pattern of the Brahmins as 'folk' is that: (i) they are possessed by the respective god/goddesses, (ii) they engage in *cāmiyāṭamam,* (iii) they perform divination. It is to be noted that these are three different moments in folk religious experience and expression. One need not result in other moments. The first moment is seen as common to all. But the other two moments are sometimes experienced but suppressed by the subject himself/herself, or by others, while other times they are not at all experienced by the subject.

Brahmin's Aiyan Kovil at Valliyoor

Dalit's CM Temple: The Source of Aiyan Kovil CM

The Worship of CM

Originally three different kinds of CM were worshipped by three families, i.e.; the Anadaraman family, Panankudi, Pannayar family and the Nondiaiyar family. But, at present, only the first two types continue. The CMs worshipped by them are called Ayyaṉ Kōvil Cuæalai and Civapaṉaiyaṭiyār. The former is worshipped by the VAOs (village administrative officers) families and the latter by a landlord who came to Valliyoor from a place called Panagkudi, as mentioned above. The descendants of these two families regard CM as their *kula teyvam*. The Brahmins here attach special significance to the worship of folk deities such as Mutāraman, Cuṭalaimāṭaṉ, and some Cāstā(s) besides the worship of major deities. They worship CM not only during important rites of passage such as birth and marriage but also for various other occasions such as the sowing of first seed for the crops, erection of a new building, house warming, digging of well, etc., and also during the big festivals such as Tīpāvāḷi, *poṅkal*, etc. The CM temple is situated on the north while his *pūṭam* faces the west. Both the CM deities worshipped by the Brahmins are strictly considered to be only theirs as they alone have a right over them, because they alone pay the temple tax or festival tax. Some of the Brahmins maintain that the worship of folk deities is not unique to the Brahmins of Valliyoor alone because, as children, they have heard from their elders that the Brahmins of Kerala[138] at Ernakulam and Cochin had engaged in *Āṭu tuḷḷal vaḻipāṭu* (worship).

The Worship of Māṭaṉ(s)

They also have belief in different types of *māṭaṉ(s)* (male folk deities) as other Sudras and outcastes do. For instance, the Brahmins here worship '*Mantaimāṭaṉ*' near the water tank. When a cow delivers, they cook '*poṅkal*' in his honour and make offerings to him. An elderly Brahmin[139] recalled the past days when the Brahmins worshipped *māṭaṉ* / *Ammaṉs* at the backyard of almost all their houses. Some of them continue to worship such *māṭaṉ* even now once in a year. Pate also notes, "and in some cases spirits of the lower type have found their way into the circle of a Brahman's domestic gods. A pyramid of mud is found in his backyard, and to it, under the directions of the householder and at his expense, offerings of liquor and flesh are made."[140] Speaking about the religious behaviour of the Brahmins of Tirunelveli, he comments, "In regard to its spiritual masters aboriginal Tinnevelly (*sic*)has undoubtedly 'led captivity captive'. "[141]

Vīra Vaḻipāṭu (*Worship of the Valiant*)

They also worship the dead who were murdered unjustly or faced a heroic death. *'Pōti Kōvil"* at Valliyoor is one such instance. The Brahmin family of Murugan temple *pūcāri,* who once planned the murder of another *pūcāri (*Nampiyāṉ *Pōti*) continues to worship him in a folk temple built for him, and this temple is called *'Pōti Kōvil"*[142] This indicates that Brahmins, like any other subalterns, also worship *"Kōlaiyil Utita Teyvaṅkaḷ"* (Gods born out of murder).[143]

Conclusion

As seen in this chapter, the measures taken by the British to rationalize revenues in the district through the *ryotwari* system and survey of land, provided new opportunities of land holding to people of different castes more in the dry zone and in the mixed zone than in the wet-zone. The *mirāsitār(s)* in these zones found themselves in less secure terrain than their counterparts in the wet zone. The oppressed sections in these areas on their part began to experience fluidity within the erstwhile rigid caste system. These findings are important for our discussion on ritual power in the later part of the work.

Further, as we have seen, the overall literacy and their higher rate of urbanisation among the Dalits of Tirunelveli during 1991-2001 has placed them [specially the Paḷḷar(s)] at a better level than the other Dalits in the state level. This conclusion based on analysis of hard data will have a lot of bearing on the concept of *peri-centralisation,* which will be developed in the last chapter.

The second part of the chapter, which has inquired into the profile of the villages under study, will help us locate the religious terrain of the CM cult in its social world. Further it gives us some basic information about the socio-economic-historical situations of the people which will help us answer questions such as 'why do the vegetarian Brahmins worship the bloodthirsty gods like the CM?' 'What advantage do the subalterns have in the worship of a polluting deity like CM?' etc. in the following chapters.

Notes

1. Cf. *Gazetteers of India, Tamil Nadu State, Tirunelveli District, Vol. I,* ed. Velmani, Chennai, 2002, 1.
2. Cf. *District Census Handbook, Part XII-A, Tirunelveli Kattobomman District,* Village and Town Directory, Census of India, 1991, 13.
3. For the myth, cf. *Gazetteers of India, Tirunelveli District, Vol. I,* 2-3.
4. Cf. *Gazetteers of India, vol. I, ; Tinnevelly District Gazetteer* compiled by Pate, Manonmaniam Sundranar University, Tirunelveli, 1993 (1916); A.. J. Stuart, *Manual of Tinnevelly District*, Madras, 1876 and David Ludden, *Peasant History in South India,* Oxford University Press, Delhi, 1989.
5. Cf. *District Census Handbook,* 13.
6. Stuart, *Manual* , 10.
7. Cf. Ludden, *Peasant History,* 20.
8. While the Wet Zone refers to the wet land and Dry Zone to the dry land, the Mixed Zone is the combination of both the dry and the wet lands.
9. '*Pramatfyam*(s)' refer to villages granted to Brahmins as royal gifts and inhabited by them, often exempted from taxation.
10. Cf. Ludden, *Peasant History,* 22-25.
11. *Ūr* assembly is the administrative body of the village that takes care of the common affairs of the village such as irrigation system, village tax for the village festival, etc.
12. Cf. Ludden, *Peasant History,* 86.
13. Cf. ibid., 86-87. Cf. also Pate, *Tinnevelly District Gazetteer* and Stuart, *Manual.*
14. Ludden, *Peasant History,* 90.

15. *Ibid.*, 91.
16. *Talavay* is the commander-in-chief, hence also the prime minister under Vijayanagar rulers. Cf. Ludden, *Peasant History*, 262.
17. *Pāḷaiyakāraṉ* refers to a military chief or commander of a fortress, popularly known as *Pāḷaiyam*. *Pāḷaiyakāraṉ(s)* were independent rulers who controlled a cluster of quite a number of villages through military power. They were supported by the kings like Pāṇṭiyā(s) or Nāyakās to whom they gave military support on regular basis or during the time of war. Like the kings, they too gave royal gifts to the temples and projected themselves as 'little kings.'
18. *Circār* refer to the state or government; used to differentiate land under direct government authority from that under Poligars or zamidaries.
19. Cf., Ludden, *Peasant History*, 69-72.
20. Cf. Thomas Turnbull, "Geographical and Statistical Memoirs of Tinnevelly and its Zamindaries" (C.1823) *Revenue Department Sundries*, No. 38, TNA.
21. Only two Maṟavar chiefs–Urkad and Singampatti–gained control of much good, irrigated land; these two became wealthy chiefs in a pre-dominantly non-Maîavar area at the extreme end of the Tamiraparani valley.
22. Ludden, *Peasant History*, 44.
23. *Ibid.*, 71.
24. *Ibid.*, 72.
25. Ludden notes that about four of every ten Tirunelveli residents in 1881 belonged to castes with a definite history of migration that took place after Pandya period.
26. Cf. Ludden, *Peasant History*, 42-51 and 68-74, Cf. also Pate *Tinnevelly District Gazetteer* and Stuart, *Manual*.
27. *Ibid.*, 82.
28. *Ibid.*
29. In this zone, caste status did not determine the division of labour in agricultural production process. Any caste would and could work the land. Cf.. Ludden, *Peasant History*.
30. For instance in Naduvakurichi, one of the villages of research, which is a dry zone, the researcher observed a very rich Paṟaiyar

landlord family who had held the panchayat president's post for two terms, while in the same village there are very poor Paṟaiyar(s) too.

31. Because of the state of independence, the British found it difficult to get the voluntary labour of dry zone untouchables for road work through the command of high caste families and eventually they had to use force to get their labour. Cf. Ludden, *Peasant History*, 82.

32. "Fixed capital assets such as bulls, plows, and wells would enable some families to live more independently than others and perhaps to rise as local patrons" Ludden, *Peasant History*, 83.

33. The village headmen were authorised to collect tax from local villagers by whatever means they saw fit.

34. They used the caste epithet 'Piḷḷai' denoting Veḷḷāḷar caste status.

35. By contrast outside the dry zone, salaries for village officers were in cash or kind and most of the *inām* land was enjoyed by temples or Brahman villages.

36. Cf. Ludden, *Peasant History*, 61-62.

37. Cf. *ibid.*, 94-96.

38. *Ibid.*, 96.

39. *Ibid.*, 165.

40. *Ibid.*, 167.

41. In other words, in wet zones, the *mirāsitār(s)* traced their title directly to royal charters and to traditions of Pandya hegemony while dry-farming peasants traced theirs to warrior chiefs and to generations of labour that made the land productive and their own.

42. Specific styles of dress, speech and residence, and forms of work characterised a family's position in the system. Brahmins completely avoided work in the fields, so too Veḷḷāḷar(s), except when they were tenants to the Brahmins. Paḷḷar(s) and Paṟaiyar(s) worked in the mud in paddy fields and lived in separate, 'polluted' neighbourhoods.

43. Gang labour refers to the public works such as digging of tanks or wells, laying of roads,. building of temples, etc., done mostly by Paḷḷar(s) and Paṟaiyar(s) as a group often supervised by one powerful man among them.

44. In many cases, for peasant farmers, rights to land rested upon authorisation from *mirāsitārs*. Some of them extracted labour services from them in turn, while more generally peasant families paid the cash fee called *swamibogam* which confirmed tenant occupancy rights, supplied *mirāsitār(s)* with needed income and marked *mirāsitār* superiority.

45. The superior portion (mēl) portion of the crop claimed by the landlord or by government, in contrast to the cultivator's portion, *kuṭivaram*.

46. For instance in the beginning of the nineteenth century, Poligar tribute or *Peschash*, as it was called, contributed only one sixth of the regional state revenue, while irrigated villages provided 85 percent of all state revenue from field crops. This figure becomes significant when we take into account the fact that, at that time, Poligar area had more than one third of the land in the district, while the irrigated villages (wet zone) had only about 20 percent of all Tirunelveli land. Cf. Stuart, *Manual,* 161, 182 and 194.

47. As per the policy principles devised by Thomas Munro, the *ryotwari* system defined the state itself as supreme landlord, and individual peasants as landowners (called as 'ryots'). The ryots paid annual cash rent, or revenue assessments, to the government and received, in return, a *paṭṭā,* an annual receipt that constituted title to land. Munro's plan was that the rents were to be fixed suitably low and fixed for a period of thirty years, to afford peasant farmers security from the arbitrary and mounting exactions from revenue intermediaries which he believed had damaged peasant property rights in the past. Cf. Ludden, *Peasant History, Peasant History, 240,* Nilmani Mukerjee, *The Ryotwari System in Madras,* 1792-1827 Calcutta, 1962. Dharma Kumar, *Land and Caste in South India,* Cambridge, 1965.

48. Cf. Ludden., *Peasant History,* chapters 4 & 6.

49. Cf. *ibid.,* 155 and Cf. *Settlement Registers* Complied for Tinnevelly District, TNA, Madras, 1870.

50. One District collector Lushington remarks, "The purchase of land is the first object of every public officer. As soon he comes to office he looks around for an eligible spot of ground and the deep schemes that are laid to obtain it are not perhaps to be credited and until it is accomplished the individual is restless and uneasy." (as quoted in Ludden, *Peasant History,* 106).

51. Ludden, *Peasant History,* 122.
52. Cf. *ibid.,* 179.
53. *Ibid.,* 180.
54. Cf. *ibid.,* 185.
55. *Ibid.,* 187.
56. *Ibid.,* 159
57. *Ibid.,* 159.
58. *Ibid.,* 162.
59. *Ibid.,* 163.

[60] Cf, ibid.,164-170.

61. It refers to the survey of village lands that fixed house-sites for the agricultural labourers.
62. Cf. *Gazetteer of India, Tirunelveli District, Vol. II.,* 940.
63. Cf. *Ibid.,* 924-925.
64. In Tamilnadu 1,88,380 acres of land is notified as surplus out of which 1, 63,722 acres of land have been disposed of upto 30th November 1994.
65. While doing fieldwork I heard from some people that *Dalits* have been able to acquire lands to cultivate as a result of land-ceiling act.
66. Cf. Gazetteer *of India, Tirunelveli District, Vol. II,* 927.
67. Calculated from figures given in the *Gazetteers of India, Vol. II.,* 928.
68. Cf. *Gazetteer of India, Tirunelveli District, Vol. I,* 342.
69. Cf. *Census of India, 1931, Vol. XIV Madras, Part II, Imperial and Provincial Tables,* Government Press Madras, 1932.
70. Cf. *Gazetteer of India, Tirunelveli District. Vol. I,* 342.
71. Some hold the view that word 'M*aḷḷar*' is purposely changed into 'Paḷḷar' to denigrate their social position in the caste hierarchy.
72. As cited in *Gazetteers of India, Vol.I,* 342-343.
73. The second myth is a counter discourse of *Paḷḷar(s)* that claims equality with maṟavar(s) and explains the resultant ground reality of social upheavals and unrest in this area due to the Dalit's struggles for social emancipation.

74. Cf. Ludden, *Peasant History,* 24.

75. *Ibid.,* 91.

76. As quoted by Ludden, *Peasant History,* 91.

77. *Ibid.*

78. Cf., *ibid.,* 92.

79. *Mukkudal Pallu,* ed. N. Sethukumaran, Vanathi Press, Madras, 1973. Cf. also Ludden, *Peasant History,* 92.

80. Ludden, *Peasant History,* 93.

81. *Ibid.*

82. As quoted in Ludden, *Peasant History,* 144.

83. Cf., *ibid.*

84. *Ibid.,* 175.

85. *Ibid.*

86. As cited by Ludden, *Peasant History,* 156. Cf. also: Ravindra K Jain, *South Indians on the Plantation Frontier in Malaysia,* New Haven, 1970; and R. Jayarathnam, "Indian Emigration to Ceylon," *Indian Economic and Social History Review* 4/4 (1967), 320-359.

87. Another local title given to the Dalits.

88. V Geetha and S V Rajadurai, "*Dalits* and Non-Brahmin Consciousness in Colonial Tamil Nadu", *Economic and Political Weekly* 28/39, 1993, 2091-2098. 96.

89. A.B. Athereya, *Gangai Kondan 1916-1984,* Working Paper no. 56, MIDS, Chennai. 9, 10, 32, 97 as cited in *Gazetteers of India,* ibid., 344.

90. Cf. Ludden, *Peasant History,* 218.

91. Of 423012 in the Province, Tirunelveli alone had a large share of their population (207005) already in 1931. *Census of India,* 1931.

92. Cf. Stuart, *Manua,* 17-18, and Pate, *Tinnevelly District.*

93. Cf. Ludden, *Peasant History,* 127-128.

94. It refers to tax-free grants of land given as a gift by a superior or ruler to the inferior/subjects.

95. Correspondence relating to the Revision proposed in the village establishments of each district of the Madras Presidency Part II, 1860-61 TNA. 833-834.

96. A landowner pays sometimes one-eighth of a koæai of paddy for every superficial koæai of his wet land; the landless man gives a few *annas* or a measure of grain.

97. Pate, *Tinnevelly District*, 135.

98. *Ibid.*

99. Correspondence relating to the Revision proposed in the village establishments of each district of the Madras Presidency Part II, 1860-61 TNA. 833-834.

100. Pate ,*Tinnevelly District*, 135.

101. Ludden , *Peasant History*, 341.

102. Pate, *Tinnevelly District*, 135.

103. The leader of a village or a clan.

104. Pate, *Tinnevelly District*, 135.

105. Report of S.R. Lushington, Collector of Tinnevelly to the Board of Revenue G.O. No. T.N.A. Chennai.

106. Boag, *Madras Report, Part I, Vol. XIII, Census of India, 1921*, Government Press, 1922, 157.

107. Tanjore which had 1,20,029 Brahmins stood first in the state for Brahmin population. Cf. *Census of India, 1931*, Vol. XIV Madras, Part II, Imperial and Provincial Tables, Government Press, Madras, 1932.

108. Cf. Pate, *Tinnevelly District*, 107 and 114.

109. *Ibid.* 107.

110. Lars Kjaerholm, "Myth, Pilgrimage and Fascianation in the Aiyappa Cult: A View From Fieldwork in Taminlnady," in Asko Parpola (ed.), *South Asian Religion and Society*, D.K. Agencies Ltd., New Delhi, 1986, 121-161, 126.

111. *Census of India, 1931*, Vol. XIV Madras, Part II, 107.

112. Cf. *Gazetteers of India*, Tirunelveli District, Vol. I, 331-332, Cf. also Ludden, *Peasant History* and Pate, Pate, *Tinnevelly District*.

113. Cf. Susan Bailey, *Saints, Goddesses & Kings*, Cambridge University Press, New Delhi, 1992 (1989) and Nicholas Dirks, *The Hollow Crown: Ethnography of an Indian Kingdom*, Orient Longman Limited, Bombay, 1989.

114. Ludden, *Peasant History*, 43.

115. *Ibid.*, 45.

116. Cf. *ibid.*, 130-132.

117. As quoted by Ludden, *Peasant History*, 132.

118. Cf. Ludden, *Peasant History*.

119. *Ibid.*, 86-87. Cf., also Pate, *Tinnevelly District* and Stuart, *Manual*.

120. Cf. *Temple Inscriptions of Tirunelveli District*, compiled by V.S. Subramanian, Vol. Xiii, TNA (Tamilnadu Archives), Chennai, 1986, pp 90, 92, 93, 100, 102, 104, 107 etc.

121. Ludden, *Peasant History*, 166.

122. Cf. *Census of India 2001, Provisional Population Totals, Paper-3, Tamil Nadu*, Series 34, complied by Dr. C. Chandramouli, Government Press, Chennai, 2003. 3.

123. In an interview with Balasuppu.

124. Of the total *Paḷḷar(s)* in the state Tirunelveli has the third largest group 13.3 %, while Thanjavur tops the list with 16.8 % of the *Paḷḷar(s)* in the state, and Trichy stands second with just 13.4% of total *Paḷḷar(s)* in the state.

125. It must be noted the Paḷḷar(s) have grown more *rapidly* over the last thirty years than others. In 1961 they constituted 33.15 % of all SC population in the district. They have increased their tally to 56.45 % in 1991, while the Paîaiyar(s) who made 14.26 in 1961 just moved up to 14.92 % in 1991.

126. It may be noted that for all SC population in the state the difference of the literacy rate between their rural and urban folk is 14.93, in the case of *Paḷḷar(s)* it is only 8.45 at the state level.

127. In 1971, all SC urban and urban literacy was 34.17% and 19.24% respectively at the state level with a difference of 14.93% between the two, while that of the district was 30.13% and 22.01% with a difference of 8.2. Cf. Table 4.

128. Joan P. Mencher, "A Tamil Village: Changing Socio-economic Structure in Madras State," in *Village in India*, ed. V. Madan, Oxford University Press, New Delhi, 2002, 179.

129. For further information in this section, refer *Gazetteers of India, Tirunelveli District*, Vol. I, 524-626.

130. *Fact Finding Survey Report on Tirunelveli District 1972*, conducted by Indian Overseas Bank, Madras, TNA, 50.

131. *Gazetteers of India,* Tirunelveli District, Vol. I, 574.

132. Assembly constituency is an electoral unit that covers a geographical area. The people of the constituency elect their representative, popularly called 'MLA' (Member of the Legislative Assembly), for the State assembly.

133. Cf. *Gazetteers of India, Tirunelveli District,* Vol. I.

134. The exact period of these rulers is a point of discussion among the historians. It could have been between 13th to early 14th century. Cf. Pate, *Tinnevelly District,* 55 for further information.

135. Interview given by the barber on 19-7-2002 during Koæai. He did not want the names to be recorded. Hence they are avoided in the script.

136. Cf. Pate, *Tinnevelly District,* 107-110.

137. Cf. *Ibid.*

138. Sarah Caldwell makes note of Brahmin's involvement in the folk rituals of Brahmins in *Sakta* worship which include blood, alcohol, sexual fluids and meat. Cf. Caldwell, 27.

139. A Brahmin, Ramasamy, by name, shared this in an interview held on 13th August 2004.

140. Pate, *Tinnevelly District,* 107.

141. *Ibid.*

142. Cf. In the above-mentioned interview with Mr. Muthu Arumugam.

143. Cf. Felix Wilfred, *The Sling of Utopia,* ISPCK, Delhi, 2005, 143.

Chapter 3

The Ethnography of the CM Cult

Introduction

In this chapter we focus on CM's *koṭai* rituals, describing the phenomena based on participant observation of the festivals as celebrated by four groups, i.e., Brahmins at Valliyoor, Maîạvar(s) at Vijayanaryaṇam, Illatu Piḷḷaimār(s) at Kayatar and Paḷḷar(s) at Naduvakurichi. Before we do that, we will clarify what people mean by *koṭai*, which is an expression typical of the southern districts of Tirunelveli, Tuticorin and Kanyakumari in Tamilnadu. Then we move on to focus on the core rituals or the most basic rituals that characterize the celebration of *koṭai* for CM. Finally, this chapter attempts to analyse the *koṭai* rituals through network analysis and explores the key loci/sources of ritual power, the site of demonstration, the channel of its distribution and the mode of its appropriation.

The Meaning of *Koṭai*

Koṭai is a popular term in the southern districts of Tirunelveli, Tuticorin and Kanyakumari. It refers to the celebration of a festival of a god(dess) that can be called 'minor' or a god(dess) of 'inferior divinity.' Reincihe considers the institution of *koṭai* as characteristic of Tirunelveli and holds that the term *koṭai* is reserved for some festivals that unite the local sanctuary of either a goddess or a god and a group of people who have some relationship with her/him. By reducing all types of *koṭai* to their lowest common denominator, it stands for 'carnivorous offering' or 'bloody sacrifice.'[1]

The literal meaning of the term '*koṭai*' is 'offering,'[2] and this refers to the various kinds of offerings that people make to gods and goddesses. One of the pioneering Tamil folklorists, S.D. Lourdu, holds that, in Tamil literature, it also refers to the gratuitous acts of kings. The term '*koṭai*' implies a reciprocal relationship between the common folk and the deity, as well as a mutual exchange of gifts between them. People give 'offerings' to the deity and the deity, in return, gratuitously confers on them 'gifts'[3] such as good health, bountiful harvest, prosperity, good luck, etc. The goal of *koṭai* is tapping of ritual power, as Blackburn notes, "the conscious purpose of *koṭai* festival is to win the favour of the gods and goddesses resident in the temple, to enlist their power to produce or continue desired states and prevent or remove undesired ones."[4]

According to the tradition noted by Blackburn, *koṭai* is generally celebrated from January to May. Convention assigns Tuesdays to goddesses and Fridays to gods. However, there are exceptions to these general conventions as CM's *koṭai* at Vijyanarayanam is celebrated in June (in the Tamil month of Āṉi), and in the month of August (in the Tamil month of Āṭi) at Valliyoor. Similarly, at Naduvakurichi, *koṭai* for CM is celebrated on Tuesday and not on Friday. Besides the occasions of *koṭai*, there are other times in which special *pūcai(s)* are held in some of the CM temples.[5]

The 'Core Rituals' and 'Common Rituals' of Koæai

As Eveline Meyer notes, the character of a god/goddess obtains its fullest manifestation during the time of festival,[6] in our case, during *koṭai*. The ceremonies performed during these times are made up of rituals that reveal the deity's essential nature. These rituals are called 'core rituals.'

A cursory survey of the whole gamut of *koṭai* rituals, as celebrated by people of different castes in different places of the district, indicates that there is apparently a set of rituals that recur in one form or another in all these places, which we call the *common rituals of CM koṭai*. These have to be distinguished from those rituals that occur only sporadically as local phenomena.

The former set of rituals–common to all CM temples during the time of *koṭai*–include core rituals. As mentioned above, they are the rituals (since they are persistent) that will best characterize the CM deity. Hence, those rituals that mark the beginning and the end of *koṭai*–though they are common to all the four–are excluded from the core rituals as: (i) They mark the beginning of *koæai* of other deities, too, and hence, (ii) they do not necessarily reveal the true nature of the deity.

In the following pages we focus on the description of common rituals that include also the core rituals first. As a basic pattern we have chosen the *koṭai* festival celebrated at Kayatar, since it is more comprehensive, i.e., it contains the greatest variety of *koṭai* rituals observed by the researcher. We shall deal with the variations of *koṭai* festival rituals in other places, later on.

The Three Days *Koṭai* Rituals at Kayatar

The *koṭai* is celebrated for three days at Kayatar on the last week of Tamil month Māci. It begins on Friday evening and ends on Sunday afternoon. The CM of this temple is considered to be the clan deity of the Illatu Piḷḷaimār(s) of this village. Hence the people of this community, wherever they are, make it a point to attend *koṭai*. They come here for these three-day celebrations from all over the state and from cities like Mumbai. In the following pages, we will describe the three-days *koṭai* of Kayatar.

The Sequence of Three Days Koṭai *Rituals at Kayatar*

The k*oṭai* rituals at Kayatar may be graphically presented as follows:

The Figure (1) given below is a presentation of the rituals of *mūṉṟunāḷ koæai* (three-day *koṭai*) and their sequence. This will provide an idea of the types of rituals that make up the body of *koṭai* festival and the sequence in which the rituals are performed within the ritual complex, as observed in Kayatar.

In Figure (1), numbers one, two and three mark the beginning of *koṭai*. Numbers eight, nine, ten and eleven are the core rituals, while numbers twelve and thirteen mark the end of *koṭai*. Together, all the above make the common rituals of CM *koṭai*. Though the diagram presented here is basically of the three-day *koṭai*, it can be applicable to a one-day *koṭai*, too. Numbers one, two, eight, nine, ten, eleven, twelve and thirteen constitute a one-day *koṭai* as observed in Naduvakurichi. The core rituals found in a three-days *koṭai* (eight, nine, ten, and eleven) are also performed in the one-day *koṭai*. But the folk theatrical performance such as *kaṇiyāṉkūṭṭu* and *villupāṭṭu* seen in all three major *koṭai*'s were absent in the one-day *koṭai*.

1
Kālnāṭṭu (Erection of Pole)

2	3
a. Bringing of Tirttam b. *Pālkuṭam* c. Mounting of *kumpam*	a. *Kāppu* Kaṭṭutal b. Villupāṭṭu c. Kaṇiyāṉkūttu

4	5	6	7
Morning Sacrifice	a. *Kaṇiyāṉ Kaivettu* b. Animal sacrifice c. Utiram *lāṭṭu*	a. Wearing of *Vēṭṭai* dress b. Sacrifice of cock c. *Kaṇiyāṉkaiveṭṭu* d. *Pūtaṉṉēr*	a. *Cāmiyāṭṭam* b. Divination c. *Villupāṭṭu* d. *Kaṇiyāṉ* kūttu

8	9	10	11
a. *Poṅkal* b. *Kaṇiyāṉ* kūttu c. *Villupāṭṭu*	*Paṭaippu* and Blood Sacrifices a. Offering of cooked rice and the cooked meat of pregnant animals b. Sacrifice of goats c. Sacrifice of pigs d. *Utiram*	*Maiyāṉampōtal*/Vēṭṭai a. wearing of the dress b. *Kaṇiyāṉ pūcai* c. Offering of cooked food d. Kaṇiyāṉ *kaiveṭṭu* e. *Tiraḷai*	a. *Cāmiyāṭṭam* b. Divination c. Villupāṭṭu d. *Kaṇiyāṉ* kūttu

12	13
Kāppuaṟuttal	Eighth Day *Koṭai* - Tiṭṭukaḷittal

Figure 1

Different Parts of Koæai Rituals at Kayatar

For our description we divide the *koṭai* rituals at Kayatar into two parts: (1) 'Common rituals' which are common to all *koṭai* rituals of CM (2) 'Other Rituals' which are found only in few places.

Common Rituals of CM Koṭai

As mentioned above, in any *koṭai*, apart from the core rituals, there are always other rituals such 'Beginning Rituals' and 'End rituals' that make the totality of the ritual complex of *koṭai*. All three categories will be dealt with in the following pages.

Beginning Rituals of Koṭai

In the celebration of koæai there is always a set of rituals that marks its beginning so that preparation for *koṭai* would start in full swing, and, from now on, a greater participation and special involvement is expected of the members of the group that celebrates *koṭai*

Kālnāṭṭu

Kālnāṭṭu, which means the erection of the pole, marks the beginning of *koṭai* in all village festivals of the southern districts. Eight days before the beginning of *koṭai*, the village leaders, along with *cāmiyāṭi(s)*, carry the pole (*kāl*) in a procession from Mutāramaṉ/Civā's temple in the village. Two types of *mēḷams* (drums) accompany this procession and the pole is installed inside the courtyard of the temple at the end of the procession. Kāl is a bamboo pole painted red and white. The *navatāṉiyam* (nine grains) are put on top of the pole, and an iron ring is fixed on the top with mango leaves tied around. From then on, the *cāmiyāṭi(s)* observe a fast and keep themselves pure, meaning, they abstain from sex and the consumption of meat and liquor.

Mounting of Kumpam

Mounting of *Kumpam* is the very first ritual unit in the three day celebration of *koṭai*, *Kumpam* is basically a pot (silver or clay) with holy water (*tīrttam*) inside and coconut on its top surrounded by mango leaves. This ritual has two parts; bringing of the holy water from another temple, and the mounting of *Kumpam* itself

Bringing of Tīrttam (holy water) and pālkuṭam[7]

Tīrttam (holy water) is brought by the *cāmiyāṭi(s)* and *pūcāri(s)* (priests) in a procession that starts from the Mutāramaṉ temple in the village on the evening of the first day of *koṭai*. After performing the *pūcai* to Mutāramaṉ, the procession of *tīrttam* (sacred water) begins. The *cāmiyāṭi(s)* and the people who celebrate koṭai carry the ritual implements and the regalia for *vēṭṭai (ritual hunting)* such as dress, cap, belt, etc., in the procession. Some devotees who kept vows to carry the *pālkuṭam* (milk pot) also join them. The village elders, mostly Illattu Piḷḷaimār(s), and women also follow the procession. While carrying the *tīrttam* and *pālkuṭam* men shake their body back and forth as if they were under the sway of a powerful external force beyond their control. Once they reach the temple precincts, *tīrttam* and *pālkuṭam* are taken inside the courtyard of the temple. This is followed by a bath in the temple well, after which they carry from the courtyard only half a dozen *kumpams* (pots) to a place hundred meters in front of the temple. At 6.00 p.m., the *pūcāri* of the temple performs *āratti*[8] in all four directions. Now only the *cāmiyāṭi(s)* carry the *kumpams* back to the temple while *mēḷam* and other musical instruments are played. Then, all the men and women come inside the temple, and the *cāmiyāṭi(s)* place the *kumpams* in front of the main altar.

Mounting of Kumpam[9]

First, *āratti* is once again performed for the deities, followed by the ringing of the bell. When the bell rings, the hosts of men standing close to the deity raise their left hands and shake their wrists. *Mēḷam(s)* are played. Now the first *pūcai* is done to a deity called Civaṉaṭainta Perumāḷ (whose *pūṭam*–nearly a conical shaped altar–alone is red). This *pūcai* involves cleansing of the altar, first, with water, and then with milk. Now *āratti* is done to the deity first, and to the people next. The tradition

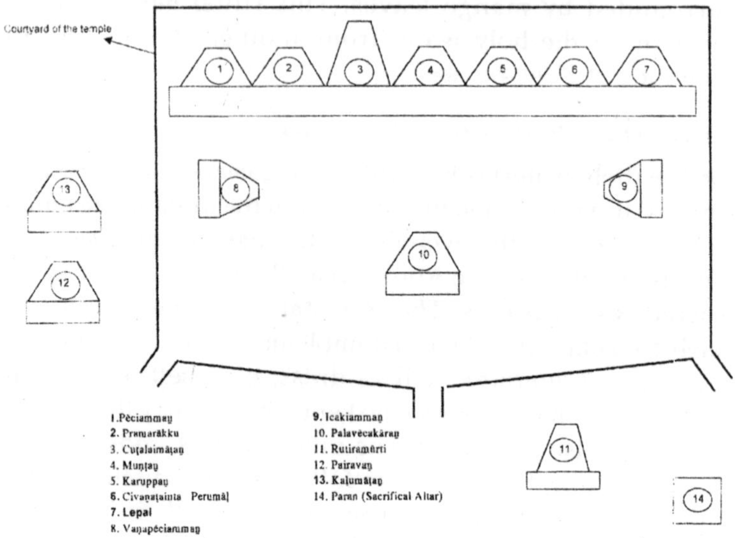

Figure 2: CM's Temple at Kayatar

here is that this deity gets the first respect, Pēcciammaṉ next, then Cuṭalai and Karuppaṉ. Any ritual done to these deities during *koṭai* is always done in this order.

Then, all *pūṭams* are consecrated first with water and then with milk. Again *āratti* is done first for the gods and then for the people. Sandalwood paste is applied on the *pūṭam,* and *kuṅkuma poṭṭu* (saffron round mark made on the forehead) is also given to all the deities. A handful of rice grains are kept on the top of all *pūṭams*. Then the main altar is incensed.

Kumpams are mounted on all *pūṭams*. As mentioned, this is done to Civaṉaṭainta Perumāḷ first. Then a red shawl is tied around the *pūṭam* and another is merely put on the *pūṭam* like a garland. A red rose garland is also given to the deity. While this is being done, the pitch of the bells and mēḷam increases. The same ceremony then takes place for Pēcciammaṉ, next for Cuæalai and finally for Karupan. The only difference is that all these latter deities get light yellow shawls, while CM's *pūṭam* gets silk dothies that are more decorative and grand. Once the ceremonies to these four deities are over, all other *pūṭams* (altars 7, 8, 9 etc... Cf. Figure 2) are given the same ritual simultaneously.

When the mounting ceremony gets over, Kaṇiyāṉs (a special type of folk ritual functionaries) come to the courtyard of the temple. They are seven in number. First, comes the *kaiveṭṭu* Kaṇiyāṉ (Kaṇiyāṉ who pierces his forearm for giving blood to CM) who leads the ceremony, followed by others. The four main *cāmiyāṭi(s)* are seated, bare-chested, with their *tirunāru* (holy ash) container. Kaṇiyāṉ brings a *kumpam* and places it on a winnowing pan in front of the *cāmiyāṭi(s)*. *Kumpam* here is a mud pot with rice grains inside it, on top of which is a coconut, surrounded by mango leaves. Placed inside the winnowing pan are betel-nuts, *kāppus* (a special amulet meant for this purpose), coconuts, turmeric, plantains, rice grains, a small container of turmeric water, and a wooden mask (popularly called *pēy-mukam,* meaning, 'devil's mask') which is garlanded. This is followed by the *Kāppukaṭṭutal* (tying of kāppu) ceremony, which we will describe a little later.

Depiction of Māvicaki's Murder by CM at Kayatar Temple

Description of Core Rituals

As mentioned earlier, the core rituals that will be described here are the most important part of *Koṭai* for the CM. Any Koṭai celebration for this deity will be seen incomplete without these ritual enactments. Now the core rituals for the CM consist of (a) *Vēṭṭai/Maiyāṉam Pōtal, (b) Aruḷvākku Collutal/cāmiyāṭṭam, (c) Paṭaippu and (d) Poṅkal.* The sequence of these ritual vary from place to place. The order followed at Kayatar is as follows:

Poṅkal[10]

The cooking of *poṅkal* was done around 6.00 p.m. in front of the temple. Almost all families of the Illattu Piḷḷaimār(s) cook *poṅkal*. It is generally understood that people cook sweet *poṅkal*. If one cooks white rice, that has to necessarily be complemented with the gifting of an animal (goat or cock). While this is going on, *Kaṇiyāṉ* kūttu (folk theatre performed by the Kaṇiyāṉs) is performed, followed by *villupāṭṭu*.[11] Around 8.00 p.m., two pigs which are tied and garlanded are brought to the sacrificial altar in front of the temple. (Cf.3.2)

The Cāma Koṭai

Cāma koæai refers to the rituals performed at midnight in front of CM's image at the cremation ground. The rituals held at that time are as follows:

Paṭaippu

Just before midnight, the veil of the CM's image is removed. The scene to be enacted on the CM's altar is the killing of pregnant Māvicakki by Kāḷipulayai in a *paraṇ* (altar), as narrated in the myth sung by the folk artists (we will deal with the myth in the next chapter). The images here are made with the help of plantain stems, which are very artistically decorated (see the picture above). To denote this, the pregnant sheep, the pregnant chicken, egg, dry-fish, etc., all are offered to the deity. Then the people bring all the goats that have been donated to the temple. Thereafter, a Tēvar cuts the goat's heart open and the CM *cāmiyāṭi* puts his head into it. He is then covered with a towel. It is believed that the CM *cāmiyāṭi* drinks the blood of these goats. Then the *cāmiyāṭi(s)* and other important people proceed to the outer altar where three pigs are sacrificed. There again it is believed that the *cāmiyāṭi* of *CM* drinks the blood of pigs under cover of the towel. He then returns to the main courtyard where people bathe him with ordinary water first, and with rose water next.

Vēṭṭai/Maiyāṇam Pōtal[12]

Now, all *cāmiyāṭi(s)* wear the dress appropriate for *vēṭṭai,* i.e., a ritual hunt that involves going to the cremation ground for a special ritual to be performed by the Kaṇiyāṉ either at midnight or at noon. Carrying torches and *veṭṭaruval* (a kind of sickle), only the cāmiyāṭi(s) accompanied by a select few proceed right up to the cremation ground. I was allowed to remain with the Kaṇiyāṉ who had already reached the ritual site. Kaṇiyāṉ spread the plantain leaves on the ground and placed three coconuts, betel leaves, incense sticks and a mud-pot surrounded by mango leaves on its top. The *cāmiyāṭi(s),* who brought with them a mud container with rice, meat, eggs and *pappad,* place it there as an offering to the spirits at the cremation ground. Now, Kaṇiyāṉ, having performed *āratti* in three directions with the incense sticks, requests all the *cāmiyāṭi(s)* to sit. He then takes the coconut, cuts it into half and places the pieces on a plantain leaf. This is followed by the cutting off the head of a cock which is rotated over the whole group by the Kaṇiyāṉ. He then rotates the beheaded cock thrice over the head of each of those seated in front of him. Finally, he throws it to the ground. Then Kaṇiyāṉ takes a knife, stands up, shouts out something and pierces his forearm. His blood oozes out, and this blood from his hand is smeared onto the four leaves kept in the four different directions. In the meantime, plantain leaves are given to all four *cāmiyāṭi(s)* and plantain pieces are placed upon them. Now Kaṇiyāṉ sprinkles water on his hand and cuts his hand once more, and drops his blood over the plantains put on the leaves of the *cāmiyāṭi(s).* They are to taste these bloody plantains. They smell it, some pretend to taste it, but all begin to yell. Some twist their tongue as if they relished the blood, put their tongue out and ask for more as if their thirst for blood is insatiable. I heard someone making sounds like a pig. The bodies of a few were shaking back and forth, while others standing beside them were trying to hold them and control their movements. Then Kaṇiyāṉ asks them whether this is enough for them. They all respond with a loud "yes!" Now eggs are given to the *cāmiyāṭi(s)* while Kaṇiyāṉ takes a small water pot containing petals of different flowers, which is popularly known as *pūtaṇṇēr* in Tamil. Then Kaṇiyāṉ, along with the *cāmiyāṭi(s)* goes down to the other side of the cremation ground, shouts out something, and asks the *cāmiyāṭi(s)* to throw the eggs in different directions. They also sprinkle the *pūtaṇṇēr* in different directions, and finally they all return to the temple site. Thus the ritual of *maiyāṇam pōtal* came to an end.

Aruḷvākku Collutal (Divination)/ *Cāmiyāṭṭam* (God-dance)

The next event in the *koṭai* is the aruḷvākku collutal/kuṟi collutal (divination) of *cāmiyāṭi(s)*, which is the most important and the most popular part of the *koṭai*. From the cremation ground, the *cāmiyāṭi(s)* all come back to the temple site. Now, the *cāmiyāṭi(s)* get fully possessed and begin to dance, which is known as *cāmiyāṭṭam*, literally meaning, 'god – dance.' As they all dance, they are given a torch in their left hand. Some become extremely ecstatic. As they yell and scream, they are given the *tirunāru* (sacred ash) in their right hand, and all the people throng to them. The *cāmiyāṭi(s)* apply *tirunāru* on their foreheads. Some devotees bring them lemons cut in half, which the *cāmiyāṭi(s)* squeeze, rotate around their heads and throw away. Others bring cocks. The *cāmiyāṭi(s)* cut off the cock's head, rotate the beheaded bird over the people and throw it to the ground. A similar motion is undergone for those who bring eggs.[13] The *cāmiyāṭi(s)* hold the hands of devotees tightly and yank them back and forth. They talk to some folks, instructing them what to do. They tell them things like, "You must go to any *Ammaṉ* temple for nine consecutive weeks, keep fast for a year on all first Fridays, and pray to God. When you come here next year, your problem will be solved." Among the *cāmiyāṭi(s)*, there are some who are very powerful for divination. People throng to them in large numbers. A *cāmiyāṭi* said to a woman, "You should never bring a lemon for god; come empty-handed and pray to god!"

As this is going on, the *villupāṭṭu* commences in another corner. Someone explains that it is this music that is so powerful, on account of which the god descends on people and enables the *cāmiyāṭi(s)* to perform divination. Some *cāmiyāṭi(s)* go there and dance very energetically to the tune of *villupāṭṭu*. This is followed by *kaṇiyāṉkūttu*. The rush for divination keeps on increasing, because the common folk believe that the *cāmiyāṭi(s)* are very powerful after vēṭṭai. This goes on till early morning (around 6.00 a.m,). The *kaṇiyāṉkūttu* and *villupāṭṭu* also continue till then.

End Rituals of Koṭai

Sharing of Paṭaipu

After divination, around 7.00 a.m. the cāmiyāṭi(s) go to bathe in the common tank of the village. They worship the deity once more and eat a portion of the paṭaipu offered to the deity. In some cases, this paṭaipu is also distributed to all the families who have paid temple tax for koæai. For the ordinary devotees, the end of koæai is marked by the cooking of a chicken, pig or goat which is offered as nērccai (votive offering) to CM. The meat is shared with the relatives and friends who have been invited to their homes for the feast. In those places where kāppukaṭṭutal (tying of kāppu) has marked the beginning of koæai, it is kāppuaîuttal (untying of kāppu) that significantly marks the end of the celebration of koṭai rituals, as we shall see later.

Eighth Day Koṭai

The eighth day *koṭai*–also called *T-ṭṭukaḻittal*–marks the end of koṭai rituals definitely. All those who were involved in koṭai festivals come together and thank CM for the successful completion of koṭai. At Kayatar, some Muslims sponsor the meal that day.

Other Rituals of Kayatar

'Other rituals' refer to those rituals that are found not in all *koṭai*, but in some places where three-day *koṭai* is celebrated. This indicates that they are not a very essential part of *koṭai* rituals. Narrated below are rituals of this type, observed at Kayatar.

The Ceremony of Kāppukaṭṭutal

This ceremony 'Kāppukaṭṭutal' refers to the Kaṇiyāṉs' tying of special kinds of amulets on the hands of *cāmiyāṭi(s)*, which they keep for the three days of koæai. Kāppu here is a thread that strings together betel, a piece of turmeric and a steel ring. This ceremony never takes place without the help of Kaṇiyāṉs. This ceremony took place as described below: All cāmiyāṭi(s) sit in front of CM altar while the Kaṇiyāṉs arrive on the spot. A Kaṇiyāṉ known as *aṇṇāvi* (lead singer) starts his song and a musical instrument called *makuṭam* is played by two other Kaṇiyāṉs. Now, the *kaiveṭṭu* (one who cuts his hand) Kaṇiyāṉ gets *tirunāru* from the *cāmiyāṭi(s)* and sprinkles it over the materials he has brought. This is followed by applying of *tirunāru*, and then *kuṅkuma poṭṭu* (saffron round mark) on the forehead of all Kaṇiyāṉs and the *cāmiyāṭi(s)*. He then applies turmeric water and sandalwood paste onto the bodies of the *cāmiyāṭi(s)*. Next, taking mango leaves from *kumpam* in their hands, two Kaṇiyāṉs standing on the either side of the *cāmiyāṭi(s)*' wave the mango leaves from left to right. Then they exchange places and wave the mango leaves from right to left. After this, the *kaiveṭṭu* Kaṇiyāṉ rotates the mango leaves over the head of each *cāmiyāṭi*. This is followed by the Kaṇiyāṉ cutting bananas into two which he rotates over the head of each *cāmiyāṭi*. Some *cāmiyāṭi(s)* shout and scream, showing signs of possession. Similarly, he rotates the coconut twice over their heads and then breaks the coconut and keeps it on the winnowing pan. Now comes the central part of the ceremony, the tying of *kāppus*. Kaṇiyāṉ now takes the five *kāppus*, puts them into water and incenses them. Next, he puts rice grains into the hands of all the *cāmiyāṭi(s)*. He takes a *kāppu* and ties it to the *kumpam* first and ties the *kāppu* to all the *cāmiyāṭi(s)*. This is the climax of the evening ritual.

When this takes place, people shout, bells ring, the Kaṇiyāṉ sings in a feverish pitch and all Kaṇiyāṉs dance and go nearer to the *cāmiyāṭi(s)*. Some women begin making *kuṟavai*, a typical sound usually made by women by twisting their tongues for any auspicious occasion in the village. Then, gradually, Kaṇiyāṉs stop their songs and recede into the background.

After this, the *cāmiyāṭi(s)* also dance. Some yell in an ecstatic fashion. People rush to get *tirunāru* from the *cāmiyāṭi(s)*. They sometimes close their eyes and act as if possessed by an external divine power. Some are so fully possessed and agitated that they need to be controlled by others, who hold them from back. All men and women go to them to get blessings. With this, the rituals of the day come to an end. Half an hour later, the *villupāṭṭu* started in which the stories of CM and other stories were sung. After this, *Kaṇiyāṉkūttu*, another popular ritual theater of the area, began. While this went on, the main *pūṭams* were being decorated elaborately. The four main deities' altars were given the shape of the respective images of the deities. This was done very beautifully with the help of plantain stems.

Civaṉaṭainta Perumāḷ *Pūcai*

The next day, early in the morning, rituals started with the killing of a red-coloured goat inside the courtyard, sacrificed to the deity Civaìaæainta Perumāḷ. After this there was no ritual till 12.00 noon, apart from *villupāṭṭu* singing around 10.00 a.m.

Ucci Koṭai

At twelve noon, the *ucci* (noon) *koṭai* starts. All the five *cāmiyāṭi(s)* are seated on the ground facing the people. Only the temporary *paraṇ* (altar) is made in front of Cuṭalai's *pūṭam* and the CM is already veiled. The Kaṇiyāṉs come into the courtyard, two of them clad as women. The *kaiveṭṭu* Kaṇiyāṉ bring a winnowing pan that contains a coconut, a garland and a tumbler of rice. He brings an *ural* (pestle) and keeps it in the centre. He applies *tirunāru* on the forehead of all Kaṇiyāṉs and the *cāmiyāṭi(s)*, while *aṇṇāvi* (the lead singer among Kaṇiyāṉs) starts his song to the accompaniment of *makuṭam*.

The *kaiveṭṭu* Kaṇiyāṉ then rotats his right leg around the *ural* (pestle), wears a garland on his neck, and a head-gear on his head with a towel. Now the Kaṇiyāṉ applies sandalwood paste on his owṇ body first and then on the *cāmiyāṭi(s)*, and traces *kuṅkuma poṭṭu* on their forehead which is followed by the village representatives garlanding the *cāmiyāṭi(s)*. Then he cuts a plantain leaf, puts it on the *ural* and sits on it. Sitting thus, he also cuts more leaves. He has to cut twenty one leaves for twenty-one gods. As the *aṇṇāvi* stops singing, the *kaiveṭṭu* Kaṇiyāṉ wears the wooden mask bearing the figure of CM. He climbs on the *ural*, with a knife and a leaf. He begins gyrating and shouting out as if calling out to CM. Now he removes the mask, sits on the *ural* and with a knife he pierces his left forearm. With the blood oozing out from the incision, he smears some leaves kept in front of him. Now, five *cāmiyāṭi(s)* are given leaves in which the smashed plantains are put. Then the Kaṇiyāṉ applies water on his left hand and cuts the same hand once again and drops his blood on the smashed plantains which the *cāmiyāṭi(s)* eat hungrily. This is followed by the slaughtering of a goat, and the *cāmiyāṭi* is said to drink the blood of the goat under cover of a towel.

Ucci Vēṭṭai (Noon Ritual Hunting)

Then the *cāmiyāṭi(s)* wear a special dress consisting of black coloured half-pants and a similar type of cap, and proceed to the cremation ground along with the Kaṇiyāṉs. en route to the cremation ground, they carry torches with them. Only a few are allowed to go the whole way. It is said by the Kaṇiyāṉ, that they go to a higher place at a cremation ground where a cock is beheaded and rotated around the heads of the *cāmiyāṭi(s)* and thrown away. Once again he pierces his arm and offers blood to the gods. Then they descend to another spot where *pūtaṇṇēr* is sprinkled in all four directions.

Aruḷvākku (Divination)

While returning from *vēṭṭai* in the afternoon, people crowd around the *cāmiyāṭi(s)* for *aruḷvākku* . This goes on for about 45 minutes. After an hour or so, people begin to gather o listen to *villupāṭṭu* and *Kaṇiyāṉkūttu*. The *cāmiyāṭi(s)* who were so ecstatic regain some degree of normalcy after their bath. Within an hour, they begin to look after the affairs of the *koṭai*. One of the important events in that afternoon is the lunch which they provide free to all those who come.

Kāppuaṟuttal

The *koṭai* ends around 7.00 a.m. when the *kāppuaṟuttal* takes place. The Kaṇiyāṉ who tied the *kāppu* thread cuts it and removes it from the *cāmiyāṭi(s)*. Then *cāmiyāṭi(s)* go to take bath, come back and eat the *paṭaipu* offered to the deity. Then the common meal begins to be served from 10.00 a.m onwards and continues till 2.00 p.m.

Variations at Other Places

At Vijayanarayanam

The sequence of every *koṭai* has its own unique ordering of rituals. *Kālnāṭṭu*, which is seen in all *koṭai* rituals, is also performed here eight days earlier. But, unlike what happens at Kayatar–where the bringing of *tīrttam* and *kāppukaṭṭutal* took place on the first evening–*mākāppu alaṅkāram* (i.e., the smearing of the deity with rice flour) marks the beginning of three-day *koṭai* here. This is followed by *kuṟi collutal*. Yet *kāppu kaṭṭutal* was present but that was performed on the eve of the second day instead of the first day. Similarly, *kutiaḻaippu*,[14] which was performed on the evening of the first day as a mark of beginning of *koṭai* at Valliyoor, was performed on the second day. Likewise, it is not the early morning sacrifice to Civaṉaṭainta Perumāḷ that marked the beginning of the second day *koṭai* ritual; rather, it was *paṭikaḷaital* (removing of rice flour paste)–which is done as a ritual–that initiated the *koṭai* rituals on the second day. This was followed by twenty one *apiṣēkam(s)* (consecrations) done with twenty one ingredients such as milk, honey, tender coconut water, rose water, etc. At noon, an ordinary *pūcai* was performed followed by the event of divination. In the afternoon, the ritual that was celebrated with great grandeur was the carrying of *pālkuṭam* that followed *kutiaḻaippu*. The description of some rituals of variation at Vijayanarayanam is in place here.

Mākāppu Alaṅkāram

This term *mākāppu* denotes the layer of paste of rice that covers the divinity for the *pūcai* on the first evening of the feast. *Mākāppu* signifies "great protection." Reiniche deciphers three interpretations in this ritual. This rite of beginning, which is also an invocation, is meant to make the god/goddess favourable. The rice paste signifies prosperity, and makes white the god/goddess, who, in ordinary time, is black.[15] This protection preserves the stains of divinity, while pacifying (role of the paste); consequently, it makes it lenient towards faults of its devotees (in the ritual, for example) and protects them.[16] It is to be noted that at the moment of *mākāppu pūcai*, the *cāmiyāṭi(s)* get possession, and the people approach them for divination.

Preparation for Pālkuæam (Milk Pot)

Around two o clock in the afternoon, all the *pālkuṭam carriers* (i.e., all the men who carry *pālkuṭam*-miklpot) arrive at Civā's temple where their family members gather to accompany them in the procession. Their relatives bring new dhotis and help the men–who are going to carry *pālkuṭam*–to wear the dhoti inside the Civā's temple. People of different castes and different villages gather there and enter into the temple. Some even walk in with their slippers on. This seems to be a day when the rules are relatively relaxed. On the verandah of the temple all the *pālkuṭams* are kept along with plantain leaves upon which rice, coconut, betel nut, incense, etc., meant for *pūcai* are kept. *Pālkuṭam* here is a copper pot with milk inside. Those who have made vows to CM for some reason or the other carry this milk pot on their head in procession for three hours. The person who is to carry the *pālkuṭam* fasts for a week, i.e., will eat only once daily, will neither drink milk nor eat any milk products. The men who carry *pālkuṭam* stay either in the Civā's temple or CM's temple itself ever since *kālnāṭṭu*. This year they stayed in the *CM*'s temple itself.[17] Those families that donate milk to the *pālkuṭam* carriers that day also fast for eight days.

Kutiaḻaippu

Kutiaḻaippu means inviting the deity for the *koṭai* that is done by performing a *pūcai* in front of the household which is responsible for bringing *CM* to the village. At 2.30 p.m., the *cāmiyāṭi(s),* the administrative head of the temple and elders go with *mēḷam* to Sāmpān's residence where the *tirunāru* basket is kept. From there they proceed to the house of a Āsāri (carpenter) where the above-mentioned *pūcai* takes place. *Mēḷam* is played outside that house and the *cāmiyāṭi(s)* get into an intense trance. Some women also get into trance. One or two divinations take place there. From there, the group goes around the village and reaches the Pēcciammaṉ *cāmiyāṭi's* house at Perumāḷ temple street. There again, a *pūcai* is done inside the house. The *mēḷam* players who are neither willing to enter the house nor encouraged by the villagers to enter inside, are forced by some men in the house to play the *mēḷam* inside.[18] After the *pūcai,* the Pēcciammaṉ *cāmiyāṭi* once again starts divining for two to three cases, to which other *cāmiyāṭi(s)* eventually show their displeasure. From there, *pālkuṭams* are taken to the Civā's temple. There, the two men who carry *pālkuṭam* get into an uncontrollable and intense trance in the beginning. However, this subsides after a while. Finally, the select group arrives at the Civā's temple. Then the priest of the temple does *pūcai* around the *pālkuṭams*. *Pālkuṭams* are mounted on the head of the concerned devotees while the *mēḷam* is once again beaten.

The Procession of Pālkuæam

The procession of *pālkuṭam* is a spectacular event in the village. The local villagers, as well as other devotees, join this big procession, which is led by an elephant. Sankara Pandian (the one who will cut goats and pigs during the night ritual) sits on the elephant up front. As the procession moves on, men and women clad in festive garments join the procession, some joining in just in front of their houses. Four sets of *mēḷams* and two groups of *karakāṭṭam* (a folk troupe) add life to the festivities. At the next street, the procession that is already moving dead slow stops for ten minutes at the corner house where more *pālkuṭams* join the procession. Once more, the procession stops after a while near the household that is responsible for bringing CM to another temple (the adjacent temple to the main temple where rituals were recorded by the researcher), and more *pālkuṭams* join the procession from this house. Eventually the procession takes three hours to reach the CM temple. At 6.15 p.m. the procession reaches the temple where the *pālkuṭams* are taken down from the heads of the devotees inside the temple. Now the procession of *pālkuṭam* will shortly culminate in milk *apiṣēkam*.

Kumpāpiṣēkam

Another variation that is very significant to Vijayanarayanam is the *Kumpāpiṣēkam*. At 7.00 p.m. Vedic-style mantras are recited just in front of the CM altar around a fire groomed out with five types of wooden logs. While two Brahmin pūcāri(s) recite Sanskritic mantras, they pour ghee into the fire with the help of a betel leaf rolled like a spoon. In front of the fire, a lamp is kept over a leaf full of paddy. Nine mud *kumpams* are mounted on the rice which is spread out. Besides this, other coconuts and bunches of banana are placed there. Now in front of CM, where Vedic fire sacrifice takes place, ten plates are placed upon which are kept coconuts, plantains, pineapples, apples, grapes, the cap and the belts with bells (meant for *vēṭṭai*). Once this is over, the Brahmin priests go over to the CM altar (this is the only time Brahmin priests enter the altar of CM) and start *apiṣēkam*, first, with water. They then pour milk from all *pālkuṭams* (a portion of this milk is collected and poured back into the *pālkuṭams*). Then they do the *apiṣēkam* with tender coconut, saffron powder, curd, sandal water, etc. Finally the water from the *kumpam* is poured onto the deity and things such as *veṭṭivfr* (a particular root), *tarpa pul* (a kind of grass), garland, etc., which are in the *kumpam* are offered to the deity. This gets over by 8.15 p.m. This type of sanskritised *pūcai* is a unique feature of Vijayanarayanam. Then a big curtain is drawn in front of the altar to facilitate the decorations being done inside. From now on, the devotees from various villages come in queue to offer coconuts, flowers, etc., in a basket. They take holy ash from the *cāmiyāṭi(s)* and men who are meant for distributing it. There are moneyboxes fixed in many places for people to drop small donations.

Besides the sets of rituals described above, the rituals that were absent in three-day Vijyanarayanam *koṭai* were numbers five and six (in Figure 1) that took place at Kayatar. However, the rituals of numbers eight, ten, eleven, twelve, thirteen and fourteen are more or less similar to what was seen earlier in Kayatar except that Kaṇiyāṉ also pierced his tongue for giving blood besides piercing his forearm.

At Valliyoor

The *koṭai* at Valliyoor has some definitive variations with the sequence of rituals described in Figure 1. The element of *pālkuṭam* (i.e., 2b in Figure 1) was not part of group two rituals (beginning of *koṭai* ritual) which took place on the eve of the first day of *koṭai*, but rather it was conducted on the morning of the second day as a separate but an elaborate ritual performed only by children accompanied by women singing some Tamil hymns. Instead, the new element in group two rituals was *kutiaḻaippu* that was treated with great significance. Further, rituals of the *kāppukaṭṭutal* (3a) and *kāppuaṟuttal* (12) by Kaṇiyāṉs were also absent at Valliyoor in spite of the fact that Kaṇiyāṉs were present there to perform *Kaṇiyāṉk%ottu*. This indicates that Kaṇiyāṉs, who call themselves *cāmikkucāmi* (i.e., 'god of gods')[19] were not very central figures to the ritual corpus at Valliyoor.[20] Instead it was the barbers (the traditional servant caste) who were included as ritual co-functionaries at Valliyoor. This was quite evident when an accompanying barber for the *vēṭṭai* ritual was garlanded like the Brahmin *cāmiyāṭi* before the event. Similarly, Kaṇiyāṉs were excluded in numbers five, six and eleven. Subsequently, elements 5a, 6c 10b, and 10d were also absent at Valliyoor. Further *ūṭṭu* (5.c) and (9.d) were also absent at Valliyoor. The obvious reason is that the Brahmins, being vegetarians, cannot perform this, which necessitates drinking the blood of animals. Yet there is a tendency towards outward manifestation of non-vegetarian behaviour that is evident in the smelling of cooked meat.

Further, the ritual of number nine[21] takes place at Valliyoor after *vēṭṭai* and the ritual of 'divination' takes the form of 'blessing' at Valliyoor. The *cāmiyāṭi* does not analyse any issues of the common devotees and suggest any solution to their problems, but gives individual blessings to his family members and to the ritual co-functionaries such as Barbers, Sāmpān(s) and Tēvar(s). A common blessing is given to the general pubic after *vēṭṭai*.

At Naduvakurichi

As for the one-day *koṭai* at Naduvakurichi, all the elements of common rituals of CM *koṭai* were present. As mentioned earlier, the Paḻḻar's CM at Naduvakurichi is called Kaḷḷattiāṉ as his *pūṭam* is placed near the Kaḷḷatti tree. Another significant thing here is equal importance given to another deity called 'Putiyamuttu'. They say Kaḷḷttiāṉ and Putiyamuttu are twins. Hence, unlike other places, major core rituals of *koṭai* are performed for two deities, i.e., Kaḷḷattiāṉ and Putiyamuttu.

As regards the rituals, in group two (of Figure 1), the element of bringing of *pālkuṭam* was missing. Instead, a new element of painting of symbol on the *pūṭam* was grafted to the group. Being a one-day *koṭai*, the rituals of 4, 5, 6, 7, were missing at Naduvakurichi, Similarly, it has to be noted that the elements of Kaṇiyāṉ *kaiveṭṭu*, *Kaṇiyāṉkūttu* and *villupāṭṭu* were totally missing here. Since they have two main deities, they have two sets of vēṭṭai and divination. Another very unique thing about Naduvakurichi is the firing of crackers after *vēṭṭai*. Further, the element of *pāriveṭṭai,* which precedes the sharing of offering that marks the end of *koṭai,* is another variation at Naduvakurichi. Having said this, let us describe some of the variations at Naduvakurichi.

Painting of Symbol on the Pūṭams

After the bringing of *tīrttam* at 6.45 p.m., the temple *pūcāri* of a particular Dalit family collects water from the *poṅkal* pot, and mixes a light red colour (*kāvi*) powder in it. He first draws a symbol of a mere red line on the Civaìaæainta Perumāḷ's *pūṭam,* and then he draws the same symbol on the Pēcciammaṉ's *pūṭam*. However, he draws a different symbol on Kaḷḷattiāṉ 's *pūṭam*. He then comes to Putiyamuttu's *pūṭam* and draws the same symbol that was drawn on Kaḷḷattiāṉ's *pūṭam*. The *mēḷam* is played while all this goes on. Four male *cāmiyāṭi(s)* and one female *cāmiyāṭi* worship and prostrate before the deity. Their way of worship is different from other places. Here, they first put their folded hands above their heads, and then they cross their hands (meaning, place the right hand on the left shoulder and left hand on the right shoulder) and put their head down. They begin to kneel in the same position. As they kneel, they bend their left leg, stretching the right leg backwards, and finally they prostrate. They repeat the same actions thrice or more times till the painting gets over. From then on people can come to receive holy ash from the *cāmiyāṭi(s)*.

Firing of Crackers

While, in other places, silence is supposed to prevail during the ritual of *vēṭṭai*, at the *koṭai* of Paḷḷar(s), there is an infringement of such a common rule: the firing of crackers–every now and then during *vēṭṭai*–is given significance. At the same time, the two female *cāmiyāṭi(s)* standing a little distance away dance mildly with baby-dolls in their hands, while *mēḷam* is played to accompany their dance. After an hour or so when the Kaḷḷattiāṉ-*cāmiyāṭi* comes back from *vēṭṭai*, he bursts crackers. It is a big spectacular show. It goes on for half-an-hour or so. Similarly, when Putiyamuttu *cāmiyāṭi* comes back from *vēṭṭai*, he too ignites a series of crackers kept in the open field. The firing of a series of crackers after *vēṭṭai* is said to be one of the distinguishing features of the *koṭai* of Dalits in Naduvakurichi village. They spend about sixty-five thousand rupees for the crackers, the bursting of which lasts for about an hour.

Pārivēṭṭai[22]

At 7.30 a.m. one of the *cāmiyāṭi(s)* is tied with a chain around his chest and taken into the field by Kaḷḷttiāṉ *cāmiyāṭi*. There he hands him over to Putiyamuttu who drags him further, and hurls a sickle over his head, as if he is going to kill him. In fact, this is said to be a symbolic act of killing. The chained man falls down on the ground and rolls on the ground for a while. He lies down lifeless for a while, to indicate that he is dead.

Depiction of CM's Essential Nature Through Core Rituals

It is to be noted that core rituals, together with their myths, are the distinguishing mark of CM. The core rituals contain a form of worship which is no doubt very old and which must have always been considered too significant to be discarded. They reveal a typical trait of the deity that they embody.

The Intractable Nature of CM

As we will see in the origin myth of CM, the intractable nature of CM is one of his characteristics. He is adamant and wants to have everything according to his own way even if it means expulsion from Kailācam, the highest abode for the gods and for humans. Even Lord Civā had to condescend to CM's demands, when he decided to create Kaṇiyāṉ and offer him the human blood sacrifice and the pregnant animals. These animals prefigure the sacrifice of Māvicakki that highlights the theme of CM's destructive power not only over the wicked, but also over his/her progeny. Thus the core ritual of sacrifice (human and animal) while enacting the myth reveals the nature of CM as *tuṭiyāṉa teyvam* (active and very powerful a god) and as a god of controlling power over the wicked.

CM's Protective Power and Power of Encompassment Revealed in Vēṭṭai

Through ritual performance, the core ritual of *vēṭṭai* establishes CM's protective power. His protective power is recognised as such by the people through his power of control over evil forces. Through *vēṭṭai* it is believed that CM overpowers all the malevolent spirits lurking in the uncultivated land and living in the cremation ground. By the control of such spirits it is believed that CM protects crops, cattle and human beings from the scourge of diseases and *pēy(s)*, and ensures the well being of the village. Further, the ritual of *vēṭṭai* also reveals the power of encompassment of CM. Though he is a temple deity inhabiting the borders of the village separating the inhabited part of the village from the uninhabited forest (*kāṭu*), yet, he has the power to encompass the lives of the people, the fields and he can also control the spirits in the *kāṭu*. This power of encompassment is demonstrated in the ritual of *vēṭṭai*. Unlike the sacred powers of other gods (which Shulman mentions),[23] which have to be limited and channeled to proper courses so that their power becomes accessible and auspicious, CM's protective power is demonstrated and established not through forms of limitation but through the act of 'encompassment' such as *vēṭṭai*. And this *vēṭṭai* is invariably followed by divination. It means that in the ritual complex of ko*ṭai* rituals, chronologically speaking, the god's power is made accessible to the people after the demonstration of his power as encompassing, not as limited, as noted by Shulman.[24] As will be seen in the next chapter, the major theme of *protective power of CM* and the sub-theme of *CM's power of encompassment* are the key thematic concerns that run through all the constituents of the cult.

Availability of CM's Protective Power to the People at Divination/ Tirun•ru

As Eveline Meyer observes, from devotee's point of view, rituals may not be much more than an occasion to collect as much sacred power as possible.[25] This appropriation of ritual power is mediated either through divination or through *tirunāru* (holy ash). Both make available to people the protective power of CM. As the interpretative meaning of divination would be dealt with later on, it is enough to mention that the core ritual of divination once again reinforces and reinstalls the theme of protective power of CM in the minds of the folk and "present opportunity for the participants to re-establish the harmony in their lives which had been disrupted by physical and mental ills."[26]

CM's Communion with People in Paœaipu and Poṅkal *(i.e. Prasātam)*

The ritual elements of *paṭaipu* (cooked non-vegetarian food) and *poṅkal*, etc., signify a reciprocal relationship between the CM deity and the people, because these 'offerings to the god' become *prasātam* (sacred food) when consumed by the worshippers. Since more about it will be dealt with in the fifth chapter, it is enough to mention that the performance of offering such as sacrifice, etc., is not only meant to reveal the essential nature of CM as the protective power, but underwrites the most basic relationship between CM and the people. It attempts to provide logic to the protective power by locating it in a system of relationship between the deity and the worshippers. It does this by creating a reciprocal relationship with the deity, the protective power and the devotees, the protected, through the ritual elements of *paṭaipu* (the cooked non-vegetarian food) and *poṅkal*. Even the objects of blood sacrifices such as the goat and pig will be cooked and consumed by the villagers. Thus, this also would be turned into *prasātam*.

Interpretation of Koṭai Rituals Through Network Analysis

Network is a collection of 'nodes' or 'points' connected by lines. In our diagram (Figure 3), node is a point of ritual moment in which a series of intersections of two ritual movements, indicated by lines with arrow marks takes place. It underlies the ordering of sequence of ritual events. Each node, as ritual centre, embodies various ritual events, and is often characterized by twin ritual movements: centripetal and centrifugal. It is constituted by a centripetal ritual movement that moves the ritual network into a node and a centrifugal ritual movement that moves it away from a node to another node. For example, let us take the node of worship in figure 3.3 It is the centre of ritual events such as 2, 4, 6, 8, 14 and 18. The ritual event of *āratti/pūcai* (2) is marked by a centripetal ritual movement towards the node of worship at this juncture. This centripetal ritual movement consists of preparatory rites such as the drawing of symbols on the *pūṭam*, personal worship of *cāmiyāṭi* and his getting blessing from Ammaṉ *cāmiyāṭi*, and the movement of devotees towards the place of worship, etc. This ritual event is also marked by a centrifugal ritual movement that progresses towards another node of 'offering' wherein *poṅkal* is cooked. This movement consists of gathering

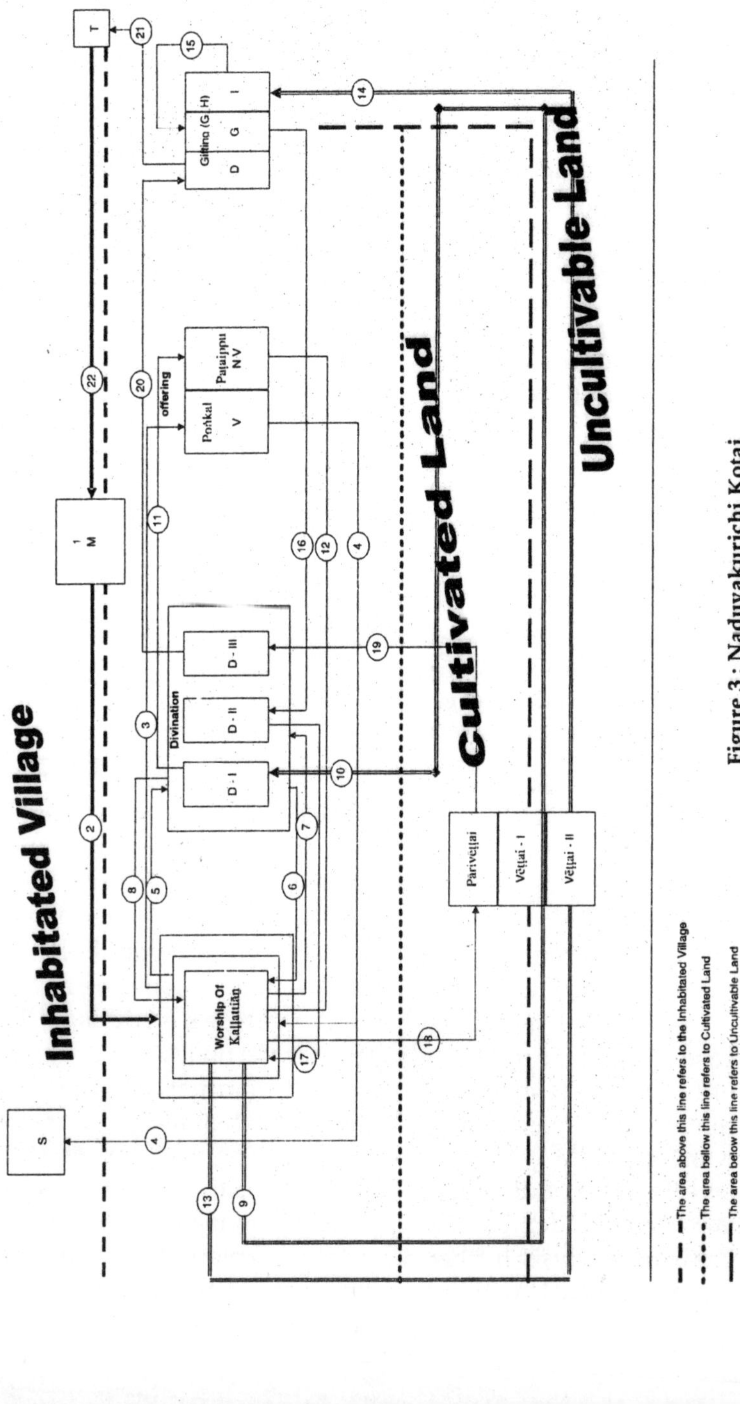

Figure 3 : Naduvakurichi Koṭai

Explanation for Figure 3

1. Procession from Mutāramaṉ Temple
2. *Pūcai* (worship)
3. *Poṅkal*
4. Mounting of *Kumpam* and garlanding of the source
5. Divination
6. *Pūcai*
7. Divination
8. *Pūcai*
9. *Vēṭṭai I*
10. Divination I
11. *Paṭaippu* (Non-veg)
12. *Pūcai*
13. *Vēṭṭai* II
14. Inspection and acceptance of offering
15. Gifting of offerings to the Drummers
16. Divination II
17. *Pūcai*
18. *Pārivēṭṭai*
19. Divination III
20. Distribution of offerings
21. Bath in the lake and eating of *Paṭaippu*
22. Back to Mutāramaṉ Temple

of firewood, placing of rice and water in front of the *pūṭam*, and applying of turmeric on the vessel, etc. It is to be noted that the centrifugal ritual movement of one node becomes a centripetal ritual movement of another node. Thus the above-mentioned centrifugal movement of node 'worship' becomes a centripetal ritual movement for the node of 'offering'.

A first look at the figures of the network analysis of the koæai at all four places indicates that the nodes that are most important (i.e., around which most of ritual activities are centered) are common to all the four. They are the node of worship of CM (*pūcai*), the node of offering, the node of *vēṭṭai* and the node of divination. It is to be noted that all four have already been identified as 'core rituals' in the previous pages. Network analysis further helps us to explore the function of these core rituals within the dynamics of ritual power.

In the discourse of dynamics of ritual power of the CM cult, one has to distinguish between its various elements, such as source of ritual power, generation of power, display of power, distribution and appropriation of power. Source of ritual power refers more to a place/locus that is vested with ritual power. Other elements such as generation, display, distribution and appropriation of ritual power are related to the ritual performances. The common folk worldview relates some nodes more to one of these elements than to others. For instance, the node of worship of CM's *pūṭam* is seen as the most basic source of ritual power, while divination is perceived as the nodal point of distribution and appropriation of ritual power. Similarly, *vēṭṭai* is associated both with the display of ritual power and with the generation of ritual power for subsequent acts of divination. The element of ūṭṭu/Kaṇiyāṉ *kaiveṭṭu* in the node of 'offering' apparently has to do with generation of ritual power. The other elements in the node of 'offering,' at first sight, seem to be unrelated to the dynamics of ritual power at *koṭai*. But they presume a most basic fundamental reciprocal relationship between the deity and the devotees. If not for the belief in the reciprocity, the dynamics of ritual power cannot take place. In fact, the node of 'offering' underlies, reinforces, reinstates, embodies and enlivens this most basic fundamental relationship between the deity and the people. It confirms and constructs a set of such beliefs in the folk worldview that upholds and facilitates the whole range of dynamics of ritual power that takes place.

In the above Figure (3) of Naduvakurichi, the most important nodes are 'worship', 'offering', 'divination' and '*vēṭṭai*'. Of all these, the node of 'worship of *pūṭam*' seems to be more important than the other nodes as six ritual events take place there. This reveals the fact that it is the most fundamental *source of CM's power*. But this source is a permanent source of ritual power. It always exists there for the common folk to approach it and appropriate it. Hence, from the viewpoint of ritual power *during koṭai*, as recounted by the folk, the node 'divination' is very significant, though only five ritual events take place there. This is so because it functions as a ritual site, immediate, instantaneous and transient, wherein ritual power is displayed, distributed and appropriated. The *cāmiyāṭṭam,* its ritual concomitant, which is not shown in the diagram, is an important outlet that *displays ritual power* very effectively. The major divinations such as divination I, Divination II and Divination III are followed by centrifugal movements from *Vēṭṭai* I, *Vēṭṭai* II and *Pārivēṭṭai,* respectively, thus underlying the commonly-held folk belief that *vēṭṭai* is the immediate source of power for 'divination'. The firing of crackers constitutes the centrifugal movement between *Vēṭṭai* I and Divination I. The igniting of fireworks at Naduvakurichi is the unique characteristic of Paḻḻar's *koṭai* festival, which gives voice to the ascendancy of the marginalized whose voice had been silenced within caste hierarchy for centuries.

The Valliyoor Figure (see, 4), too indicates that the node of worship of CM's *pūṭam* is the most important one, as the highest number of centripetal ritual movements (fourteen times) occur there. The other significant nodes at Valliyoor are those of blessing and of offering, both witnessing to an equal number of inward movements, i.e., seven. Though formal divination does not take place at Valliyoor, it takes the form of blessing and a kind of *aruḷvākku* . Out of seven occurrences there, five of them were centrifugal movements from the node of offering (that too sacrifice) and obtained by the ritual co-functionaries as a token of gratitude for performing sacrifice for the Brahmins. The most important *aruÀv□kku,* i.e., the very first one after *vēṭṭai,* is reserved for the family members at the VAO's house but coupled with the ritual of *pūcai* and *āratti* there.

In fact the ritual element of *propitiation* is more evident at Brahmins *koṭai* than in other cases, as it takes place five times within the temple precincts, and once at *maiyāṇam*. Besides the slaughtering of animals, it also took the form of throwing of boiled eggs. It took place many times. The very beginning event of three-day *koṭai* such as bringing of *tīrttam* featured also as a propitiation ceremony, as the *cāmiyāṭi* clad in *vēṭṭai* dress threw boiled eggs for different gods/spirits at many places during the procession. Perhaps the Brahmin's *koṭai* at Valliyoor is the

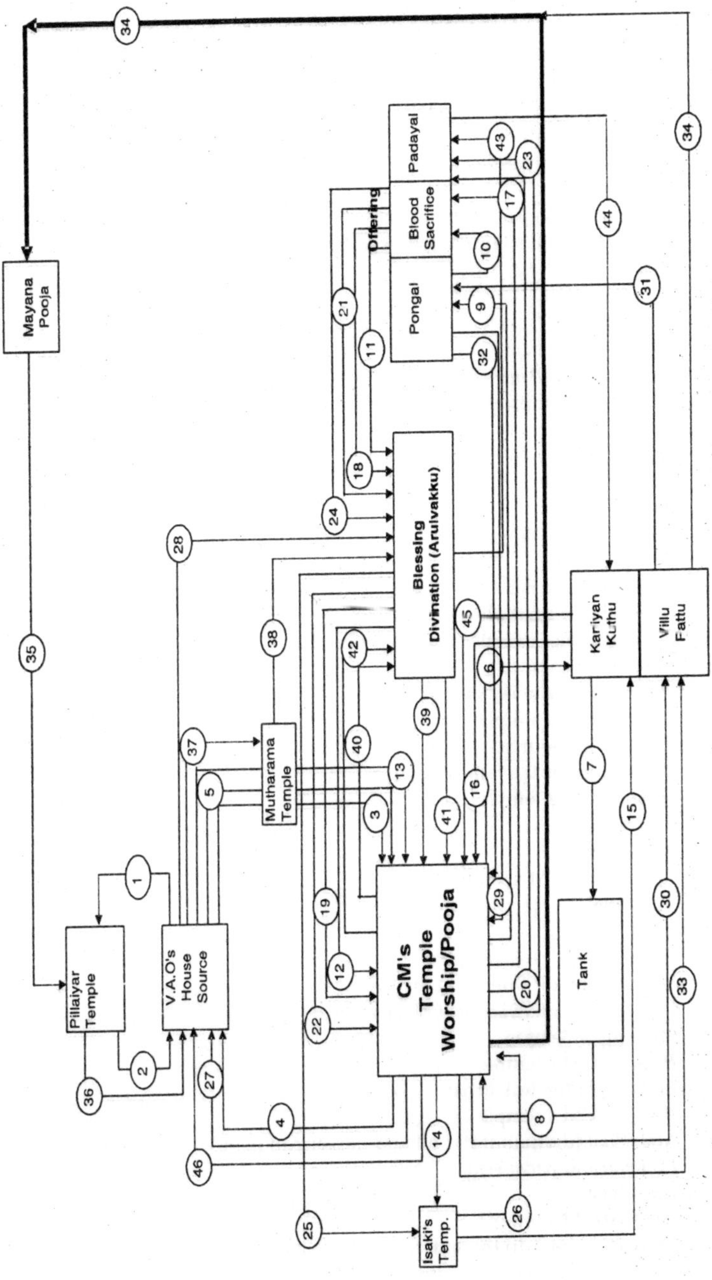

Figure 4 : Valliyoor Koṭai

Explanation for Figure 4

1. Procession to Piḷḷaiyār temple
2. *Pūcai* at home
3. Procession via Mutāramaṉ temple to CM's temple
4. *Kutiaḷaippu* at neem tree
5. *Pūcai* at CM's temple
6. Kaṇiyāṉkūttu
7. Bringing of *kumpam* from the tank of saravanpoighai
8. *Pūcai???* at CM's temple followed by mounting of *kumpam*
9. *Poṅkal*
10. Blood sacrifice
11. Blessing
12. Mākāppu alaṅkāram
13. Carrying of *pālkuṭam (milkpot)*
14. Lighting of lamps, *mavilakku*
15. Kaṇiyāṉkūttu
16. Milk *apiṣēkam*(consecration)
17. Blood sacrifice
18. Blessing
19. *Pūcai* for Ladasanyasi
20. Blood sacrifice
21. Divination for Barbers
22. *Pūcai* at CM's temple
23. Blood sacrifice at Icakiammaṉ temple
24. Blessing
25. *Pūcai* at Icakiammaṉ's temple
26. *Pūcai* at CM's temple
27. *Pūcai* to the source
28. Divination for the family
29. Pūcai at CM's temple
30. Villupāṭṭu
31. *Poṅkal*
32. *Apiṣēkam* at CM's temple
33. Villupāṭṭu
34. *Vēṭṭai*
35. *Pūcai* at Piḷḷaiyārēs temple
36. Distribution of *Tirunāru* at the source
37. Distribution of *Tirunāru* at Mutāramaṉ temple
38. Blessing of Sampāṉ
39. *Pūcai* at CM's temple
40. Blessing of the folk artist
41. *Pūcai* at CM's temple
42. Aruḷvākku (divination)for all and blessing of people with *Tirunārui*
43. *Paṭaippu* and *paraṇ veṭṭu*
44. Kaṇiyāṉkūttu
45. *Pūcai* at CM's temple
46. Procession back to the source

only event wherein the carrying of *t-rttam*, the very beginning of three-day *koṭai* takes the structure and form of propitiation. The noon worship at the house was followed by such propitiatory rites once again. Unlike as in other places of *koṭai*, the offerings and sacrifices made at Valliyoor seldom took the form of *prasātam* among Brahmins. This further proves Fuller's point that where there are no *prasātam* produced for the consumption by human beings, the offerings become mere "rituals of propitiation, appeasement or exorcism, which serve to separate the worshipper from an angry deity or a malevolent demon."[27] While this highlights the greater emphasis that Brahmins give to the rite of propitiation, it also clearly indicates that the idea of 'propitiation' is of utmost importance for the Brahmin's celebration of *koṭai* the reasons of which will be explored in the last chapter. Another significant node that is given more importance here than in other places is that of worship at the source, i.e., the VAO's house, which clearly demonstrates to the public a clear link between the CM and this family, the reasons of which need to be investigated.

As regards Kayatar (see, Figure 5), both, the nodes of worship of CM *pūṭam* and that of offering have equal importance, as both occur six times. If we also consider sacrifices of the *maiyāṇapūcai* held twice, once at noon (*ūcci koṭai*) and at midnight (*cāma koṭai*), the node of 'offering' plays a more significant role than in other places, thus indicating the priority given to the reciprocal relationship between the deity and the worshippers (Illatu Piḷḷaimār[s]) over other things. This is further evident from the fact of the common meal served by the temple administration during *koæai*, which was not seen in other areas of research.

As regards Vijayanarayanam (see, Figure 6), all the three major nodes such as 'worship at CM's temple', 'divination' and 'offering' all play an equally important role, as each one occurs six times. As in other places, there is a link between worship of CM (source of power) and divination (distribution of ritual power), as seen in 2, 4, 18. Even divinations 7 and 9 have to do with *kutiaḻaippu*, which is a ritual about conceptualisation of the source of CM at the temple. Further,

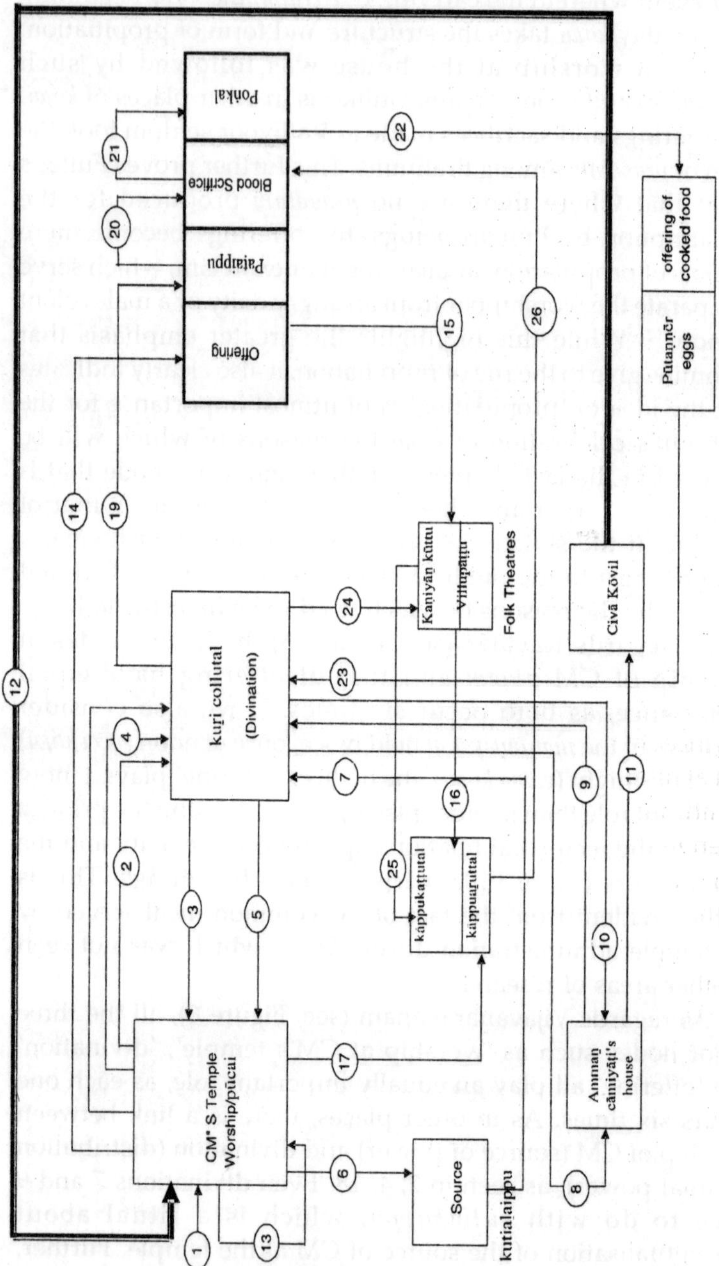

Figure 5 : Vijaya Narayanam Koṭai

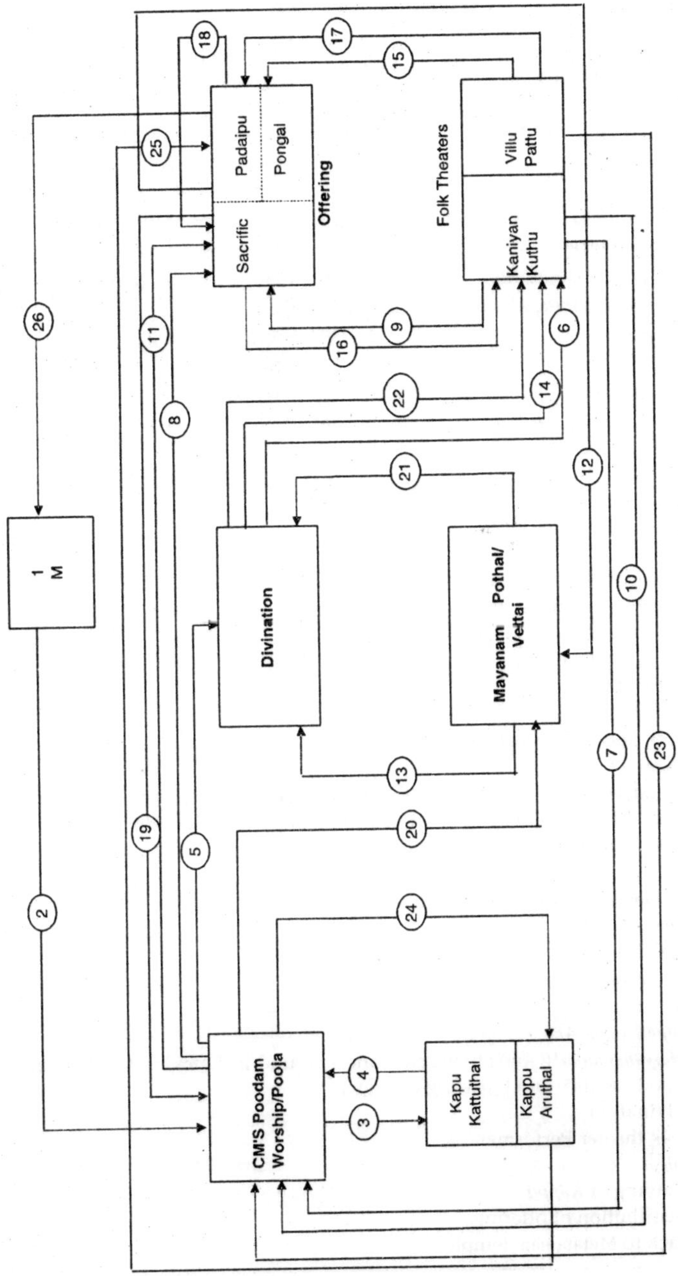

Figure 6 : Kayatar Koṭai

Explanation for Figure 5

1. Mākāppu *Pūcai*	2. Divination
3. Twenty one type of *Apiṣēkam*	4. Divination
5. *Pūcai* at a house linked to origin	6. *Kutiaḻaippu*
7. Divination	8. *Pūcai* at ammaṉ *cāmiyāṭi's* house
9. Divination	10. Starting of *pālkuṭam*
11. Procession to Siva's temple	12. Grand Procession of *pālkuṭam*
13. *Kumpāapiṣēkam*	14. Offerings of devotees
15. Folk theatre- *Villupāṭṭu*	16. Tying of *Kāppu* (amulet)
17. *Dīpa/Doūpa Arātaṉai* (a form of *Pūcai*)	18. Divination
19. *Paṭaippu*	20. Sacrifice (animal/human)
21. *Poṅkal*	22. *Maiyāṉampōtal*
23. Divination	24. Folk theatre
25. Untying of *Kāppu*	26. Distribution of offering

Explanation for Figure 6

1. Procession from Mutāramaṉ Temple
2. Mounting of *Kumpam*
3. Tying of *Kāppu* (Protective Amulet)
4. *Pūcai* (Worship) at Pūṭam (altar)
5. Divination/ *Cāmiyāṭṭam*
6. Kaṇiyāṉpāṭṭu (song)
7. *Pūcai* at Pūṭam
8. Sacrifice
9. Folk Theater performances
10. *Pūcai*
11. Blood sacrifice (includes also Kaṇiyāṉs piercing of forearm)
12. *Maiyāṉampōtal* (Going to the cremation ground-includes human/animal blood sacrifice and throwing of eggs)
13. Divination
14. Villupāṭṭu(parallel performance)
15. *Poṅkal*
16. Folk Theater performances
17. *Paṭaippu*
18. Sacrifice
19. *Dīpa/Doūpa Arātaṉai* (a form of worship)
20. *Maiyāṉampōtal* (Going to the cremation ground-includes human/animal blood sacrifice and throwing of eggs)
21. Divination
22. Folk theater Performances
23. *Pūcai*
24. Untying of *Kāppu*
25. Distribution of offering
26. Back to Mutāramaṉ temple

as mentioned earlier, here too, the most important ritual moment of divination, i.e., 23, the climax event of *koṭai* derives its credentials of ritual power par excellence from *maiyāṇapūcai*.

Based on the above dynamics of ritual power, ritual can be defined as follows: *ritual is a network of power wherein different sets (families) of performative*[28] *acts interact with each other in relation to a locus/source of power (called ritual nodes) through the mediation of ritual specialists* or *worshippers*. The object of folk ritual network is to unveil the power: to make the latent, evident; to render the inaccessible, accessible; and to cause the dormant to become torrential. Sequentially, ritual is a movement from one/less powerful place to a another/more powerful place, from one/less powerful event to another/more powerful event, from a less manifest source of power to a more manifest source of power; or, conversely, from the more unmanifest source to the less unmanifest source of power. Ritual also functions to control the evil and unwanted powers, but in its functionality of control of evil powers, it moves in the manifestation of such control from a more powerful evil source to a less powerful evil source. Thus, folk ritual becomes a network of events consisting of different moments and movements of discrete activities between spaces that are sacred and a-sacred, social and a-social. Ritual power, as mentioned in the framework of ritual power, has the ontological dimension on one side, and other dimensions such as existential, material, and socio-political dimensions, on the other. Because of their association with the supernatural, i.e., the ontological dimension, rituals can become transformative on other planes, as Deflem notes that rituals have "their powers to act upon and change the persons involved in ritual performances."[29]

Conclusion

In this chapter, we have described the ritual complexes of *koṭai* celebrations in all four villages. The rituals that are found in all the four places are termed 'common rituals' and they give us an idea about the most basic structure of *koṭai*. 'Common rituals' consists of 'core rituals,' which are the most essential components specific to *koṭai* for CM. The emergence of core rituals as the most significant rituals is confirmed by the method of triangulation through another technique of data analysis, namely, network analysis. Network analysis has further explored the function of these core rituals in the dynamics of ritual power. Besides, the description of core rituals has led to the interpretation of essential characteristics of CM, i.e., the intractable nature of CM, CM's protective power and CM's power of encompassment. As will be seen in the next chapter, these characteristics will also form the common underlying themes of different constituents of the CM cult.

Notes

1. Reiniche, *Les dieux*, 147.
2. Cf. Stuart Blackburn, *Singing of Birth and Death*, University of Pennsylvania Press, Philadelphia, 1988, 37.
3. Cf. In *A Study of Sudalaimadasamy Cult in the Tirunelveli District of Tamilnadu: A Minor Project Report submitted to the UGC*, St. Xavier's College, Palayamkottai, 2000, 65.
4. Blackburn, *Singing of Birth*, 38.
5. These occasions at Vijayanarayanam are the feasts of Kārttikai, Mahācivarāttiri, etc. Besides, the first days of the Tamil months of *Tai, Cittirai and Vaikāsi* are some of the days in which special *pūcai(s)* are held. Further, the last Friday of every Tamil month is marked by the cutting of goats and *aṉṉatāṉam (free-food for all)*.
6. Cf. Eveline Meyer, *Ankalaparamecuvari Cult*, Steiner Verlag Wiesbaden Gmbh, Stuttgart, 1986, 105.
7. *Pāl kuṭam* in this case was a silver pot with milk with which they wash the main deities.
8. *Āratti*, refers to the ritual waving of camphor flame. In folk ritual complex it need not always refer to the culmination of *pūcai* as Fuller observes (Cf. C.J. Fuller, *The Camphor Flame. Popular Hinduism and Society in India*, Princeton University Press, N.J., 1992, 73), because often the folk *pūcai* begins with an *āratti*.
9. *Kumpam* at this place was a silver pot.
10. *Poṅkal* is boiled rice, often cooked with sugar and spices.

11. *Villupāṭṭu* refers to singing of folk songs to the tone and rhythm of a bow-like instrument.
12. Strictly speaking, *maiyāṇam pōtal* (going to the cremation ground for a special ritual), the most important ceremony of *koṭai* needs to be distinguished from vēṭṭai (ritual hunting), While *maiyāṇam pōtal* involves just going to cremation for *maiyāṇa pūcai* presided over by Kaṇiyāṉ, *vēṭṭai* is an elaborate ritual that lasts for more than an hour. It is literally ritual hunting of village borders. The cāmiyāṭi goes all alone to village boundaries, visits the folk temples situated on the banks of rivers or tanks, and offers things such as eggs or garlands to all the gods and spirits along the way, the climax of which is the *maiyāṇa pūcai*. *Maiyāṇam pōtal* is done with ritual co-operation/leadership of Kaṇiyāṉ, while in the *vēṭṭai* Kaṇiyāṉ is conspicuously absent. But in most of the ritual contexts people use these terms interchangeably.
13. It is believed that the eggs that *cāmiyāṭi(s)* throw to the ground will not break; and, if they break, various explanations are forwarded. For instance, some say that it indicates that bad times are to befall the person who has come for divination, or, others say that it indicates disbelief on the part of the devotee, or, it could even mean that the *cāmiyāṭi* is not powerful.
14. *Kutiaḻaippu* literally means 'inviting (*aḻaippu*) from one's home (*kuti*).' In the context of *koṭai*, it means performing the ritual of *pūcai* at the house of 'someone' who was responsible for bringing CM to that particular temple and inviting CM from there to the temple by rekindling CM's presence at the point of origin.
15. Reiniche, *Les dieux*, 161.
16. Further the author notes that, to make this paste, each family must give a measure of paddy. During the Tamil month of *kārttikai*, the paddy is peeled with the pestle by a woman who has reached menopause.
17. When they stay in the Civā's temple, all (even Dalits,) can stay at the temple of Civā. It indicates that during *koṭai* the notion of sacred space is redefined even in the temples of major gods.
18. In my view this indicates that the prominence that the Veḷḷāḷar(s) enjoyed earlier is no more in force, but that is what the Veḷḷāḷar *cāmiyāṭi* was trying to regain by asserting himself in the performance of rituals.

19. Kaṇiyāṉs call themselves so, because they say that they are very essential for invoking CM's presence on *cāmiyāṭi* and to perform human blood sacrifice at *koṭai*. They were created for this purpose in Kailācam and performed such rituals for CM already at Kail□cam after which CM consented to come down to the earth.

20. The Brahmins' rejection of Kaṇiyāṉ's ritual primacy is one of the things that brings about similarity and unity of ritual complex between Brahmins and Dalits since both do not employ Kaṇiyāṉ as ritual co-functionaries. While the former does that, because accepting them as 'god of gods' would defy their *varna* status as the divine mediators in Sanskritic Hinduism, the latter do not employ them because they do not need any human ritual help for performing *koṭai,* as they have internal authority in themselves to have direct access to the power of CM available in the impure realm of cremation ground. Though Brahmins do not have such an internal authority (which is evident in their seeking help of barbers at vēṭṭai), yet they are forced to imitate the Dalits in this behaviour, out of 'socio-religious status' compulsion given by Sanskritic Hinduism. Here the religious behaviour of Brahmins in the subaltern religious realm, guided by the 'dictates' of Sanskirtic Hinduism, makes them to imitate the lowest of all groups, i.e., Dalits. Thus it reveres the logic of Sanskritisation where the ultimate point of reference for the imitation of behaviour is the Brahmin *varna.*

21. Ritual nine refers to *Paṭaippu* and blood sacrifices as noted at Figure 1.

22. The ceremony of pārivʃææai is present in many places all over Tamilnadu. Eveline Meyer notes that this ceremony is of somewhat mysterious nature: "The ritual is a hunt, but what is hunted, who is doing the hunting and how it is done varies from temple to temple." Meyer, *Ankalaparamecuvari,* 245. Cf. also Gustav Oppert, *On the Original Inhabitants of Bharatavarsa or India,* Westminster/Leipzig, Harrassowitz, 1983.

23. David Shulman, *Tamil Temple Myths,* Princeton University Press, Princeton, New Jersey, 1980, 347-352.

24. He notes that 'power', to remain auspicious, has to be either limited (bounded) or to be isolated from the source of impurity, as many temples (which are built) aims at isolation. But such an isolation is not possible. Purity is an ever-receding goal as long as life on earth is eagerly desired. Hence violence, death and

impurity become integral parts of ecstatic worship of Civā. But this touch of impurity is cleansed through acts of self-sacrifice as noted by Shulman (*ibid*). But, in contrast to this trend, there is neither attempt of isolation from the realm of impurity nor concept of purification through sacrifice of self present in the case of the CM cult, which has maintained its autonomy in spite of CM's identification with Civā.

25. Meyer, *Ankalaparamecuvari*, 225.
26. *Ibid.*
27. C.J. Fuller, "Sacrifice (Bali) in the South Indian Temple," in *Religion and Society*, ed. V. Sudarsan *et al.*, B.R. Publishing Corporation, Delhi-23.
28. The thesis does not employ structuralist approach towards rituals, as it studies primarily the performance of rituals, rituals in action. For structuralist school, a symbolic object, gesture or word as such has no meaning, but became meaningful only in co-relation to each other. This approach confines the meaning of symbols, words and actions to the domain of '*structures of thought*'. But the kind of approach needed for the study of ritual corpus like *koṭai* should assign primacy to *performances* and its meaning systems as shown by victor Turner. Mathieu Deflem has indicated how Levi's Strauss' structuralism is not so relevant for Victor Turner's study of Nedumbu rituals. Cf. In "Ritual, Anti-Structure, and Religion: A Discussion of Victor Turner's Processual Symbolic Analysis," *Journal for the Scientific Study of Religion* 30/1 (1991), 1-25.
29. *Ibid*, 5.

CHAPTER 4

A FOLK HERMENEUTICS OF THE CM CULT

Introduction

This chapter, entitled 'A folk hermeneutics of the CM cult,' attempts to understand the religious phenomenon of CM-worship from the people's viewpoint, and tries to explore the recurring themes of various aspects of the CM's cult by privileging the thought-patterns of the common folk. Accordingly (subsequently), the chapter holds that what constitutes the CM cult are the five major components, namely, (a) the origin myth of CM, (b) the temple myth, (c) *cāmiyāṭi(s)*, (d) the devotees and (e) the *koṭai* ritual, by deploying the common underlying structures, themes and narratives of all five components. To achieve this end, as mentioned in the first chapter, it employs the *holistic structural-content analysis of the narrative method* to analyse and interpret the first four components of the CM cult, namely, the origin myth of CM, the temple myth, the life stories of *cāmiyāṭi(s)*, and those of the devotees. Further, while understanding *koṭai* ritual as a performative narrative, it moves on to enlist the main themes of different narratives of *koṭai* rituals described in the previous chapter and see how they synchronise with the major themes of the cult.

Origin Myths

Origin myths refer to the stories of origination of CM in the highest heaven of Kailācam, the abode of Lord Civā, and his descent to the world. These stories speak about the different circumstances connected with CM's birth and the reason why he was expelled from heaven. The different myths given below are the documented texts of oral narratives. They are the English translation of Tamil texts. The structure and contents of the narratives are maintained as they are found in the original texts, because they are significant for the analysis. The analysis, in the later part of this section, reveals the underlying themes common to all three myths.

Different Myths

Myth A[1]

In the beginning, Lord Civā creates Pramaṉ and Viṣṇu. Later, through Pramaṉ, he creates the whole universe: its planets, different worlds, hills and oceans. Takkaṉ is created as one of his assistants in the creation of the world. A few years later, Takkaṉ takes Vetavaḷḷi as his consort, and rules the state of Takkā. As a result of his fasting and penance, he receives as a boon from Lord Civā that he begets a daughter. Meanwhile, Pārvati doubts Civā's capability of feeding each and every living being (*paṭiyaḷattal*) every day. One day she locks an ant in a casket, and when she opens the box the following day, she finds the ant grasping tiny grains of paddy with its mouth. Becoming furious over the suspicion of his wife, Civā orders that she be born as a daughter to Takkaṉ. Pārvati is born as the daughter of Takkaṉ. When she comes of age, Civā comes to marry her. Though Takkaṉ insults Civā in the beginning, he later repents and decides to give his daughter in marriage to Civā.

During the marriage ceremony, as Pārvati is walking around the ritual fire, she begins to sweat profusely. Civā directs the drops of her sweat to the fire, out of which is born Pramacakṭi. Subsequently Pramacakṭi's birth takes many manifestations from Pārvati's feet, from her hair and from Civā's hair. Having taken many forms in Pramacakṭi, she implores Civā that she begets a male child. Civā asks her to spread her *muntāṉai* (the border) of her *sari* in front of the thirty-second pillar at *maṇimaṇṭapam*[2] in Kailācam. As she unfolds the border of her *sari*, Lord Civā shakes the lamp from which a flame of fire falls onto the *sari*. Immediately the flame turns into a lump of flesh. Civā shapes that into a child called CM.

CM is an unusual child, who, even in childhood goes to the cremation ground to eat carcasses. Both, Pārvati and Civā detest him, and decide to expel him from heaven and send him to earth. He asks for a female companion and gets one called Cuṭalai Māṭati. Further, CM demands that he must be given *koṭai* if he has to leave. Dissatisfied with the vegetarian kind of offerings, he asks for blood-sacrifice plus *kaṇiyāṉāṭṭam* (dance of Kaṇiyāṉ)[3] accompanied by the music of *makuṭam*.[4] Kaṇiyāṉ is created and made to dance with Intirāṇi and other female Apsaras.[5] From Intirāṇi's anklet, a pearl falls and from there comes another Kaṇiyāṉ. He performs a goat-sacrifice and also a human blood sacrifice by piercing his tongue with a knife and letting it bleed.

Having received *koṭai* at Kailācam, CM leaves for Kasi, and proceeds from there to Trichy and to the Mīnācci temple at Madurai. Finally, he reaches Arumugamangalam. Then he goes to Pakavati Ammaṉ temple at Kanyakumari and reveals himself to the goddess Pakavati. She keeps him as her guardian. Thereafter, CM expresses his wish to go to Kerala. Pakavati Ammaṉ tries to prevent him from going there by explaining to him that there are dangerous sorcerers there. Nonetheless, CM is hell-bent on going there and vows to overpower them all. Assuming the form of a mendicant, he comes to the village where the most powerful sorcerer called Kāḷipulayaṉ and his daughter Māvicakki reside. CM, wanting to meet the latter, assumes the role of a snake-charmer but Māvicakki does not come out of her house. Then he goes disguised as a beggar to her house where she meets him. He decides to rape her. Later, at night, he enters her private chamber assuming the form of a lizard, and rapes her during her sleep. She complains to her father Kāḷipulayaṉ. In spite of his attempts to identify him through sorcery, he fails to locate his whereabouts. Meanwhile, CM comes back to Pakavati Ammaṉ to continue his service as a guardian.

Back at the Pakavati Ammaṉ temple, CM continues his work of working havoc on the people of Kakachi hill[6] by destroying their crops. When they complain to Kāḷipulayaṉ about these destructive developments, he decides to bring CM to the spot by performing *koṭai*. When *koṭai* is performed, CM comes there as a bee and stings Kāḷipulayaṉ on his cheek, and demands that he sacrifices his pregnant daughter. Still unsatisfied, he asks for the sacrifice of the king's (Ramarajan's) elephant. Kāḷipulayaṉ concedes that too. Getting to know Kāḷipulayaṉ's role in the death of his elephant, the king decides to kill Kāḷipulayaṉ. Finally he returns to Pakavati Ammaṉ's temple. From there once again he proceeds from place to place such as Kalidaikurichi, Trichendur and so on.

Myth B[7]

In order to test Lord Civā's power, Pārvati requests him to give sustenance (*Paṭiyaḷattal*) to all living beings. Before he could begin his mission, Pārvati hides two ants in her sari at her waist. When Lord Civā returns from the earth, she asks him if he gave sustenance to each and every living being on the earth. Civā says, "Yes. I did!" Pārvati challenges him and asks, "Did you give sustenance to these two ants?" Civā says, "Yes!" for them too. When Pārvati releases the ants from her sari, she finds that they too have had their feed. Now Civā orders that she does forty-one days of penance, to be cleansed of the sin incurred by her suspicion. Pārvati also agrees to it and begins her life of penance and mortification in the north of Kailācam, and continues this for twelve years. Later, Civā and Nārataṉ (his mentor) go to visit her and request her to give up her penance. She agrees only on condition that her request will be met. When Civā inquires about her wish, she asks for a child to be born without the co-operation of the husband. Civā promises to grant her this favour.

Now, as instructed, Pārvati goes to the northern fort at Kailācam and stands in front of the fort, and spreads her *muntāṉai*. At that time, without her knowledge, Civā blows out the lamp there and a spark of the flame falls from there onto Pārvati's *muntāṉai*. This is transformed into two lumps of flesh.

With the help of clay, Pramaṉ adds nose, eyes and limbs to the masses of flesh and moulds them into two infants. Civā gives 'life' to them and Pārvati names them 'Cuṭalai' and 'Muṇṭaṉ' and begins to bring them up.

Sometime later, a thousand dead bodies are being cremated in '*Tillai*' (the cremation-ground at Kailācam). At that time, Cuṭalai tells Muṇṭaṉ that their mother's milk will not fill their stomach and hence asks him to accompany him to the cremation ground. Thus, both go there to eat the carcasses and furtively come back to their cradle. When Pārvati gets the smell of carcasses from them, she gets upset and complains to Civā. When he suggests that they be sent to heaven, she refuses. She also rules out Civā's suggestion that they be given a *koṭai* at a cremation ground on earth. But, Cuṭalai makes demands for a female companion, and is given one named Māṭati. Besides, he demands that *koṭai* be performed on Kailācam itself before he goes down to earth. He demands animal sacrifices of goats and pigs, and the blood sacrifice of human beings. In this situation of demands, Civā lays twenty-one plantain leaves. He calls Kaṇiyāṉ to make *pūṭams* (a kind of altar) made of clay, and asks him to give 21 drops of blood by piercing his tongue and hand. Finally CM gets the power of destruction and creation, and leaves Kailācam.

From Kailācam, CM goes to Kanchi and to the north. There he descends on a mosque, throws goat and cow bones on the streets of the *Leppai(s)*-Muslims. When they satisfy him by erecting an altar and performing *koṭai*, he leaves them and goes to Kasi. From Kasi he goes to Madurai, disturbs Mīnācci Ammaṉ (famous female deity in Madurai) till she recognises him and offers him *koṭai*. Thereafter, he goes to Kuttalam, Papanasam, Sengottai, Ariankavu, Ramarajan kottai, Pechiparai and finally reaches Kanyakumari.

At Kanyakumari, he knocks at the door of Pakavati Ammaṉ. After a long conversation, Pakavati makes him realise that she is his mother, and asks him to guard her seven big baskets of jewels. If he does so, he will get the first part of *pūcai* while she will receive the latter part of the *pūcai*. Besides, Cuṭalai demands twenty-one *pūṭams* and the customary sacrifices due to him.

From there he goes to Salem, plays havoc on a dominant caste group called Kairālya Piḷḷaimār(s). They perform *koṭai* for eight days. At this juncture, the seven Pulayā rulers in Kerala suffer from the humiliation of non-issue. Hence, the youngest of them, Kāḷipulayaṉ, makes penance. As a result, on the tenth month, a child is born in a pitcher. The child is named 'Māvicakki'. When she comes of age, she looks so pretty that the Pulayā(s) build a fort to guard her. They realise that they need more jewels in order to get her married. And through sorcery they come to find out the seven baskets of jewels at Pakavati Ammaṉ temple. A Pulayā comes to steal the jewels from there when CM is away for a *koṭai* at Salem. Realizing the intention of the Pulayā, CM hurries back to Kanyakumari. Sensing his arrival, the Pulayā leaves the temple hastily. Nonetheless, CM takes a vow to behead the Pulayā(s) within seven days.

After this, CM requests his mother to give him permission to go to Kerala to destroy the Pulayā(s). She refuses to give him permission, as they are dangerous sorcerers. But CM insists and finally manages to get her blessing and permission to go there. Thus, he goes to Kakachi hill, where he destroys the crops of Eṭṭuvīṭṭu Piḷḷaimār(s) who approach the great magician Kāḷipulayaṉ. When Kāḷipulayaṉ tries to identity the cause of it, CM appears before him and demands that the eight months pregnant Māvicakki be sacrificed for him. Now, through magical spells, Kāḷipulayaṉ shuts CM in a small case. However, CM soon releases himself and hits him hard after which Kāḷipulayaṉ accepts to perform *koṭai* and to sacrifice Māvicakki for him. He later curses Pulayāēs lineage for seven generations and returns to Pakavati Ammaṉ who appreciates him and in turn requests him to be her guardian for twelve years.

Myth C[8]

In Kailācam, all the gods and goddesses are happily seated with their consorts. As per the requests of gods, Lord Civā asks Pramaṉ to create the world. Pramaṉ takes a handful of clay and creates the land and the oceans. Subsequently he creates the whole universe, all the stars and the different planets. He also creates plants, insects, animals and human beings. Now Lord Civā sustains and protects all beings on earth. One day, when Lord Civā descends to earth, goddess Pārvati is left alone. At that time Praman̲ happened to visit Kailācam. Mistaking the five-headed Praman̲ for Civā, Pārvati gets up and adores him. When Praman̲ tells her the truth, she repents. However, when the real Lord Civā comes, she does not undertake her routine rituals of honour and respect. When the infuriated Civā asks the reasons for slighting him, Pārvati explains to him what happened.

Fuelled by uncontrollable anger, Civā sets out to remove Praman̲'s fifth head. As he manages to sever the head, it gets stuck to his hand. As a result, Civā is afflicted by *Pramakatikōcam* (which, in Sanskritic Hinduism, refers to the sticking of Praman̲'s fifth head on to the hand of Civā, which makes the latter mad). Civā goes to the cremation ground, applies ashes on his body, and dances there for seven and a half years. Finally, when he returns to Kailācam to get united with his wife, Pārvati, she begs for a boy-child but not with the aid of any man. Civā asks her to go to the thousand-pillar *maṇṭapam* - where a lamp of Civā burns at the thirty-second pillar - and to spread her *muntān̲ai* there. When Pārvati does so, three drops of flame fall as pearls on her *muntān̲ai*. She immediately wraps it with her *sari* and brings it to Mount Kailācam. When she opens her *sari* at Kailācam, she finds three *muṇṭam(s) ū* masses of flesh - therein. When she complains to Civā about it, he asks Praman̲ to transform that into three children, Pecciamman̲, Cuṭalai and Muṇṭan̲.

Pārvati embraces her children lovingly, feeds them with her breast milk and puts them to sleep in the cradle. But, Cuṭalai–attracted by the smell of the burning flesh of the dead at the cremation ground–asks others to accompany him to the cremation ground. Dressed as demons with skull cap, belt, etc., all three go to the cremation-ground, dance happily with the demons, and eat the carcasses of the dead. Having enjoyed a big feast there, they stealthily return home and sleep in their cradle. When Pārvati comes to know about it, she gets upset and complains to Lord Civā. Her complaint is that the three are not fit to be in Kailācam, hence must be sent down to earth. When Civā asks Cuṭalai to quit Kailācam, he demands a *koṭai* from Lord Civā who concedes to his demand, builds an altar at the cremation ground and performs *koṭai* for them. But Cuṭalai, unsatisfied with this gesture, presses for human blood sacrifice. Civā was confused over what to do; but, Pārvati hits upon the idea of asking Kaṇiyāṉ, who was born out of pearls from her anklet, to give a human blood sacrifice. Kaṇiyāṉ pierces his right forearm and gives three drops of human blood to Cuṭlai. Now Cuṭalai leaves Kailācam, passes through the great oceans at night, goes to Mecca, and gets a *pūṭam* there by the *Leppai(s)*-Muslims. From there he goes to thousand and eight Civā temples and one hundred and eight holy shrines. Then he goes to Sivalaperi and gets a *pūṭam* by Sanniyāci Kōṉār. From there he proceeds to Athisankanallur, and thereafter to the Pakavati Ammaṉ temple to be her guardian.

During this time, a magician Kāḷipulayaṉ wants to build a fort for his beautiful daughter Māvicakki to keep her safe. However, he does not have enough money. With the help of magic he comes to know about the ornaments at the Pakavati Ammaṉ temple and robs them. Now Cuṭalai resolves to exterminate the whole generation of Kāḷipulayaṉ who has challenged him as guardian, and goes to Kerala bidding farewell to Pakavati Ammaṉ. There he takes different roles of magician, snake charmer, etc., but cannot locate Kāḷipulayaṉ and his daughter. Finally, he takes the form of a mendicant and goes begging from place to place, door to door. Thus he comes to the fort of Māvicakki, and when she comes out to give him alms, he confronts her and reveals his real intention of taking revenge on her. He takes it as a challenge to do it within seven days. When she reports this to her father, he appoints four guardians at four doors for protection. However, on the seventh day, Cuṭalai takes the form of an ant and enters her bedroom, assumes the form of a handsome groom, rapes her and disappears. Next morning she fearfully reveals to her father what had happened the previous night. Through his magical ink he identifies the culprit as Cuṭalai and vows to kill him within seven days. In the meantime, Cuṭalai goes to sevenhills and ruins different crops of Palliyars. They approach Kāḷipulayaṉ to identity the cause of the havoc and to eliminate it. Kāḷipulayaṉ fixes a day to perform a big ritual. On the day that he was performing it, Cuṭalai comes to the scene, slaps him, and says that he will be overpowered only if he performs a *koṭai* at Kakachi hill where Kāḷipulayaṉ has to sacrifice his pregnant daughter, Māvicakki. He further warns that if he does not perform it, he (Kāḷipulayaṉ) himself will be killed.

Kāḷipulayaṉ fixes a day and performs this elaborate *koṭai* wherein he sacrifices a pregnant goat, pregnant pig, pregnant chicken, etc. This he does on six different *paraṉ(s)*-raised altars, and on the seventh *paraṉ* he has to sacrifice his own pregnant daughter. He cuts open her body, takes out the liver and the seven months old baby and offers it to Cuṭalai. Besides this, Cuṭalai wants to kill Kāḷipulayaṉ himself. With this intention Cuṭalai enters the right leg of the king's elephant. As result, the elephant is limping. Meanwhile Cuṭalai also appears to the king Ramarajan in a dream and tells him that the only remedy for his elephant's leg is that it has to stamp on the head of Kāḷipulayaṉ. At the appointed time, as instructed by Cuṭalai, Kāḷipulayaṉ is caught, put into a pit and his head is made to stick out. Now the royal elephant is led to step over the head of Kāḷipulayaṉ, and the head of Kāḷipulayaṉ gets cut off from the body, rolls and reaches the feet of the elephant, i.e., Cuṭalai. At this point, Cuṭalai grants a boon to Kāḷipulayaṉ that he too would be worshipped along with him as *Pulamāṭacāmi.*

Having accomplished his mission of wiping out Kāḷipulayaṉ and his generation, he returns to his place at Pakavati Ammaṉ temple. From there he further travels to different places such as Uikadu, Rettiyar kovil, Arumguamangalam, Polikarai, etc.

Analysis of the Myths

Before we set out to analyse the various structural units of the myth, we are confronted with the question : What exactly is the connection between the frame and the next episode? At first sight, it seems to be a stereotype beginning,[10] having no connection with the rest of the story. A closer look shows that in Myth C, Pārvati's mistaking Brahma for Civā can be construed as the result of the failure of Civā to protect his own wife. This incident is followed by Pārvati asking for the male child (a sign of protection for a mother in the Hindu worldview) and establishes the link between the frame and the episode, i.e., it is Civā's failure to protect his wife and subsequent separation between Pārvati and Civā for seven years that led her to ask for a male child. This is also implied in Myth A and Myth B in which Pārvati's question to Civā, "Did you give sustenance/ protection to all?" is in fact an indirect dig at Civā's failure to protect his wife. Thus the theme of "Suspicion of Power of Protection" sets the tone for the main theme of "Power of Protection of CM" for the myth and for the cult, as we will see.

Structural units and their themes	*MYTH A*	*MYTH B*	*MYTH*
Prelude[9]	Creation of Praman̲/Viṣṇu & the universe (AC) Creation of Takkan̲ and his request		Description of Kailācam Creation of universe by Praman̲ (AC)
The Frame Suspicion of Civā's Power of Protection & Sustenance	Suspicion of Civā's power of Sustenance and protection (AB) Punishment (AB): expulsion from heaven and marriage with Takkan̲ Birth of Pramacakṭi	Pārvati questions Civā (AB) Punishment (AB) and atonement thr' tapas for forty one days (given by Civā)	Civā descends to earth for the protection of creation. Pārvati mistakes Praman̲ for Civā When real Civā comes, no respect. Angry Civā removes B's fifth head Pramak*atikōcam*
Birth of CM	Pārvati asks for male child (ABC). From the flame (ABC). Spreading of *muntān̲ai* (ABC). One Child (Muṇtan̲)	Pārvati asks for male child (ABC) From the Flame (ABC) Spreading of *muntān̲ai* (ABC) Two Children	Pārvati asks for male child (ABC From the Flame (ABC) Spreading of *muntān̲ai* (ABC) Three Children
Eating of the carcasses/ expulsion Disbelief in mother's power of protection and sustenance	CM goes to the cremation ground (ABC)Asks for a female companion (AB)	Mother's milk insufficient- expressed CM goes to the cremation ground (ABC) female companion (AB)	CM goes to the cremation ground (ABC) cap, dance with *pey*

Contd...

Structural units and their themes	*MYTH A*	*MYTH B*	*MYTH*
***Koṭai* at Kailācam** Intractable power of CM	Animal sacrifice-kaṇiyāṉ's blood (ABC) Kaṇiyāṉ born off anklets	Animal sacrifice-kaṇiyāṉ's blood (ABC) Description of kaṇiyāṉ's activities	Animal sacrifice-kaṇiyāṉ's blood (ABC) Gets power to Create and to destroy
Descent into earth CM's power of Encompassment	Kasi (AB), Trichy, Madurai (AB), Arumugam,	Kanchi, North, Mosque (BC), Kasi (AB) Kuttalam, Madurai (AB)	River, sea, Mecca at North (BC), Mosque (BC)
Guardian of Pakavati Ammaṉ	Explains who he is B Makes him as her guardian (ABC)	Knocks at Gate B. explains who he is Agreement of second Bali (offering) B Makes him as her guardian (ABC)	B Makes him as her guardian (ABC)
CM as Power of Protection & Destruction **Circumstances of CM's trip to Kerala**	Trip undertaken on his own in spite of warning of Evil powers Pakavati persuaded to give permission (AB)	Māvicakki born out of tapas Insufficiency of JewelsAttempt by Kāḷipulayaṉ to steal in CM's absence CM hastens-prevents it Pakvati persuaded to give permission (AB)	No money for Kāḷipulayaṉ to build fortress for Mav. Jewels stolen in CM's absence Vows to finish off P's descendants
Encounter with Māvicakki	Snake-charmer -AC Mendicant -AC M. under heavy security-AC Form of Lizard Rape–AC		Snake-charmer -AC Mendicant –AC Takes a bet to rape her M. under heavy security-AC Rape-AC
Havoc at Kakaci Hill	Plants, fields are ruined at one time. People/Pillaimars approach Kāḷipulayaṉ- for sorcery ABC	Plants, fields are ruined at one time. Piḷḷaimār(s) approach Kāḷipulayaṉ- for sorcery ABC	Plants, fields are ruined at one time. Piḷḷaimār(s) approach Kāḷipulayaṉ for sorcery-ABC

Contd...

Structural units and their themes	*MYTH A*	*MYTH B*	*MYTH*
***Koṭai* by Kāḷipulayaṉ** Intractable power of CM	Appears on his own (ABC) Demands Sacrifice of MV and Other blood sacrifices (ABC) Demands King's elephant. Pulayaṉ killed by king	Appears on his own (ABC) Demands Sacrifice of MV and Other blood sacrifices (ABC). Pul. tries to put him in a casket Overpowers him *Koṭai* kept Curses pulayaṉ's lineage	Appears on his own (ABC) Demands Sacrifice of MV and Other blood sacrifices (ABC) Enters into elephants legs -Kills himCM grants him Apotheosis"
Back to Kottaram and proceeds to different places CM's power of Encompassment	Proceeds to different places from there (ABC)	B. requests him to guard him for twelve years. Proceeds to different places from there (ABC)	Proceeds to different places from there (ABC)

Figure 1

Furthermore, the mode of birth of CM, namely, from the flame, underlies the power of CM, which is often symbolised as fire. It is to be noted that CM's power in this locality is often characterised as fire by the people. "*Ēmatta neneccā Cuṭalai cāmi pocikkiṭuvār*" (if you are insincere, CM will burn you to ashes). The child born–not out of her husband's sexual union– but out of a flame is a symbol loaded with meaning. It is to demonstrate Pārvati's disbelief in Civā's power of protection, on the one hand, and, to show, on the other, her intention to have a more perfect power of protection in CM as he was born without Civā's co-operation but from fire.

The myth further speaks of Pārvati's complaint about CM because he ate carcasses. It may be because the flesh of the dead is impure. But the underlying reason is that the child goes to the cremation ground because it finds its mother's milk (blood) insufficient (explicitly stated in Myth B), and therefore eats the flesh and drinks the blood of the dead. It explicates the child's disbelief in his mother's power of protection and sustenance. Subsequently CM is forced to seek another source of vitality. It also indicates CM's unquenchable thirst and insatiable hunger resulting out of the enormous power the child needs for its sustenance, which the mother's milk could not provide.

The imagery of the cremation ground and *koṭai* near *maiyāṉam* is an anomaly because no death can occur in Civā's Kailācam, the supreme abode of *moksa*. His association with the dead and with the cremation ground has to be established even in Kailācam, so that it can be sanctioned here on earth. It is to justify that the modes of CM worship on earth are the continuation of the privileges he was given even in Kailācam.

The myth further shows that CM is the intractable power that demands and has things according to his way. He makes even Civā give *koṭai* and manages to go to Kerala by persuading Pārvati who warns him of his trip to Kerala. This reveals the mother's role of protection. It also points to the impending dangers CM has to face in Kerala where his power would be challenged, on the other.

In Myth B CM does not rape Māvicakki, because Kāḷipulayaṉ, scared of CM, leaves Kottaram without stealing. There he recognises CM's power, while the extent of anger in Myth C is described as more furious than in A and B because Kāḷipulayaṉ steals the jewels, underestimating CM's power. However, he destroys the whole generation of Kāḷipulayaṉ so that there will be no future threat to Pakavati Ammaṉēs wealth. In all three versions, he is not controlled by sorcery. When he is sought through sorcery, he comes to the spot on his own, challenges them and demands *koṭai,* etc. - all indicating the supremacy of his power. Towards the end of his mission, Pakavati Ammaṉ requests him to guard her for twelve years. This reveals the theme of recognition and reinforcement of his Protective Power.

The story of CM ends by stating that he goes further on from Kottaram to different places as he did before. This shows the encompassing dimension of CM's power. In contrast to the idea of "controlled, limited and encompassed power" of folk gods,[11] CM is believed to manifest his ever-present encompassing and subsuming power. His granting of apotheosis to Kāḷipulayaṉ is another instance of encompassment into the characteristics of 'divinity' aspect of major gods, as it is the prerogative only of major gods to grant apotheosis. It is an instance of a minor god's appropriation of stereological function of major gods.

Further, unlike the other demon gods who were tamed and put at the feet of higher gods, as Waghone has noted,[12] CM remains fairly independent and autonomous. His episode in Kailācam shows that he forces even the greater gods and higher powers to his way. Madeleine Biardeau has shown that after the 10th cent. C.E., through the *bhakti* movement, demon gods were made to realise their dependency on major gods, and to acknowledge with gratitude their place at the Lord 's feet. It is interesting to note that in spite of being co-opted into Sanskritic Hinduism, CM has resisted the dominant trends of historical religious developments in India. The myth, while highlighting his defiant character, points to the incongruence between the other (so-called) minor gods who are controlled by the major gods in the final analysis and CM who controls the major god Civā.

Though the myth reinforces the dominant idea of a minor god's (and in this case CM's) symbiotic relationship with the higher gods, he is never made to surrender his independent nature to the likes of gods. It is not loyalty and obedience that wins for him a domain of rule under his control. It is his intractable disobedience and defiant character that establishes an indisputable domain of power for himself.[13]

Further, the theme of "The Power of Protection of CM" is seen all through the myth. This power is neither unqualified nor unconditional. It is qualified by CM's power to destroy evil or to make people realise the presence of his power. It is conditional because it is accessible only to those who seek him and recognise him.

Thus, the origin myth is a story about power and its characteristics, about what constitutes and enhances and preserves power–namely, ritual, honour and the display of a certain brazen audacity of CM to hold on to his intractable and unconventional ways. If one has to interpret the central issue of the story from the folk's vantage point, this is a story that pre-figures the compelling and protective power of CM in the service of the folk life-world. It is a power that is also manifest in the politics of social power in the region of Tirunelveli district, as we will see in the last chapters. Like so many folktales, this one articulates a distinct vision of god, a vision endowed with attributes of autonomy of CM characterised by highly specific cultural expressivity. We have here the rudiments of a folk counter-system, with its own semantics and values, yet subtly linked to that of the heavenly court at Kailācam, that is inhabited by supernatural gods of major religions.

In the following pages, we will see how the major theme of CM's power of protection and other sub-themes, as evident in the origin myth, are further realised through the emergence of more sub-themes and delineated as such in other components of the cult such as temple myths, life-histories of *cāmiyāṭi(s)* and devotees and in the *koṭai* rituals

Temple Myths

The village folk in Tirunelveli district do not experience the powers of CM in the abstract but through their concrete historical times and geographical spaces. It is the local temple of CM in each village that makes it possible for the village folk to concretely experience the power of CM. In this section, different such experiences of the people are presented first in the form of stories, and analysed later to find out the predominant characteristics of the powers of CM, which are common to all the temples

Different Temple Myths

Each local temple has its own story which speaks about how the local village community encountered the power of CM for the first time, which led eventually to the establishment of CM's temple. These stories have survived as collective memories of the village folk through oral traditions passed on from one generation to the other. In this sub-section, we will see four such stories that are directly related to the villages under study.

The Myth of the Kayatar Temple

During the 14th cent. C.E., one of the viceroys of Nāyakā(s) called Veṭṭu Perumāḷ brought a big tree from Kerala by a bulla cart in order to erect a flagpole at the Kōtaṇṭarāmaṉ Akilāṇṭēṣwari temple at Kayatar. CM too came along with the tree from Kerala. The supportive stones of the tree, which fell down from the cart while transporting the tree, are worshipped even today at the Ayaṇār temple near Kayatar and narrated in the *villupāṭṭu* tradition of the same temple. The deity who came along started giving trouble to the village. He appeared to someone in a dream and demanded that he be stationed on the riverbanks near the cremation-ground. According to one account, the car of the Kōtaṇṭarāmaṉ Akilāṇṭēṣwari, which was pulled along the main streets, got stuck in a street facing the CM temple and the car could not be moved further. On that occasion, CM descended on one of the villagers and claimed that he be propitiated first by human blood sacrifice by piercing the thigh of a person. To this day, to mark this, a symbolic human blood sacrifice is made during the car procession by piercing the thigh of a Panṭāram (seller of flowers in the temple) on the last day in the month of *Paṅkuṉi* every year.

The Myth of the Naduvakurichi Temple

A Dalit lady, Āvuṭaiācci, brought a fish from the river and was about to cut the fish when the fish spoke up: "I have come to bring good fortune, don't kill me!" The frightened lady released the fish in the waters running alongside a Brahmin's house. Thereafter, that Brahmin family began having difficult times for two years. When they approached the soothsayer, he told them that CM had come home, and if he were worshipped, all misfortunes would vanish. Thus, the Brahmin family concerned put up a *pūṭam* (altar) in front of their house, under a Kaḷḷatti tree (hence, the deity is called Kaḷḷattiāṉ), and gave *koṭai*. The deity did not accept it because the offerings were only vegetarian items. Then, by lots they decided to ask the Paḷḷar to give *koṭai* to Māṭaṉ on their behalf. They gave a children's burial ground for this purpose. The Dalits put up an altar there for Kaḷḷattiāṉ.

The Myth of the Vijayanarayanam Temple

Once upon a time, two persons, namely, Pēciappatēvar and Āṇṭisāmpāṉ, from Vijayanarayanam, went to Sivaleperi to buy two pairs of bulls (one for Pēciappatēvar and the other for Paccayaṉāsāri). After striking a deal with a man from Kerala, they exchanged the rope as a customary sign of purchase of the cattle. However, they did not pay anything to the owner. The owner complained to CM in a temple at Sivalaperi. As they were leading the bulls back to their houses, the bulls died one after the other. Further, when they sat to eat their food, the cooked rice in the lunchbox turned bloody. When they returned home to Vijayanarayanam, trouble began in their homes: first, Paccayaṉāsāri's bulls disappeared from the cattle-shed, and, after three months, Pēciappatēvar himself died. Soon thereafter, troubles began in the village: people got dysentery and vomiting, many cattle died of an unknown disease, strange sounds and shouting were heard at night. The villagers approached sorcerers to identify the cause. No soothsayer could identify it. Eventually, the people gathered together in a place and asked the *kōṭaṅki* (fortune-teller, in Tamil) to identify the problem. Although the fortune-teller had a lot of trouble in doing his job, the people asked him to persevere in his mission. Finally he was led to the cremation ground. As they proceeded towards the cremation ground, a lizard spoke up and narrated the whole chain of events from the purchase of cattle at Sivalaperi till the latest troubles in the village. Thus, the root problem was identified. The lizard asked them to erect a temple for CM at that very spot near a single palm tree. From that day onwards, the worship of CM was started at Vijayanarayanam and the deity is called *ottapaṉai Cuṭalai* .

The Myth of Valliyoor Temple

One hundred and fifty years ago, the VAO (Village Administrative Officer) of Valliyoor, a Brahmin named Anandaraman, went to Sri-Vaikundam. On the way back, his eyes fell on a stone-tub in the CM's temple that belonged to the Dalits (see the picture below). As he wanted to take it home, he ordered his workers to take it away and put it in his cart.

However, CM came along with it. Thereafter, troubles began at home: dysentery, vomiting, strange noises at night, etc. Mr. Anandaraman's family sought the help of a soothsayer. He identified the coming of CM to their house and asked them to recognise him in order to avoid any further troubles. Thus, the Brahmins started worshipping CM near their cattle shed and the Brahmin's temple is known as Ayan Kovil (the picture below):

Analysis of The Myths

What marks the origin of all the four temples is the encompassing power of CM, a theme that already figures in the 'Origin Myth of CM'. Analysis of the above temple myths shows that, often, a person or persons who suffer injustice or who do injustice mediate this encompassing protective power of CM. The other temple stories collected by the researcher register the cases of people who plead to CM for the redress of wrongs. At the behest of those who suffered loss (as in the case of Vijayanarayanam) or on his own (as in the case of Valliyoor), CM appears on the scene to take revenge on those who do wrong.

The protective power of CM turns hostile until it is identified and recognised, respected and honoured. He conceals his power and makes his presence felt by playing havoc in the lives of people, even in the places where apparently no wrong is done, as in the case of Kayatar or Naduvakurichi. CM does this not because he needs propitiation but, as one of the villagers shared with the researcher, "because he has to reveal his power and establish his dominion over the area so that no future wrong will take place." The myths show that people come to know about CM's presence either through the *involuntary mechanics* of dream or hallucination, wherein he reveals his presence in the village, or, through *voluntary mechanics* that people employ such as soothsaying to identify the cause of misfortune in their lives. Subsequently, once the power of CM is identified or recognised, it is installed in a *pūṭam* (altar) to make sure that the protective power of CM is localised. This also serves to

Different Themes of the structural units	*Kayatar*	*NaduvaKurichi*	*Vijayanarayanam*	*Valliyoor*
Origin: Encompassment	CM comes along with the flag pole.	Through Fish	Unpaid pair of bulls *Aniyāyam*-unjust behaviour Intervention of CM sought	The stone-tub carried from Dalit's temple- Unjust behaviour
Havoc: Power of Protection turns as hostile and destructive	Concealment of power-unrecognised havoc	Misfortune	Manifestation of its hostile/retaliatory nature Bulls die-blood in rice etc.	Misfortune in the family
Mechanics of identification	Dream- Involuntary mechanics	Soothsayer: Voluntary mechanics Good fortune assured	Hallucination (Involuntary mechanism) Soothsaying (Volunt. mechani) Re-assertion of power by establishing its superiority	Sorcerer (Voluntary mechanism)
Altar established Power recognised Re/assertion of power of superiority	Altar made near river and worshipped Blocking of Car	Altar near the house Veg-offer Demand of blood sacrifice/ assertion of its true nature	Altar near the place identified by lizard	In the house near neem tree Demand of blood sacrifice/ assertion of its true nature
Reinforcement of power through extraneous localisation: Further encompassment	Piercing of thigh during annual car procession Veṭṭu Perumāḷ's story: Gone to Devakottai.	Escape in accident Job Transfer	Various miracle events worked outside by *ottapaṉai* at Sirumalanchi, etc.	Outside TN and India

Figure 2

impress upon the minds of the people that CM is not a transient power but a permanent source of protective power. The myths further show that, in most cases, there is reassertion of his power where he will further reveal his true nature or his superiority over other deities. Subsequently, the myths (at kayatar in the temple myth itself and in other places through other instances recounted by the villagers) reveal that there is reinforcement of his protective power through *extraneous localisation* where he shows further encompassment of his protective power elsewhere.

Life Histories of *Cāmiyāṭi(s)*

The powers of the supernatural beings are made available to the common folk through some mediation. The mediation, in the folk religious terrain, often takes place through human beings. Such human beings are called *cāmiyāṭi(s)* in the southern districts of Tamilnadu. *Cāmiyāṭi(s)* are, undoubtedly, powerful medium who facilitate the experience of the powers of local deities for the sake of others. But this is possible for them only because they themselves have experienced the powers of these gods in their own lives. Hence their god-experiences are important for the study of the power of gods. In this section, first, we propose to narrate some of such encounters of the powers of CM in the lives of *cāmiyāṭi(s)*. Later, these lifehistories will be analysed in order to explore the common patterns of the experiences of the powers of CM that turned them towards him.

Different Stories

1. *Ayyadurai:* Ayyadurai alias Sudalaikannu is a sixty-seven year old *cāmiyāṭi* from Vjiayanarayanam. He is the most popular *cāmiyāṭi* in *ottapaṉai* temple at Vijayanarayanam. His family has been associated with the temple for many years as his father was a key figure to maintain the continuation of *koṭai* at a time when it was about to be stopped due to conflict between the families that were celebrating *koṭai.* Ayyadurai's father and brother were *cāmiyāṭi(s)* here. As a child, Ayyadurai used to come to the temple with his parents. However, he remained indifferent to the god. From the age of thirty-five,

he started worshipping CM, but, even then, he never thought of performing *cāmiyāṭṭam*. At that time he was running an illegal business of smuggling rice. Though the police caught many of his business-associates during raids, somehow or the other, he escaped. He attributes this to the special protection of CM. Once, while transacting business, CM took possession of him. From then on he showed more interest in worshipping CM. This went on for about ten years. At present he is fully involved in serving CM and this is his sole occupation. Sudalaikannu is always seen in and around the temple: the 'all in all' of the temple. He remains a kind of charismatic figure respected by all the devotees and villagers. He says, "CM has always been very close to me and protects me wherever I go." His villagers invite him to Chennai, Coimbatore, and even to Mumbai, to offer special *pūcai* to CM when they start a new business or when they inaugurate a new house. When he goes to other temples, the *pūcāri(s)* (priests) and *cāmiyāṭi(s)* automatically identify him without any prior knowledge about him.[14] He describes this as "*Paravalāṉa cakti vāyinta teyvam* " (Tamil, meaning, "the encompassing power of God").

2. *Muthurajan:* Mr. Muthurajan, the present *panchayat* president of Thirvenkatanathapuram, is a sixty-year-old *cāmiyāṭi* from a place called Sirumalanchi. He comes from a family that owes strong allegiance to a vegetarian religious sect called *Ayyā Vaḻi.* As a vegetarian, his father did not show any interest in the meat-eating gods of the village like Cuṭlai, Ammaṉ, etc. One day, his father, who had gone to the market at Vadacheri did not return from there. His uncle, who went to look for him, eventually found his whole body entrapped in a marsh except for his head, which was swamped by flies. He pulled out his body that appeared lifeless, put it on the bullock-cart and returned to Sirumalanchi. As the body was being brought in the cart, it received a 'stone belting', which is generally attributed to be the handiwork of evil powers. As the cart neared the CM temple, the attack stopped, and the body began to revive. Muthurajan's father came back to life. Even since, CM began to come upon his father occasionally. In addition, other deities also descended on him. In this way,

Muthurajan's father was drawn into accepting the role of CM's *cāmiyāṭi,* though he continued to follow *Ayyā Vaḻi.* However, his father began to be afflicted with a strange viral fever and disease that made him lame in one leg. His leg was operated upon, and hence he was unable to walk. When *koṭai* came that year everybody was wondering how he would perform *vēṭṭai* and *cāmiyāṭṭam.* To everyone's surprise, he stood up miraculously due to an enormous power that was mysteriously infused into him. He performed the ritual. Subsequently, he was seriously ill and about to die in another *koṭai,* but god CM revived him and gave him the necessary strength and power to perform his duties as *cāmiyāṭi.* Being prompted by the god that he would die at a particular time, he announced that a particular *koṭai* would be his last. He actually did so, as predicted: dying at 2.00 a.m after performing *koṭai* rituals.

As a young boy, Mr. Muthurajan was a non-believer and did not believe in *cāmiyāṭi(s)* and *cāmiyāṭṭam.* In fact, he told others that he regarded them as uncivilised, although his father, the *cāmiyāṭi,* would get his power from CM only in his presence during *koṭai.* After his father's death, he continued his work outside the village. But, once, before Ammaṉ *koṭai,* he had a dream where he saw CM clad in a yellow dress giving him a key. A few days later, when Ammaṉ *koṭai* really took place, Muthurajan became possessed, wore a yellow dress voluntarily and carried the *tīccaṭi* (fire pot) and walked on the fire. The *tīccaṭi* fell on his leg burning it badly. His leg got badly wounded just like what happened to his father. Subsequently, in 1980, he lost his job because he did not have the SSLC (High School) certificate. In 1980, during this period of vulnerability, CM came upon Muthurajan for the first time.

Since Muthurajan was jobless, he attempted to write the SSLC exams 8 times between the years 1980 to 1984, but he did not pass the exam. Even though people tried to help him in the exam hall, he just would not pass. Disappointed, he gave up. However, after a few years, CM appeared to him in a dream and asked him to appear for the exam. As he received orders from CM that year, he says, "Miraculously, I was able to answer very well, and even wrote things that I never studied." Anyway he passed the 10th standard exam in 1993. He got a job in 1994 and retired as VAO (village administrative officer) in 1999. After his retirement, he was asked by CM in a dream to file his nomination for the local body elections. Strangely, although he was comparatively a weak candidate–when compared to the other opponents who were economically and politically very powerful–he won the election miraculously. Moreover, the margin of victory too was a big surprise for him. It is CM who has chosen him to be his servant for the people. He worships CM in the temple once in two years. On one Friday every month, he undertakes a strict fast in his home, during which people take advice from him. "It is CM who puts words in my mouth," he testifies. People telephone him all the way from Mumbai and even Singapore to request him to pray for them to CM. He prays for them and their intentions are fulfilled. Wherever he goes, he is recognised by people who treat him with great respect. He attributes all this to the power of CM, an '*apāra cakṭi*' (enormous power) that does only good to people in the final analysis.

3. *P.S. Sudalaimuthu:* Sudalaimuthu, an āsāri (carpenter) by caste, comes from the near-by village called Kalakadu. He is an ex-army man. His grandfather was jointly responsible for bringing CM to Vijayanarayanam village. Hence, he considers *ottapaṉai Cuṭalai* (special name of CM in Vijayanarayanam) as his family inheritance. His grandfather and father had been *cāmiyāṭi(s)* in the temple for many years. He was not much involved in CM's worship. He was possessed by Mundan only three years after his father's death. Though he often got into a 'trance,' he was never divinised. He was not recognised as a *cāmiyāṭi* in the beginning. For the last five years, he has been tying a '*kāppu*' (amulet tied for protection) and is recognised as a *cāmiyāṭi* by everyone. People approach him for various needs such as sickness, childbirth, etc. Whenever he himself is in confusion, CM appears to him in dreams and instructs him what to do or not to do. He feels the protective presence of Vijayanarayanam's CM in his village. When he feels lonely, he applies holy ash of CM and he strongly feels his presence within himself.

4. *S. Sudalaikannu:* Mr. S. Sudalaikannu, a Tēvar aged 65, residing at Vijayanarayanam is another *cāmiyāṭi* who has been performing this function for the last fifteen years. As a *cāmiyāṭi* he represents CM. *Cāmiyāṭṭam* is the hereditary service of his family to CM and to the village. He is the only son of his father who died when he was fifteen years old. After his father's death, many tried to take up that role. They did not succeed. In fact, it is said they all met with sudden death. Like other *cāmiyāṭi(s)* he too was not exceptionally involved in the devotion of CM. At one *koṭai,* Sudalaikannu was possessed by god. In a trance he went to the ritual space on his own, rather unconsciously, and demanded that he should tie *kāppu* for CM. When CM possesses him, he utters aruḷvākku (divination). "I do not remember later on what I said earlier in trance. In divination I do not know what I say. The moment I realise that 'I' am saying something, I stop to divinise," explains Mr. Sudalaikannu Ever since he started dancing for CM, he feels that CM has been accompanying him wherever he goes and protecting him from many accidents during his journeys.

5. *Arjunan:* Mr. Arjunan, a Sāmpāṉ (Dalit) of Pattarpuram, is a 27-year-old driver in Mumbai who comes every year to Vijaynarayan to perform *cāmiyāṭṭam.* He has been a *cāmiyāṭi* in this temple for the last five years. Like others, his family is also involved in this function for many generations. His great grandfather was Āṇṭisāmpāṉ who was jointly responsible, with others, to bring CM to the village. From childhood onwards, he used to come to the temple to worship CM and to do service. After his father's death, due to illness and poverty, he underwent lots of hardships very early in life. When he was in two minds to go to Mumbai to seek his fortune and make his life, CM appeared to him in a dream and instructed him to go there. He has been doing well ever since. He firmly believes that it is CM who has brought fortune into his life, and has been protecting him in the new unknown place. CM had saved him miraculously in a fire accident in the slum in Mumbai.

Different themes of the structural units	*Vijayanar-cāmiyāṭi*	*Sirumalanchi-Cāmiyāṭi*	*P. S. Sudalai muthu (Muṇṭaṉ cāmiyāṭi at V.Nara.*	*Sudalaikannu*	*Arjunan*
Involvement of Family	Grandfather/father had a special interest	*Ayyā Vaḻi* family Father– *Cāmiyāṭi*. Leg-infected-and operated upon.	CMis his family's inheritance. Grand father responsible for bringing CM.	For three generations	For five generations
Period of personal non-recognition of CM's power	Indifferent	Atheist, non-involvement	Less personal involvement	No special Involvement	From childhood onwards used to go to the temple
Period leading to recognition of CM's power: Fortune/ misfortune	Smuggler, Miraculous protection Came on him outside	DifficultiesLost job Favours: SSLC passes/ elected president against all odds	Sudden death of the father- lots of trouble.	Death of father. Subsequently death of 4 other *cāmiyāṭi(s)*.	Illness, poverty
Recognition of power	*cāmiyāṭṭam* for last 20 yrs. "CM is all for me".	*cāmiyāṭṭam* for last yrs 15 He is all powerful in my life	The deity possessed him only after 3 yrs of his father's death. Ever since good fortune. Social and Ritual sanction (*kāppu*) only for the last 5 years	Non voluntary Personal assertion Asked to go to Bombay	Dream appearance: Fortune promised.
Reinforcement of power through extraneous localisation: (a power of encompassment):	Unexpected recognition by other *cāmiyāṭi(s)* in other temples (CM and Non-CM)	Unexpected recognition by other *cāmiyāṭi(s)* in other temples (CM and Non-CM)	Presence is felt in his village, Kalakadu. Accompaniment of god's power through holy ash in loneliness.	CM has saved him number of times from dangers during his travel accident there.	He protects him in Bombay. He was miraculously saved in a fire

Figure 3

An Analysis of the Life Histories of the Cāmiyāṭi(s)

The analyses of the life histories of the *cāmiyāṭi(s)* show the phases of non-recognition of CM's power, recognition of CM's power, and CM's power of encompassment through extraneous localisation, which underlie their relationship with CM. The myths show that, though the families of the *cāmiyāṭi(s)* were involved in the worship of their respective CMs, almost all the *cāmiyāṭi(s)* were often indifferent to, or little involved in, the deity. Through such narratives of indifference, they indirectly ascertain that it is not they who on their own usurped the role of *cāmiyāṭi*, but CM who has chosen them. Even now the *cāmiyāṭi* of Sirumalanchi remains least interested in the day-to-day affairs of the CM temple, but maintains a certain degree of personal devotion to CM because he says that it is a benevolent power that has come to uplift the standard of the common man's life. The myths further indicate, except in one case (Ayyakannu), that it is the period of misfortune or personal affliction as Nabokov has noted,[15] that has led the *cāmiyāṭi(s)* to committing themselves to CM as his servant, thereby recognising the role of his power in their own lives. It is through giving them suffering and pain that he brings them to him, not exactly to trouble them, but to raise them higher, as one *cāmiyāṭi* opined. Some stories indicate that the personal recognition of CM's power has the other side of social recognition of *cāmiyāṭi* as a valid mediator of CM's power to the village folk. Further, the life histories of the *cāmiyāṭi(s)* unfold the fact that the theme of *extraneous localisation* of CM's power is realised in their lives too, whereby not only the protective power of CM is felt as omnipotent, but, through this, their-*cāmiyāṭi(s)'* mediatory powers are also recognised and expanded.

Life Histories of Devotees

Like the *cāmiyāṭi(s)*, another set of people who are believed to have been specially touched and transformed by the power of CM are some select devotees. These villagers, in turn, by believing in the power of CM and exhibiting it through rituals, contribute towards the continuation of the cult of CM. As the devotees are the important players of the cult, the life stories of some of the devotees are presented below, and analysed later, so as to explore what kinds of experiences of CM's powers drive them towards him and make them significant constituents of the cult.

Different Life Stories

1. *Jesu Raj:* aged twenty-five, came to Sirumalanchi from Vadalivalli, a neighbouring village. He is working in Mumbai. A few years ago he had severe stomach ache, diarrhoea, jaundice and back pain for more than a year. The medical treatment undergone in Mumbai did not bear any fruit. He prayed to different gods in Mumbai, but the situation did not improve. As he was growing desperate, some of his friends from Tirunelveli residing in Mumbai suggested that he could pray to CM at Sirumalanchi as he is a very powerful deity. Heeding his friends' advice, he prayed to CM at Sirumalanchi and kept a vow to cook *poṅkal* and slaughter a goat as sacrifice during *koṭai* if he got healed. Since he was miraculously healed, he had come there to fulfil his vow. He had also spoken about it to his friends and relatives. One of his cousin's sons at Tirupur had been suffering from a brain tumour. Jesu Raj had asked him to make a vow to CM at Sirumalanchi. They are already beginning to experience positive signs of the child getting healed faster than expected. They have kept a photo of CM in their house at Tirupur and strongly feel the protective presence of CM there.

2. *Kanmani Ammal:* Kanmaniammal from Kurivkulam is a sixty year old lady who has been coming to Valliyoor for the last six or seven years. Her son had two children who died in their childhood, one after the other. Kanmaniammal's son was childless for five years. Kanmaniammal came to *Ayyaṉ Kōvil Cuṭalai* at Valliyoor and prayed to him. She vowed that she would cook and offer *poṅkal* every year if a child was born to her son. A male child was born soon, and she came to the temple to fulfil her vows. Similarly, her daughter at Ambasamudram had been facing financial problems and ill-treatment from her husband. She asked her to pray to CM at

Valliyoor, and she is feeling the protective hand of CM there as her situation is significantly improving day by day.

3. *Muthu:* Twenty-eight year old Muthu is from Vijayanarayanam. He now works at Tiruvananthapuram. Ten years ago, he was afflicted with a strange viral fever which no doctor could heal. In such a situation of despair and hopelessness, some of his relatives asked him to go to a CM temple. He prayed to CM and kept a vow that he would carry *pālkuṭam* (a ritual of carrying milk pot) every year if he got healed. Ever since, he prays to CM to be cured of all sicknesses. As CM heard his prayer, he carries *pālkuṭam* every year in fulfilment of his vow. He says that CM protects him at Tiruvananthapuram. He often experiences CM going in front of him seated atop a white horse.

4. *Murugan:* Twenty-three-year old Murugan hails from Tirunelveli. He has passed the 10th standard and is now working with a daily newspaper company. He has been coming to CM's temple from childhood onwards as it is his *kula teyvam* (clan diety). When his mother was struck by a strange fever, he earnestly prayed to CM that, if his mother were healed, he would carry *pālkuṭam* to CM every year. As the mother got healed, thanks to the protective power of CM, he has been regularly carrying *pālkuṭam* for CM for the last ten years. Besides, every year they cook *poṅkal* once and offer a blood-sacrifice of a goat during *koṭai.* Since CM is their *kula teyvam,* they perform the ear-piercing ceremony in CM's temple, keep the first copy of a marriage invitation at his feet to get his blessings, come first to his temple to thank him soon after the marriage, etc. He is so devoted to CM that he feels CM resides in his heart. He also feels accompanied by CM wherever he goes.

5. *Murugan:* Another Murugan whom the researcher met is a forty-two-year old goldsmith from a village called Kunthankulam. He has been frequenting the CM temple for the last six years. He himself is a *cāmiyāṭi* of Ayyanar. When his business was going from bad to worse, he was told by the villagers to pray to the CM of Naduvakurichi. After praying to CM, his business picked up. Now he says he is doing well,

Different themes of structural units	*Jesu Raj*	*Kanmani ammal*	*Muthu*	*Murugan*	*Murugan*
Period of Misfortune -Failure of other powers -Non-Recognition of CM's power	Stomach pain, diarrhoea, jaundice, back ache- no cure of doctor	Death of two grandchildren Went to doctors No children	Peculiar viral fever afflicted him ten years before. No treatment was effective	Peculiar sickness of the mother	Loss in businesses
Acceptance of CM's power & Removal of Havoc: Manifestation of CM's power	Heard of this deity through his relative. Came here. Met *cāmiyāṭi*. Kept vow. Healed	She prayed to God. Chid born	Asked by his relatives to pray to CM. Kept vow.Healed	Prayed for the mother. Kept vow. Mother healed	Many of his villagers have received avours from CM; he too prayed to CM; business picked up
Performance of Gratitude to CM's Power	*Poṅkal* now and cutting of goat for *Koṭai*	*Poṅkal*	Carrying of *Pālkuṭam*	*PālkuṭamPoṅkal/* fastingAnimal-sacrifice	*Poṅkal*, coconut and offering of flowers
Encompassment of Power	He had told his cousin at Tirupur to pray to CM. His child suffering from head tumour is getting healed miraculously.	I have prayed to him for other needs of my daughter too. Already she feels protected by him at Ambasumudram.	Experience of CM in white horse at Tiruvananthapuram.	CM's presence fills his heart. Feels accompanied by CM wherever he goes	CM comes a police man- protect him- leads him in the darkness. CM appears as child -wakes him up in sleep to save in dangers.

Figure 4

thanks to CM. He feels a strong accompanying presence of CM in his life. When he returns at night to his village all alone in the dark, he sees CM as a policeman going before him. He recollects dreams where CM had often come to him as a child and woken him from sleep and saved either him or his cattle from the danger of snakes and wild animals.

The Analysis of the Stories

The analysis of the life histories of the devotees shows that, as in the case of *cāmiyāṭi(s),* it is more misfortune than fortune that brings them to CM. In the case of devotees, this period of misfortune is characterised by the failure of other powers (different gods and goddesses, or medical treatment, etc.) to save them from misery. Their acceptance of CM's power of protection is always accompanied by their personal commitment to CM, often expressed by the keeping of vows. Once they personally commit themselves to CM, there is a gradual revelation of CM's power, wherein the manifestation of CM's power of protection is realised through the disappearance of pain, suffering and misery, either in one's life or in the life of someone for whom the vow was made. This is followed by acts of gratitude such as preparing *poṅkal,* undertaking *pālkuṭam,* etc., that is nothing but the celebration of CM's power of protection in one's life. Finally, the analysis holds that, like in other constituents, the theme of the encompassment of CM's protective power is enacted in the lives of devotees too.

Analysis of Rituals

Since the various elements such as *paṭaipu* (offering of cooked meat of pregnant animals), blood sacrifice (animal, human), etc., already prefigured in the origin myth, the *koṭai* ritual becomes one more instance of the commonly held notion of "ritual as the enactment of the myth", and subsequently they are a mechanism of remembrance of various themes of the Origin myth. The core rituals, as we have shown in the previous chapter, depict the true nature of CM such as the intractability of his character, his power of protection, his

		Underlying Themes of Koṭai rituals
Core Rituals	Vēṭṭai / Maiyāṇam *pūcai*	1. CM's power of Protection 2. His Control of Evil Powers 3. His Power of encompassement
	aruḷvākku collutal/ kuṟi collutal	Manifestation of CM's Power and appropriation of CM's power of protection
	Blood Sacrifice *Paṭaippu* *Poṅkal*	1. Re-enactment of intractable power of CM 2. Commemoration of CM's destructive power over evil forces
	Sharing of Offerings	1. People's consumption of the deity's offering.
Other Rituals	1. Kāppu Kaṭṭutal 2. *Mākāppu Pūcai* 3. *Kutiaḻaippu*	Seeking of CM's power of protection Making the power of protection favourable Refreshing the folk memory about the Recognition of CM's Power of Protection.

Figure 5

power of encompassment, appropriation of CM's power of protection and his communion with the people.

All these ritual elements reinforce and inscribe the same theme of CM's power of protection, which we have seen manifest in the original myth and subsequently in other components such as local temple myths, in *cāmiyāṭi* stories and in the stories of devotees.

To elaborate it more, the very idea of *Kāppu kaṭṭutal* (Kayatar and Vijayanarayanam), i.e., the tying of protective amulets as a symbol of protection and safeguard against the release of tremendous energy[16] instil in the mind the very purpose of *koṭai,* namely, seeking CM's power of protection. This is done by kindling and releasing the power, manifesting it to subdue other evil powers, tapping and appropriating it, worshipping and surrendering to it, all these done through *koṭai* rituals. In similar vein, *mākāppu pūcai,* which was described in the previous chapter, reminds people of the true nature of the deity as powerful and dangerous, on the one hand, and makes him favourable and protective for the worshippers, on the other. The ritual of *kutiaḻaippu* is another example that recalls the original context of CM's relationship with the village, the local temple and the local village folk. By re-establishing the connection between these three entities at the level of the consciousness of the people, it once again refreshes the locally constructed historical memory about the protective power of CM and its recognition by the elders of yesteryears in the village.

All these indicate that these elements of *koṭai* ritual reveal the major theme of power of protection and the other sub-themes from the above narratives of temple myths, the life stories of *cāmiyāṭi(s)* and those of the devotees. These are enacted through *koṭai* rituals that install them in the memories of the people, establish the validation of such themes, and ensure their continuation by transforming them into beliefs, through the mechanism of ritual performance.

Conclusion

This chapter has shown that the five elements, namely, (a) the origin myth of CM, (b) temple myths, (c) the *cāmiyāṭi,* (d) the devotees and (e) the ritual of *koṭai* together constitute the CM cult. They are all necessary components. The chapter has inquired into what is common to all of them and what in the folk worldview holds them together to constitute CM. Through such a query, it has explored the common underlying themes that inform the logic of the constitution of all the five narratives into a single whole.

The following chapter will show that the main theme of the protective power of CM and the sub themes have their recurrences in the various stages of *koṭai* ritual discussed in the next chapter. For instance, the various sub-themes such as non-recognition/suspicion of CM's power of protection, period of misfortune/havoc underscore the pre-ritual stage, while ritual-stage marks the context of acceptance of CM's power, involve acts of efforts to remove the misfortune through the power of CM such as divination or performance of gratitude (*poṅkal* or sacrificial slaughter of goat) that witness continuation of the power of CM in the lives of the people. The post ritual-stage is the re-acceptance and re-recognition of the protective power of CM, as we shall see.

Notes

1. Myth A is taken from Shanmugasundaram, *Cuṭalaimāṭaṉ,* 57-60. To distinguish the myths from the main body text of the thesis, this myth and other two myths are given in single space.
2. A hall supported by artistic pillars.
3. *Kaṇiyāṉ*s are a social group of tribes who regard themselves as a priestly class in the folk religious terrain.
4. A musical instrument played during *koṭai.*
5. The *Apsaras* are the heavenly female beauties whose chief is called Indirani.
6. It is to be a hill over which Kāḷipulayaṉ is said to have magical control.
7. Myth B is taken from D. Lourdu. *A Study of Sudalaimadasamy Cult.*
8. Myth C is taken from the manuscript written by an *aṇṇāvi* Kaṇiyāṉ Thirumalaisamy from Tirunelveli for the purpose of the present work.
9. I regard the creation of the universe and the description of Kailācam in myths A and C as 'prelude' because they are ways of starting a story in Indian tradition by the folk artists. The details have no direct bearing on the rest of the plot.
10. The same frame is seen in some myths, e.g., Kattāvarāyaṉ's myth. Cf. David Dean Shulman, "Outcastes, Guardian, and Trickster: Notes on the Myth of Kattāvarāyaṉ," in *Criminal Gods and Demon Devotees,* ed., Hiltebeitel, State University of New York Press, Albany, 1989, 36-67.
11. Cf., *ibid..*
12. Cf. Joanne Punzo Wahorne "From Robber Baron to Royal Servant of God? Gaining a Divine Body in South India," in *Criminal Gods,* 405-426.
13. One wonders if this is what makes him a suitable god for Brahmins, who were also seen as disloyal to Sanskritic Hinduism. They not only became disloyal to Sanskritic Hinduism by worshipping CM, but their disloyal character was covered up and legitimised through their worship. Their worship of CM did construct and was constructed by the violation of social *dharmas* and religious behaviours prescribed by and assigned to Brahmins in *varna* ideology.

14. One of the ways a *cāmiyāṭi* publicly acknowledges another *cāmiyāṭi* is to give the container of the holy ash to him to take it for himself, while for others he distributes the holy ash with a blessing or *mantra* (incantation).
15. Cf. Nabokov, *Religion Against Self,* 19-30.
16. Cf. *Ibid.*, 156.

CHAPTER 5

A TRIPARTITE SCHEME IN THE OPERATION OF THE RITUAL POWER OF KOṬAI

Introduction

According to Bryan Turner, religion "is a response to the existential dilemmas, of human life, especially illness and death, but this response is itself structured and directed by religious cultures which have the effect of binding individuals together in social collectivities."[1] Along this line, the first part of this chapter, describes *koṭai* rituals, as one such structured social response to the problems of the contingencies of life by showing how *koṭai* rituals involve and imply three stages of folk encounter with their local existential problems. Further the chapter discusses about the nature of *koṭai* rituals with the analytical categories such as 'Prescriptive versus Performative' and 'Strategic versus Symbolic' and moves on to the interpretation of ritual elements such as *pūcai,* offerings, *vēṭṭai,* divination and *cāmiyāṭṭam.* Having outlined the schema of this chapter, let me now move on to the description of the three stages of *koṭai* rituals.

The Three Stages in Koæai Rituals

My analysis of the *koṭai* rituals of the CM cult reveals a scheme of three stages in its operation. The three stages[2] are: (1) The *Pre-ritual stage* where the traumatic experience of the 'negativities' of life leads to the accumulation of anxiety and fear in a human person that can be called *'territorialization of angst'*. (2) The *Ritual stage* wherein ritual power is generated, displayed and tapped to identify the causes of angst, then conditions are laid to remove them, and thus hope is instilled. This stage is marked by the *'archeology of angst'*.[3] (3) The *Post-ritual stage* where the causes of angst wither away, the impact of power begins to be felt, and faith in CM is reinforced. This stage is marked by *'de-territorialization of angst.'*

The three-stage scheme, based on the "function" of the ritual as noted in chapter I, is a phenomenological scheme, quite evident in what happens to people *before koṭai,* what they do *during koṭai* and how it alters their perceptions *after* the event. This tripartite scheme is generic, not very specific to the *koṭai* of CM alone. Hence, it can be applicable not only to most of the *koṭai* festivals of the gods/goddesses in this area, but also to the folk festivals of the deities in other parts of Tamilnadu. Perhaps, what is specific to the CM cult are some of the ritual strategies by which CM *cāmiyāṭi* generates, taps, displays and distributes ritual power to the folk. Such ritual strategies as *ūṭṭu* , *nākkuveṭṭu /kaiveṭṭu* (gashing of tongue or forearm with a knife), *maiyāṉa pūcai* (the rites of the cremation ground), *tiraḷai koṭuttal* (a kind of appeasement ritual for the dead) are specific to the CM cult. The ritual power generated by these specific rituals, as will be seen, can be a source for the emergence of new vectors of differently embedded social meanings specific to different religio-cultural landscapes. Having said this, let us move on to the elaboration of the three stages mentioned above.

The Pre-ritual Stage

This stage before the ritual period is characterized by people's experience of misfortune, suffering and trauma. Both, Blackburn, who has done a study on the singing of bow songs during the rituals of *koṭai,* and Nabokov, who has done studies on Tamil folk rituals, hold the view that one of the main focuses of both the myth[4] and the ritual[5] is human fragility and precariousness which involve anxiety, misfortune, the fact of childlessness, and the experience of death or fear of death.

These themes invariably occur in the folk theatres of bow songs[6] and *kaṇiyāṉkūttu*[7], and these are the facts of life that set the stage for the Tamil folk rituals as Nabokov has noted.[8] Making a study of the devotees coming to the folk temple in the northern part of Tamilnadu, Nabokov notes, "What all had in common, however, and often in distressing abundance was profound personal affliction. Many were at the lowest points in their lives."[9] The anxiety, fear, and suffering begin to germinate and encompass a person/family/community, constituting its territory around them, and leading to a state of angst. People find themselves in the 'grip of blindness.'[10] This pre-ritual phase can be termed the *territorialisation of angst*.

The people believe that any mishap in one's life/family/community is caused, more often than not, by a strange factor unknown and unidentifiable by him/her/them, though some people believe that it is caused by *'evāl'*, i.e., 'command', as Nabokov notes.[11] It renders its victims often socially dead, even if they are not physically dead.[12] Subsequently, anxiety is experienced in all areas of life caused by a series of death or sickness, abandonment, and all sorts of unwelcome suffering. All these point to the expansion of 'territorialisation of angst'. Besides being a state of germination of fear and anxiety, it is also a phase of the emergence of a certain compulsion for the "pursuit of power" to tackle the pessimistic and gloomy ambience in the life of an individual or a family. This phase of territorialisation of angst covertly sets the background wherein people are inevitably compelled to seek an ontological or supernatural power during the ritual stage of *koṭai*. Thus this stage provides a rationale not only for the generation of power through rituals, but also for the prominence and popularity of the cult. Further, as Nabokov observes,[13] it is this common experience and consequent sharing of misfortune that would produce in the next stage (ritual stage), a sort of bonding phenomenon, which Victor Turner called 'temporary *communitas*.'[14]

The Ritual Stage

Surrounded by the territorialisation of angst, the folk come to attend the rituals of *koṭai*. They look for a reliable and powerful agency that can throw light on their negative life circumstances, provide a solution to their problems, alleviate their pains and reinstate hope in their lives. Here, as Bourdieu notes, ritual functions as an effective cosmogonic practice for people "who cannot afford the luxury of logical speculation, mystical effusions, or metaphysical anxiety."[15] Through rituals such as *koṭai*, people are invited to believe in the protective power of the supernatural agent, CM, by witnessing his power of control over the sources of evil powers in the rural setting. The same power is also seen to have control over the lives of the people as CM's *cāmiyāṭi* demonstrates the ability to analyze the problems of the people and to propose solutions for overcoming them, and hope is finally instilled into them at this stage. Thus the ritual stage can be described to have the following elements:

1. Generation and display of power,
2. Archeology of angst,
3. Instillation of hope.

Generation and Display of Power

One of the main aims of *koṭai* ritual is to rekindle and generate the protective power of CM. It is done through rituals such as *kutiaḻaippu* (the ritual of inviting the deity) and *vēṭṭai* (ritual hunting), made available to people through concrete symbols such as *tirunāru* (sacred ash), *prasātam* (consecrated food), etc. It is witnessed also in the drinking of the blood of pigs and goats or in *ūṭṭu*[16] and impressively gesticulated and displayed through *cāmiyāṭṭam* (trance-dance), and more definitely and effectively is distributed and made available to the people through divination.

Archeology of Angst

Through divination, the 'archeology of angst' is carried out by the *cāmiyāṭi*. Divination involves the following steps: (1) Prediction of the problem; (2) Identification of the causes; (3) Proposal of condition for the removal of angst; and, (4) Instillation of future hope/assurance of return of well-being.

The first three steps constitute the 'archeology of angst' in divination. All instances of divination may not contain all the above steps, and these steps may not take place in a chronological sequence: for instance, the fourth step may precede the third or all the other steps, or in a few instances, it may be the only form of divination. However, in most of the cases the third and the fourth steps are often compulsorily present.

Now the archeology of angst begins with the *cāmiyāṭi* coming out with the *prediction of the devotee's problem* at the very look of the latter. *Cāmiyāṭi* utters sentences like: "Your family is undergoing severe financial crisis," "You are suffering from acute stomach ache, headache, or back pain," "You have lost your job/looking for a job," "Your have no peace because your husband is not living with you," "You have no children," "The animals in your household are dying of sicknesses," etc. Then he would *identify the causes of their predicament.* He now makes statements like: "Some evil spirit is dwelling in your house, and you are afflicted because you are possessed by that spirit," or "You have no child because you have no faith in CM," or "Someone has cast a spell or worked sorcery on you/your family," etc.

The next step is the proposal of condition for the removal of angst. These conditions could be either pre-effect or post-effect. The form of pre-effect conditions would be like, "First, if you do (this), then you see that will happen," etc. Some examples are: "Fast every first Friday of the month and do *pūcai(s)* at my temple for one year and your stomach problem will be solved," or "You live in a bad house according to *vāstu*[17] and therefore shift from that house and all your problems will vanish" or "Give up your bad habits, they do not please CM," etc. The instances of post-effect conditions are also common. Their forms are like: "Do not worry, my son, I am your father/master," "This father/master will not desert you, he removes all your difficulties. Then you do this/that," etc. Some examples of the post effect conditions would be: "I will give you a job/You will get a promotion by the next month, and then you must give me hundred rupees," or You will bear a child by the next *koṭai*, you must ask him/her to carry *pālkuṭam* (milk pot) when s/he is twelve," or, "This will happen, and then you must offer me a pig/cock/goat," or, it could be a question to a devotee: "I'll do this for you, what will you give me?" Here the devotee is made to choose the condition(s) that he will have to honour. The last step is *instillation of hope*, which we will treat separately.

Instillation of Hope

This last step 'instillation of hope' is the point of culmination both in divination and in *koṭai* rituals, hence the overlapping. In the case of post-effect conditions discussed above, the fourth step might precede the third step. It means that the assurance of the return of well being is emphatically stated first, and then the post-effect condition is laid. The possibility of instillation of hope into the minds of devotees is dependent on the perceived degree of power manifest in the rituals and in divination. The more the power of a particular folk god like CM is perceived, the more the possibilities are open for the better degree of instillation of hope. Yet, the concluding note of the ritual is one of assurance of hope and of the return of well-being.

Post-ritual Stage

This is the stage where territorialisation of angst encountered by a devotee/family/village begins to dismantle. People begin to experience the initial signs of disappearance of fear/anxiety/and control of the evil powers that surrounded them. As "ritual process shift(ed) people to new conditions of confidence, integration or health,"[18] there is less fear and less anxiety. This is what is called 'de-territorialisation of angst.' As the power of CM is instilled in the minds of the people through rituals of *koṭai*, any disappearance of evil and appearance of good is associated with that power. By de-territorializing angst off people's lives, CM is believed to establish power over the territory of people's lives. Indeed CM is brought back to function as a guardian and protector of the village and of people's lives. If no signs of disappearance of angst occur or are seen taking place in other's lives, then the folk might attribute it to the devotee's lack of faith in the folk god. If no positive sign of good happens in the village or if any mishap suddenly occurs for the villagers, then the blame is on the imperfect/improper conduct of the ritual, or on the impure state of *cāmiyāṭi* in *koṭai,* which is said to have infuriated the deity.

Notably, in the folk religious realm, there is a period of *off-peak ritual season* that has to be distinguished from *peak ritual season*. The latter is centered on *koṭai,* where there is a torrential outpouring of the power of CM. The former is a period where the effects of peak ritual season are continued; faith in CM is reinforced through routine and minor rituals. Here too there are instances of manifestation of the power of a god, but *no generation* of the power of the god, strictly speaking. Whatever degree of manifestation takes place then, it is believed to prefigure the power of CM in *koṭai.* As the de-territorialisation begins to be experienced, people approach CM in this season to reinforce their faith in his power and show their gratitude. In case it does not take place, they come back to clarify the matter with *cāmiyāṭi* who will do so by modifying the conditions made earlier.

The above analysis indicates that folk religion functions through rituals as one of the effective means of coping with crisis situations. In the psychology of religion, this is seen as one of the significant functions of religion. Researches done in this field indicate that religious individuals are less likely to suffer from psychopathology than others,[19] less likely to be depressed and less likely to commit suicide than others. Hence religious faith appears to have a link with psychological health, much more than with illness.

Some authors like Horowitz, Parkes and McIntosh have understood religion as a schema that plays a vital role in coping. "Religious schemas are likely to be cued or activated during times when people are coping."[20] Religion functions as a cognitive schema which provides people, among other things, ways of thinking about traumatic events, thereby facilitating a faster cognitive processing of such events. Faster processing is often related to better adjustment to aversive events.[21] "Being able to cognitively process a negative event quickly and efficiently could facilitate the integration of the event."[22] Besides, religious schema provides meaning to people during crises. The search for meaning (i.e., finding a purpose for or understanding of the event) is one of the three important themes in the coping process as Rothbaum, Weisz & Synder, Silver & Wortman have noted.[23] Having found meaning through the schema of religion, a person may be more likely to experience better adjustment to the events or situations of crisis in life.[24] In the CM cult, *koṭai* ritual becomes one of the important occasions in which, through ritual elements like divination, the folk are made to experience religion as a schema for coping. This coping strategy influences people in understanding what they perceive, provides them with faster cognitive process, enables them to change their basic schemas about themselves and their world, and makes them perceive their lives with a more optimistic outlook than before.

Further studies in this field have indicated that those who have higher faith (i.e., belief and reliance, not so much on religious doctrine, but on higher power), "have significantly lower anxiety and depression scores, (they) are less likely to exhibit signs of character pathology, and have significantly higher ego strength scores than participants with lower faith."[25] The above research finding can be very well related to the folk religious phenomenon like CM, which is governed not by any coded religious doctrines and principles but by belief in a higher ontological power.

In Dialogue with Victor Turner's Analysis of Ritual Process

No discussion on rituals will be adequate without taking into account the views of Victor Turner, one of the authorities on the anthropological understanding of rituals. But to discuss Victor Turner's views on rituals, we need to take note of Van Gennep's contribution to the study of rituals, as the former is largely inspired and influenced by the latter. Van Gennep's seminal work on rituals sees a three-fold stage during *the period of rituals*. In particular his analysis of rites of passage, focusing as it does on 'transition' or 'passage' from one stage of life (season or event) to another, perceives a three-stage structure of rituals (separation, transition and incorporation) at the point of transitional rituals.

We need to point out the difference between the analysis of ritual by Van Gennep and the ritual we are studying. His analysis of life-cycle rituals is concerned with the change of status in the lives of the individuals and groups during the above-mentioned period of transition from one stage/season to another. It does not take into account the crisis situations of human beings in other contexts, in their day-to-day living conditions, and subsequently is not concerned with the rituals associated with them. Unlike Van Gennep's views, our understanding of *koṭai* rituals is concerned about all the above elements. Besides, the present analysis of *koṭai* rituals indicates that *the periods before and after* the *koṭai* ritual have a vital place in people's perception, construction and appropriation of the significance of the rituals at *koṭai.* The periods before and after the *koṭai,* when looked at from the interpretative meanings subscribed to *koṭai* by the folk, must be understood as necessary constituents of a single whole called '*koṭai*'.

While Van Gennep's analysis of rituals was founded solely on the interaction of rites of passage, Victor Turner, focusing on the rituals of affliction of the Ndembu people, has also seen the pattern of separation, transition, and incorporation. But one wonders if he has worked on them with the a-priori theory of rituals given by Van Gennep. After his death, Turner's wife, Edith, a co-researcher with him, made a study on 'tooth ritual' (Ihamba), one of the rituals already described in Victor Turner's *The Drums of Affliction,* but came out with an insider (*emic*) account of the rituals, experiencing at first hand, the spiritual healing power described by the Ndembu. This clearly indicates that there are alternative ways of looking at the rituals of affliction of the Ndembu people, different from that of Victor Turner.

One wonders as to what extent the 'processual analysis' adopted from the pattern of life-cycle rituals can be applicable to 'rituals of affliction'. The process of life-cycle rituals is initiated by the social custom performed uniformly as a routine in the lives of almost all individuals of a given society. The *raison d'être* of a life cycle ritual can be applied invariably to all cultural members of a given society. The reason why the process of a particular ritual begins in a person does not vary from one person to another. But in the case of 'rituals of affliction', the *raison d'être* of a ritual varies significantly from one person to another. Secondly, all the cultural members of a given society do not routinely subscribe to 'rituals of affliction'.

This indicates that the preceding two types of rituals work with two different starting-points. But in any processual analysis, analysis of the cause, i.e., the starting point, is very significant for the analysis of the processes, because the cause can impact upon the process, and the former can significantly alter the course of the latter. Now, in the case of rituals, the interpretative meaning of rituals is significantly coloured and determined by the aim of the ritual practitioners. Failure to assess their motive and meaning will result in the breakdown of exegetical meaning[26], which is of great importance for Victor Turner himself in the study of rituals. All this shows that rituals of affliction need a treatment different from the one adopted for life cycle rituals. The present study, which looks at the rituals of *koṭai* from the viewpoint of angst, is one such attempt.

Further, the ritual stage of *koṭai* described has few dimensions in common with the liminal period described by Victor Turner. The liminal period primarily spoken of as the characteristic of the passage of rites is one of seclusion and ambiguity (sexlessness), a dissolution of all categories and classifications, giving rise to role reversals, and stresses on the absolute authority of the ritual elders.[27] First, it has to be stated that the ritual stage of *koṭai* does not significantly witness any dissolution of categories and classifications. As regards the role reversals, *koṭai* witnesses divergent patterns. The barbers and Tēvar(s) in Valliyoor (as helpers to Brahmins), and Dalits in Naduvakurichi performed the same traditional roles in *koṭai* rituals too, while the Brahmin engages in role reversal by going to the cremation ground, and by being a *cāmiyāṭi* for a Dalit god. Thus not all ritual functionaries in all cases take to a 'suspension of normative obligations.' Unlike in Victor Turner's analysis of Ndembu elders, the absolute authority of ritual elders [*cāmiyāṭi(s)*] in the CM cult can be regarded, in most of the cases, as both moral (ritual) and secular as well.[28] However, the idea of seclusion described by Victor during the liminal period is more or less present during the celebration of *koṭai* in varying degrees and intensities in different places.

Further, the present analysis follows Victor Turner in holding 'ritual' primarily as a process. For Turner, this process evokes sentiments of mutual concern necessary for social life.[29] The present analysis of ritual, which looks at it from the viewpoint of an individual's angst, is concerned about the process that deals with the *sentiments of individual's* anxiety, fear and apprehension. It has to do with the procedures, techniques and strategies that aim at the resolution of an individual's crisis-situations in a manner that would anticipate the foreclosing of the possibilities and probabilities of crises in the life of an individual. To put it differently, the ritual-processes here are not so much concerned about the objective structures of social life as in Victor's Turner,[30] but primarily with individuals' differently situated subjectivities. But in the process, some of the polyvalent symbolic gestures and metaphorical narratives employed by the *cāmiyāṭi* during *cāmiyāṭṭam* and divination do touch upon the categories of objective social realities. What surfaces with such polysemous symbolic gestures are ambivalent social meanings, some conforming to the objective social world, while others are directed more towards subtle but concrete social transformations.

The Nature of Koṭai Rituals

Prescriptive or Performative?

Borrowing ideas from Marshall Sahalins,[31] Nabokov—who studied the Tamil religious phenomenon—distinguishes between two types of rituals: prescriptive and performative. The former type gives the participants no other option but to comply with stated procedures and aims. The latter permits everyone to make one's own performative and interpretative choices.

Prescriptive rituals' transformation of inner dispositions is intimately associated with the objective forms of the ritual. They work to make people adopt 'public' identities. They are 'totalizing' and compelling. "This is evident from start to finish: from 'warning' that programs participants for the forthcoming action to their final 'pledge' to internalize their transformation ... A series of formulaic procedures pressure participants to comply with the demands placed on them,"[32] so that ritual process becomes a form of power and coercion, as noted by Maurice Bloch.[33] The goal of these rituals is "to change their minds and to see things from an 'outsider' perspective, in which life with others is all there is"[34] as in the Tamil world people approach rituals with the perspective[35] that "life with others is not simply worthwhile."[36]

Though performative rituals follow a formal logic and coherent sequential organization, their imposition of a relatively consistent frame of reference does not produce uniform interpretations or transformations on all the participants. Nabokov sees them as paradoxical because "such open-ended rituals are encoded with strong imagery of a predominantly aggressive–even destructive–tone."[37] The performative rituals involve appropriation and manipulation of what Victor Turner calls 'dominant symbols', whose meaning possesses a certain amount of autonomy throughout the symbolic system.[38]

As regards *koṭai* rituals of the CM cult, the corpus of rituals in *koṭai* comprises both prescriptive and performative rituals. Rituals of *pūcai*, blood sacrifice, *poṅkal* and *ūṭṭu* are all prescriptive, while some of the very essential components of *koṭai* such as *vēṭṭai*, divination and *cāmiyāṭṭam* are more of the performative type. As regards the *koṭai* rituals, we have to make a distinction between the *form* and *content* of rituals. As regards the performative rituals such as *vēṭṭai* and *cāmiyāṭṭam*, though the ritual functionaries may not have a choice with regard to the structure/form of a particular ritual, yet they will have freedom with regard to its content.

As noted earlier, the performative rituals permit people to make their own performative and interpretative choices. The rituals of *cāmiyāṭṭam, vēṭṭai* and divination become prominent in this context, as they are known for their fluidity and indeterminacy. For instance, at Valliyoor, the Brahmin *cāmiyāṭi,* after *vēṭṭai,* brings to the temple a bone that he picked up from the cremation-ground. This goes against the known behaviours of purity prescribed for a Brahmin and points to the freedom he exercises in his ritual action. Further, at Naduvakurichi, one sees the Dalit *cāmiyāṭi* wearing slippers, while *cāmiyāṭi(s)* in other villages during *vēṭṭai* do not wear, rather, should not wear slippers. This choice reveals the performative characteristic of *vēṭṭai* and its ability to function as a symbol of subversion. In caste-ridden Indian society where outcastes cannot wear slippers in the presence of the high castes, the Dalit *cāmiyāṭi's* act of wearing of slippers is a violation of such norms and an act of subversion. Similarly after *vēṭṭai,* the Paḷḷar(s)ẽ bursting of firecrackers worth thousands of rupees indicates that, for the Dalits who are subjugated in the culture of silence, the crackers amplify their voices and announce to all villages within a ten km radius their celebration of *koṭai,* proclaiming the emergence of a newly-gained socio-economic status.

All this indicates that performative rituals need not always perform a negative role of 'disengagement from social roles and personal relationships'[39] as Nabokov notes, but it can also transmit socially significant meanings. These rituals need not always touch upon the personal relationship of individuals but also the social relationship of collectivities by giving voice to the subjugated knowledge of the subalterns, and to their tethered spatiality and inflicted temporalities.

My idea of prescriptive rituals differs slightly from Nabokov's not in the sense of something being prescribed to the devotee where she/he does not have the freedom to act (as Nabokov does), but in the sense of something being the norm of the already- established objective social conditions of caste hierarchy. Hence those rituals which do not follow the latter norm, can be regarded as performative. In such an understanding, what is prescriptive according to Nabokov (because the participant does not have any choice) could be performative, as some of the rituals such as divination and *vēṭṭai* need not prescribe to the norms of *varnarshrama dharmas*,[40] but defy them. Hence they can be called performative.

Vēṭṭai/ Cāmiyāṭṭam/divination, involving dominant symbols and symbolic performance, as noted by Victor Turner, are characterized by the empirical properties such as multivocality, unification of disparate significata (i.e., the underlying meanings of the symbol) and polarization of meaning. The symbols and symbolic gestures employed by the *cāmiyāṭi* during these performances are endowed with multivocality in that a particular symbol/symbolic action represents different things, actions and their meanings by the functionality of condensation. Let me explain what I mean. To recall Turner's views, the unification of disparate significata refers to the fact that the significata are connected by virtue of common analogous qualities or association in fact or thought. Polarization of meaning indicates that they possess two distinct poles of meaning: the *ideological pole* or normative pole that refers to the components of the moral and social order, to principles of social organization and the *oretic pole* or the sensory pole where the significata are natural or physiological phenomena and processes that arouse desires and feelings.[41] Now let us take the example of *vēṭṭai* dress and implements, such as the cap and the coat, *vallam* (a kind of lance),[42] *pantam* (torch), etc. They can represent CM, the king as well as the hunter. They are multivocal as they can represent all these different images, yet they are united and they all can evoke both the sentiments of the social order and of ordinary, common, and natural things. Thus the rituals of *Vēṭṭai/ Cāmiyāṭṭam*/divination, characterized by the qualities of dominant symbols and endowed with diverse meanings and multiples choices, are predominantly performative rituals.

Strategic or Symbolic?

While making an analysis of religious acts, Juergensmeyer distinguishes between the 'strategic' and the 'symbolic'. The strategic implies "a degree of calculation and an expectation of accomplishing a clear objective."[43] It attempts to leverage power in order to win its goal. The "symbolic" type refers to those rituals that are intended to illustrate or refer to something beyond their immediate target. The symbolic has to do with dramatic displays of power, performed not to achieve a strategic goal but to make a symbolic statement. Taking cue from Juergensmeyer's distinction, one can locate some of the folk rituals and performances on the side of the "strategic," and others on the side of the "symbolic." Rituals like blood sacrifice, *paṭaipu* (cooked offering), *maiyāṇa pūcai,* (rites of cremation ground) are of the strategic type. They are designed towards a clear goal to produce desired results with the ritual complex. But ritual performances like *cāmiyāṭṭam* and explosive spectacular shows such as firing of crackers are symbolic types, and need not be tactics directed towards an immediate or strategic goal but dramatic events intended to impress others with their symbolic significance. They are performed not so much to achieve a strategic goal as to make a symbolic statement. This shows that the symbolic has the potentiality to essentialize rituals as performances.

But performances can be either *performance events* or *performance acts*. Performance events are rather dramas designed to have an impact on the several audiences that they affect. Those who witness them therefore a part of what occurs. The significance and meaning of such events are symbolically multifaceted. They mean different things to different observers.

Some rituals can be performative acts. They are able to perform social functions and they have transformative import. Performative acts like verbal utterances not only represent reality but also shape it. They are symbolic actions that can contain a certain power of their own.

Folk rituals can be both *performance events* in that they make symbolic statements, and *performance acts*, in so far as they try to change things. Though ritual performances like divination might appear to be performance events, yet they are covertly performative acts. These performative acts make a difference, if not in a direct, strategic sense, yet in an indirect way so powerful as to change people's perceptions of the world. As

Austin has mentioned, the power of the performative act is related to its perception.[44] Bourdieu goes a step further and maintains that the power of the performative act is rooted in social reality and is given currency by the laws and social customs that stand behind it.[45] To sum up: the folk rituals of CM cult consist of both types, the strategic and the symbolic; the former is characterized by the 'function' role of rituals that we discussed in the first chapter, while the latter by the 'performance' role—which is actualized either through *performance events* or *performance acts.*

Interpretation of Different Rituals of Koæai

Pūcai

Pūcai, a basic form of worship in any temple contexts, basically aims at and culminates in the assimilation of the deity by the devotees. It takes place when a camphor flame is shown—a ritual called *āratti*. Fuller observes that at this point "the divine and human participants are most fully identified... God has become man and a person, transformed, has become god; they have merged."[46] This process of merger begins with what is called *taricaṉam* i.e., 'seeing' and 'being seen' by the temple deity. The reciprocal eye contact established through *taricaṉam* dissolves boundaries that normally prevail between divinity and humanity.[47] Seeing is a kind of touching and a form of knowing. "The act of *darsan* (in Tamil, *taricaṉam*) also becomes a form of absorbing, so that any objectification of a supernatural is always a form of assimilation as well."[48] The meaning of the deliberate look of *cāmiyāṭi* at CM's *pūṭam* (altar) every now and then when he performs rituals such as drinking of blood or milk and divination should be understood against this background. That is to say, *cāmiyāṭi* takes a 'look' at the *pūṭam* during rituals to establish his total identity with CM and to show that he performs a particular ritual on his behalf.

Offerings

As many scholars have noted,[49] offering such as *poṅkal* is the continuation of further realization or actualization of the theme of identity and reciprocal relations between the deity and the devotees. The offering made to CM is of two kinds: vegetarian and non-vegetarian. The former includes the offerings of fruit, flower, and coconut–all put in a basket (returned to them as *prasātam*, i.e., consecrated food meant for consumption by the human being) and *poṅkal;* the latter includes blood sacrifice and cooked meat. Though the earlier anthropologists had always looked at non-Brahmanical animal sacrifices as mere propitiation or appeasement, scholars like Fuller[50] and Nabokov have interpreted them more positively. Fuller holds that where the flesh of the sacrificial animal is cooked and transformed into meat and is consumed by human beings, it can be regarded as a positive ritual that "serves to bring the deity and worshiper close to each other."[51] From such a viewpoint, what is offered to CM–be it flowers, coconuts, *poṅkal*, or animals–all can be regarded as *prasātam.* This is so because even the goat or chicken that is killed on behalf of the village for blood sacrifice is cooked, and gifted to the deity as *paææippu* (cooked offering) and is distributed among the folk, who consume it. Needless to mention it, the individual's sacrifice of fowls, pigs or goats that are sacrificed to CM are taken home for a good family feast the following day. Thus, all the above-mentioned offerings, be they vegetarian or non-vegetarian, can be regarded as processes that establish communion or identity between humans-beings and gods.

However there are other rituals such as *nākkuveṭṭu or kaiveṭṭu* (gashing of tongue or forearm with knife), *tiraḷai koṭuttal* (a kind of appeasement ritual for the dead) and *ūṭṭu*,[52] which seem quite ambiguous. Though the *nākkuveææu or kaiveṭṭu* ritual—that is supposed to lead to the consuming of human blood by the *cāmiyāṭi(s)* and the *ūṭṭu* ritual which is equivalent to drinking of the blood of animals such as a goat or a pig might look like propitiatory rites (as they seem to appease the deity), they are more than that; they are means of deriving the power of CM by the *cāmiyāṭi* who, by performing such rituals, becomes possessed and gets powerful by establishing his identity with CM through such acts. It is so because such rituals are enactments of the origin myth of CM. Now by these rituals the *cāmiyāṭi* becomes identical with CM, and is transformed and empowered to act on behalf of CM during *vēṭṭai* and divination. Nevertheless, the ritual of *tiraḷai koṭuttal* performed at the cremation ground is primarily a ritual of propitiation of unwanted supernatural forces such as evil spirits or the dead.[53]

Vēṭṭai: Ritual Hunting

If *cāmiyāṭi* has to be believed to be powerful and to be the mediator of the power of God, he has to be *seen* as powerful. This is what happens in the case of *cāmiyāṭi* during and after *vēṭṭai*. In *vēṭṭai* he is capable of going all alone at midnight into the outer space, the forest (*kāṭu*) and into the cremation ground (all these are spaces inhabited by the powerful evil spirits), hunts them, overpowers them and de-capacitates them. Since people's problems are believed to be caused by such powerful evil spirits, *vēṭṭai*, as an act of overpowering those powers, is seen as a more powerful act by people.[54]

In *vēṭṭai*, the *cāmiyāṭi* becomes a nomadic subject wandering into the outer realm of a social body and asocial spaces, and is believed to be establishing his dominion over them. To borrow Foucault's view, there is "the use of space, temporal routinisation, and physical movement in the production of ritualized bodies,"[55] during *vēṭṭai*. It is this ritualized body and the act of *vēṭṭai* that give him legitimacy in divination to break the established frameworks of social power. He de-territorialises his outer realm, makes a definitive entry into the inner social space and engages in power-discourse that establishes new patterns of intensities some stronger than before, others not previously established, but newly articulated.[56]

David Rapport, Roger Friedland and others have held that the control of territory defines public authority and that certain groups "have historically gained their identity through association with control over public places."[57] In the context of Tirunelveli district, as we have seen in the second chapter, the holding of land in the village is closely associated with social status both in *mirāsitār* villages of the wet zone and of dry lands under the zamindari. By acquiring new tracts of land in the public place of uncultivated areas (*kāṭu*) during the new revenue system under the British, the villagers enhanced not only their economic, but also their social status within the caste system. Seen in this light, vēṭṭai is a symbolic exercise of control over the territory of the villages. It is an exercise of power not only over public space but also over the centrality of space, namely, the agricultural land, which is the source of survival and social existence in the rural agrarian economy. Indeed agricultural fields are symbols of power, and the performance of *vēṭṭai* claims control over them in a symbolic way. It is a ritual expression of the power of CM *cāmiyāṭi* to control central locations of economy-by traversing them and expelling evil spirits out of them-even when in fact most of the time ,the *cāmiyāṭi* may or may not have control over its economy, the mode of production and relations of production.

Vēṭṭai can attain a different social meaning when it is performed by a Dalit *cāmiyāṭi*. It is generally understood that land belongs to the owner of the land, the upper caste. Prosperity of the land obviously leads to the prosperity of the landowner. But very often the instrumental agency of prosperity, i.e., the labour is not with the land-owning caste/ class, but lies outside of them. It is the landless labour caste, mostly Dalits, who are the real agents of prosperity and wealth in the rural agrarian economy.

Vēṭṭai is an occasion that celebrates this hidden truth, wherein the Dalit *cāmiyāṭi*, a representative of CM, the god of Dalits, shows his control of power over the lands of the high-castes. It is a symbolic explication of the latent and the real, and an act of unveiling of the suppressed truth. Hence *vēṭṭai* is not a mere unrealistic symbolic performance leading to a display of illusion and wishful thinking of Dalits, but a strategic symbolic act that has a goal: to bring to the fore the latent truth of economy, thereby enabling symbols to point to the socially suppressed real. Performance becomes a symbolic social drama, a celebration of the latent and socially submerged economic truth. Just like evil spirits, if not satisfied, can cause havoc to the crops and to the prosperity of the landowners, so too, Dalits can become the source of havoc to prosperity if they refuse to perform labour. But, often such socio-economic upheavals do not take place because the equation of totality of power in terms of money, muscle power, wealth and education is skewed in favour of the high castes. But, whenever and wherever the low castes have gained socio-economic independence through educational qualifications and job opportunities, the balance is tilted in favour of the low-castes. There have been social revolts leading to caste clashes. At such times, *koṭai* is explicitly used as a real display of power resulting in social tension.[58] It brings to the fore the plebian aspect of ritual power, which operates as a counterstroke to the established forms of power within the caste hierarchy.

This shows that some performative acts can become more than 'symbolic'. By demonstrating the vulnerability of the power of the caste hierarchy, these performances can weaken that power, to some extent. Juergensmeyer's observation that, "Because power is largely a matter of perception, symbolic statements can lead to real results"[59] is realized in this context.

Further, as Fuller notes, Dalits are generally "associated with demons and wild/evil spirits, with whom they are supposed to be able to mediate, and all these beings are commonly said to live outside the village."[60] There is a clear symbolic opposition between the impure Dalits representing *kāṭu* (uncultivated exterior region) and the pure high castes who represent the civilized centre. Thus the Dalit *cāmiyāṭi*'s ritual hunting of both the exterior, uncultivated region and the civilized village is a clear indication of the strategic act of encompassment of the exterior and impure power of the periphery over the interior, the pure and the civilized centre - the village and its hierarchical structures. This is consistent with the Dalits' increasing appropriation of the civil and social spaces within the village.

Folk/subaltern rituals and their performances in this case are perceived to have certain social power and to have cosmic importance. They are perceived to have power to discredit the authority of caste hierarchy. The perceived inadequacy of the power of the classical deities to control the malevolent spirits and to secure the cultivable lands is ground gained by the folk/ subaltern religions.

Divination

Divination is a result of what is called in the Tamil folk world *cāmi iṟaṅutal* (descent of a god upon a person). Victor Turner calls this *dramatic plotting* by which he means the enactment of the roles of gods, cultural heroes, ancestors or demons as described in the myths by the ritual officiates.[61] In divination, which he equates with 'preaching and homiletic', the shaman or *cāmiyāṭi* engages in psychological analysis. Diviners seek to probe the hidden tensions and grudges in the community that are believed to be responsible for affliction.

All that takes place in *koṭai* is geared towards the "peri-centre"[62] of divination, wherein all, the rich and the poor, the high caste and the low caste, each one individualized in one's pathological world of angst stands awaiting the connectivity of the network of ritual power of CM. Indeed, people vie with each other for the linkup with CM power through the eye of CM *cāmiyāṭi* that would fall on them and through the touch of his hand that will impart his power to them.

To employ's Foucault's understanding of power as relations, divination is characterized by the exercise of power through images of relations like diviner-divinised, master-slave, king-citizen and father-child. The temporality and totality of that power is mediated through *cāmiyāṭi* and his empowering bodily activities. It consists not only in its actual exercising by the *cāmiyāṭi*, but through the perceived actualizing capacity of that power by the devotee and in their appropriation of that power—the activities that make them the receptacle of the power of CM.

As the body is extensively involved in the act of divination, one needs a deeper understanding of the body in order to understand the dynamics of divination, It is the surface of the body which "is the most discussed, imagined, prescribed and proscribed, disfigured, disguised and disciplined surface in the physical world,"[63] by the social, cultural and the religious universes. The human body becomes a site of inscription in almost all human interactions. People "inscribe bodies, marking them and enabling them to serve as markers; bodies serve as signifiers, just as a text in a book... They have been attributed meaning, and they can be read by others, and rewritten, they are texts, carrying knowledgeability and power."[64] Every human body is body without organ (BwO)[65] and it is a political surface upon which is inscribed the discourses of power. It is subject to spatial and temporal constraints, but this is the outcome of inscription,[66] territorialized not only by the expertise discourse of knowledge, such as of medicine, etc. but by the ordinary discourse of day-to-day life, carried out by everyday social actors such as parents, spouses, elders and caste men.

As the body of the Dalit *cāmiyāṭi* is a surface inscribed by everyday forms of the oppression within the caste system, in *cāmiyāṭṭam* the surface of BwO becomes a site where resistance to dominant discourse can occur. While the Dalit body is prescribed and proscribed, disfigured, disguised and disciplined surface in the physical/social world, and his physical movement restricted by the strict surveillance of the caste hierarchy, in *cāmiyāṭṭam* it is entitled to any free movement, knows no limitation whatsoever. The power of CM capacitates him to de-territorialize the BwO, not only of Dalits but of Brahmins/high caste men too. Subsequently, he prescribes and proscribes the surface of the body of the oppressors, thereby de-territorializing their BwO.[67]

As the bodily inscription is constituted through the twofold process of discipline, i.e., discipline on the behaviour of the physical body and on the ideal representations of belief, taste and judgment,[68] it is through the contestation and redefinition of this dual process that the subaltern *cāmiyāṭi* rewrites the bodily inscriptions, not only for himself but also for other high caste men. He redefines the bodily inscriptions for himself, by staking the claim of Brahmanical purity and by exercising a mediatory function for the whole of the village community like a priestly Brahmin. When the power of his divination pulls Brahmins/other high caste men around him, he alters their rules of discipline regarding their behaviour towards a Dalit and reverses the ideal representations of belief in the caste hierarchy. In *vēṭṭai* as well as in *cāmiyāṭṭam* he is believed to possess yogic powers.[69] That which is acquired by disciplining of the body by the twice-born is attained by the power of the folk god. It points to another instance of contestation of inscription of the body. What the cāmiyāṭi engages in is de-territorialisation of BwO "enabling it to become something other than that which it was a consequence of its inscription."[70] He launches a new play of discourse and a "deferral of meanings which prevent any discourse from having a single reading."[71]

In divination, the *cāmiyāṭi* constitutes the other. While divining he is forced to produce words that are diagnostic of the problem of the other. The *cāmiyāṭi* proposes the solution for the other, sometimes faulting her/him for her/his wrong deeds and delivering a judgment on the other like a self-styled king, master and judge. Indeed, the idiom that is employed, the costumes that he wears project him as an all-powerful king. In doing so, a subaltern *cāmiyāṭi*, deconstructs the caste hierarchy and "peri-constructs" the subjectivity of high caste devotees. "Peri-construction" of subjectivity refers to the re-constituting activity of the oppressed ego and the oppressive alter ego of the caste system, an act that takes place on the periphery of society.

Divination, then, is the diagram of a certain form of the "other-construct", an act that at once reconfigures one's identity and disconfigures the false hierarchical identity of the other in which the referent other is a high caste man. When a high caste man (Brahmin/Maṟavar) approaches a Dalit *cāmiyāṭi* for divination, the former presents himself to the dictates of a Dalit, places himself at the receiving end of a Dalit, an act of violation of the hierarchical hegemony in *varnashrama dharma.*

In divination, the devotee is "vulnerable" and seeks the intervention of *cāmiyāṭi* whom he encounters as very powerful, though temporarily, while the devotee stands powerless, helpless and hapless. This unevenness compounds his vulnerability. It is this vulnerability compounded by the perceived unevenness of power-relations or asymmetry of power, as we have noted in the first chapter, which prompts him to place himself at the receiving end of power in divination. Thus it is vulnerability compounded by unevenness that provides facticity to the operationalisation of power in divination.

This play of power becomes paradoxical when it takes place between the Dalit *cāmiyāṭi* and a high caste man; the former, a socially vulnerable entity, is entitled to compound the vulnerability of the latter–a more powerful social entity–by virtue of unevenness of power. Thus divination, to employ Bourdieu's ideas, enables the Dalit *cāmiyāṭi* "to alter the current state of the socio-cultural taxonomy, causing shifts in dominance among various symbolic schemes while simultaneously licensing such alterations."[72] This is done through the medium of a 'ritualized body,' the production of which takes place during the rituals of *koṭai*. A ritualized body, Bell notes, is a body aware of a privileged contrast with respect to other bodies. It is a body invested with schemes the deployment of which can shift a variety of socio-cultural situations into ones that the ritualized body can dominate in some way.[73] It is to be noted that it embodies and produces these schemes without bringing any of the operations to the level of explicit discourse, but restructuring the larger cultural milieu through kinds of social practice like rituals, as it was noted in the first chapter.

Three Moments of Inter-textuality in Divination

What happens in divination is inter-textuality, "the play of one text upon within or besides other texts,"[74] to employ Derrida's expression. As shown in the following diagram, I have explored three moments of inter-textuality in relation to divination: one concerns the state leading the devotee to divination, the other relates to the moment of divination itself and the third one is related to how people deal with their contingencies in the light of divination.

The First Moment

The existential angst of the folk built up through illness, anxiety, physical pain and social suffering, etc., presents itself as a formidable text, lands them in 'undecidability of existential nature', which engages in "continual deferral of meaning, the slippage of meaning which occurs as soon as one (the folk devotee) tries to pin (it) down"[75] its cause. Postmodern writers rightly point out that, in the context of deference, "The signifiers can refer not to referents (the underlying reality), but only to other signifiers," [76] the angst takes them to the *cāmiyāṭi(s)* (diviners), forming an inter-textuality between the cultural members (devotees), their situation of angst and the divination. In other words, the first moment of inter-textuality is placed in the pre-ritual stage, a period of territorialization of angst as shown in Figure 1.

The Second Moment

In divination, the second moment of inter-textuality occurs in the ritual period when the *cāmiyāṭi* engages in a discourse where his verbal text (words of divination) comes into play with the textuality of supernatural powers on the one hand and the contingencies and angst of the life-world of the devotees on the other.

The process of inter-textuality opens up the play of different other texts wherein the BwO (Body-without-Organ) of the *cāmiyāṭi* de-territorializes the BwO of the devotee and de-territorializes itself in the process. It inscribes and rewrites the BwO of caste hierarchy.[77] In the context of inter-textuality, it is often held that, "the play of one text deconstructive of another (is) itself in turn dissolved or re-read."[78] In a similar vein, the assertion-discourse of a Dalit in the form of divination in the face of a high caste man has to be understood as a deconstruction of caste hierarchy, wherein the established frameworks of hegemonic meanings are subtly broken in this second moment of inter-textuality of divination.

The Third Moment

The third moment of inter-textuality reconnects the devotee to the world of objects and relations on the basis of divination. Now the devotee plays on with a new text of life obtained in divination—which is a matrix of the intersection of two poles:

Ritual

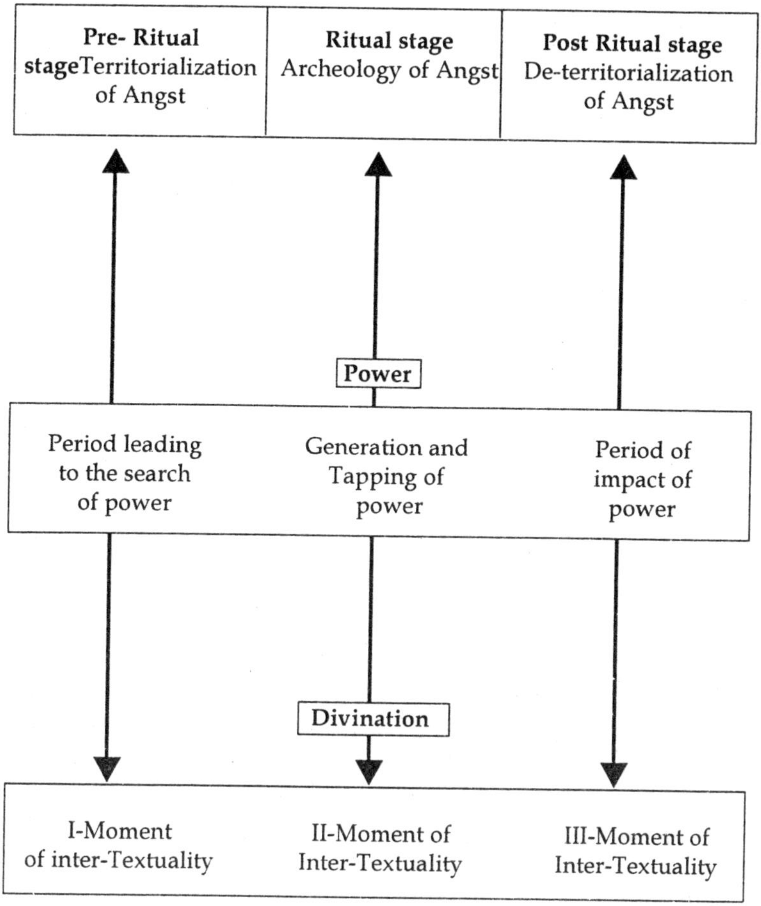

Figure 1

god (CM), the devotee and the facilitating acquaintances (sacral functionaries /family/relations/friends) at one pole; the other humans and dangerous objects of the world at another pole. The god-devotee faith relationship and the dictates of divination are the semantic axis around which the subjective world will revolve for some time.[79] Thus the third moment of inter-textuality is located in the post-ritual period, a period of de-territorialisation of angst.

Repetition and Neglect in Divination

Repetition of certain formulae and idioms are very conspicuous in divination. The themes of master-slave, king-citizen, and father-child are played in the symbolic representations over and over again. The verbal utterances such as "You are my child, worship me, do not worry, I will set right everything in life," and "I am the master, I know everything, you do what I say, go now!" are often heard.

Though it may sound mechanical, dramatic and artificial to an outsider, yet, it is one of the crucial strategies for kindling and reinforcing the social memory of such dominant themes that existed in the past, indicating "an interaction in the here and now is to be seen as a recapitulation of earlier interactions."[80] Here divination needs to be understood not only as a manifestation of power of the CM but also as a strategy for the reinforcement of such power among people. However, this kind of repetitious display of power, which brings about the interaction between the low caste *cāmiyāṭi* and a higher caste person, has the potentiality of a social play. In that social drama, the enhancement of the status of a lower caste over the higher caste takes place in that the former possesses a higher form of power over the latter, and such an exaltation is prolonged more consciously than unconsciously. The wilful neglect of the high caste people and other powerful men such as police and local village leaders in situations where the Dalit *cāmiyāṭis* make them to wait just like any other devotee thereby treating them just as"one among many," (sometimes totally neglecting them), is a tit-for-tat treatment meted out to them (the high castes), a sign of social protest. This shows that the *cāmiyāṭi,* thus, possesses a 'practical mastery' of the schemes for ritualisation, appropriates the ritual's potential to establish privileged contrast, can display it as a social act and employ it to dominate others.

As observed earlier, divination makes use of the old idiom of kingship and feudalism, and replicates 'sick ' hierarchy of power, to employ's Bell terminology. By such strategy, it may not seek to reform the old system as Bell observes, but "it functions to defy the penetration of the oppressive social world."[81] Thus ritual replication of this sort "affords a form of resistance that does not threaten the resister with physical destruction or cultural anomie."[82]

The kind of relationship that transpires between the CM and the devotee during divination, based upon control and dependency, may be seen as a "form of property relation, by which the empowered party possesses the dependent."[83] The underlying logic is that CM has the power of control on the lives of the devotees, over the village and over other evil forces. In other words, CM has the power of protection over the village, its inhabitants (human and sub-human), its inner space and its outer boundaries. But this protective power will be actualized, concretized and reciprocated only when a devotee honours his power in the form of dependency. Though the folk god was traditionally conceived to reign within the boundaries of a village like a king in his kingdom, at present, his devotees having migrated from these villages believe that he has also migrated with them as their guardian and protector. In this way, the folk believe in the evolving, disseminating, and encompassing sovereign power of their folk god.

As one of the Brahmin participants cum *pūcāri* at Naduvakurichi remarked, "It is divination that makes a big difference to the folk gods and folk cults. I cannot divinize in a Civā temple. That is what makes it more famous than great gods."[84] Divination is one thing that decisively demarcates folk cults from major religions. In divination, as noted earlier, assurances are given definitively, people know for sure that the god is concerned with their individual cases, knows the cause of fear/anxiety, etc. Divination can suggest solutions to their problems and can guarantee a bright future. What happens in the worship of major religions is that the worshippers have to presume the mind of God, believe that God is concerned about their life problems. They have to analyze for themselves the cause of their existing predicaments, fix for themselves a conditionality for the removal of anxiety/fear/suffering by means of a vow, have to trust that he (god) has "power" to remove the causes, without being not very sure about the efficacy of the process. Very often multiplicity of such vows to different gods in the major religions makes it almost impossible to relate the fruitful effect to a particular cause of 'power'. What is referred to here is the ambiguity and dilemma experienced by a devotee regarding what vow to fulfil to which god when one's suffering is removed. One's ambiguity arises from the fact that one is unable to fix an effect to a cause and an efficacy to an agency, while in folk cult the chances of such occurrences are much less, given the fact that divination emphatically embodies the link, in concrete terms, between effect and cause, agency and efficacy.

Cāmiyāṭṭam

Cāmiyāṭṭam, which literally means 'god-dance' in Tamil, is one of the important ritual performances of *koṭai*. It is significant from the viewpoint of folk religions, since it marks and displays the descent of a god upon a man or a woman. It is all the more significant from the viewpoint of the subalterns, as it has the potential to generate a new system of socio-cultural meanings, as we have seen above. As a clear manifestation of acquisition of a god's power, *cāmiyāṭṭam*it often precedes divination in the ritual sequence of *koṭai*. Sometimes, it occurs in the midst of divination too. It is also performed outside the context of divination during the course of *koṭai* rituals.

Whatever the context be, *cāmiyāṭṭam* is always accompanied by folk musical performances such as, *villupāṭṭu, kaṇiyāṉkūttu*, etc... In fact, music plays a vital role during *cāmiyāṭṭam* (trance dance) as well as during divination. As Bass notes:

"[P]ublic musical performers transcend boundaries typically created and maintained through complex systems of verbal interaction, that distinguish cosmic domains with respect to spheres of interactions, access to and control of supernatural power, varieties of intelligence and insight, and degrees of 'animacy' and 'agentivity.'[85]

Music allows people to communicate across the formidable barriers they create, the barriers, as Zuckerkandl observes "separating self from things, subject from object, agent from action."[86] In divination music is helpful "where the self-abandon is intended or required–where self goes beyond itself where subject and object come together." [87]

As regards the symbolic potential of *cāmiyāṭṭam*, a few observations are in place here. Anthropological and sociological studies have recently dealt elaborately with body and power. Body is seen not only as a site of inscription of power as shown by Foucault.[88] It can also have a vital role in the ritual strategies of resistance, as Comaroff has opined.[89] The former has shown that body mediates all actions upon which the world is constructed. Body has become the site of inscription of schemes of power and domination. It effectively constitutes both the self and the universe of which it is a part.[90] Hence the exuberant dance of a Dalit *cāmiyāṭi* is an attempt to rework and to redefine the schemes of classification of power in caste hierarchy. Thus he reconstitutes himself and the social universe of the hegemonic Hindu caste-system of which he is a part. Here, as Comaroff has shown in another context, the *cāmiyāṭi* constructs through ritual, a social body "not as an icon of microcosm of the socio-economic order," but as a "matter of parts in fractured relation to the whole."[91] The *koṭai* events of Dalits, not only simultaneously resist and discourage "the wholesale acceptance of the order of domination and subordination"[92] of the caste-system in the area, but also demonstrate that they are no more powerless thanks to the economic autonomy and political voice they have been gaining for the last few decades.

Besides, through a series of physical movements during *cāmiyāṭṭam* (and vēṭṭai), ritual practices can construct an environment structured by practical schemes of privileged contrasts,[93] which acquire a special status of dominance, as Bell notes. The construction of an environment is simultaneously the moulding of the bodies within it as values impressed upon them from without.[94] Thus the social body internalizes the principles of the environment being generated.[95] Inscribed within the social body, these principles enable the ritualized body, the *cāmiyāṭi*, to generate strategic schemes that appropriate king/master symbolisms to dominate the socio-cultural situations of caste hierarchy. Appropriating the bestowal of power by external forces such as deities like CM, which is seen as vast, legitimate, and accessible only to those in appropriate offices, the Dalit *cāmiyāṭi* engages in a subaltern ritual construction of authority which is at once a stabilization and a specific augmentation of power.[96]

Vēṭṭai and Divination as Symbolic Empowerment

The rituals of *vēṭṭai* and divination provide to the *cāmiyāṭi* what Juergensmeyer calls symbolic empowerment. According to him, symbolic empowerment refers to a perceived sense of empowerment disproportionately greater than what the act actually would have achieved.[97] It simply means that the way an action of this type is perceived achieves more than what the real action can do. Power in symbolic empowerment is obtained by the fact that the "how" of perception of an action determines the "what" of an action wherein the power of perception defines the power of action. The mode of the social perception of an action often produces more than the real effects of an action. Here, the fact that one acts in a particular manner in consonance with a social perception of an action obtains more power than what the real action could do. However, there must be congruence between who acts, where one acts, how one acts and how one is perceived. The power of this congruence seems to dominate over the power of the action itself. Subsequently, as Juergensmeyer notes, in many cases the power that the actors obtain has "real impact on their community, their relationships, and themselves"[98] as well as on those who fear them and grant them respect. As we have seen, the ritual drama of *vēṭṭai* and divination is performed with such great perfection that it conforms to the already established set of cultural stereotypes about them. Thus it enables the *cāmiyāṭi* to maintain consistency between what he does and what he is supposed to do, to such a high degree of perfection that he is perceived to be all powerful, can do what he wants, and can defy any rule or custom. Hence it makes the people fear him and grant him respect.

Vēṭṭai, Cāmiyāṭṭam and Divination: A Power Game of Manipulation, Control and Extremism.

Vēṭṭai, cāmiyāṭṭam and divination are a game of power. It is just here, in the élan with which the poor Dalit (Paḷḷar) plays his game, that his power is forged. On the one hand, this power derives from the outrageous manipulation of 'powers of danger', a creative outlet of energies acted out to de-limit the boundaries that make their existence, at best, controlled and subdued. On the other hand, the very extremism evident here in various events such as tasting of blood of hundreds of goats and pigs, and eating of their livers and of various physical movements in *vēṭṭai* and *cāmiyāṭṭam,* etc., definitely invests in it, to a great degree, certain symbolic coercive potential in the social realm. As mentioned above, he can order and reorder the social norm.

This game of *cāmiyāṭṭam* and divination is one of one-upmanship. It results in asymmetrical exchange of gifts as in all temple contexts. People gift *paṭaipu* to CM and the latter, through the *cāmiyāṭi,* claims to cure them of their sickness, and proposes to get rid of their problems and crisis. *Cāmiyāṭi* can demonstrate his power ostensibly to reject the offering, but not the devotees. Similarly divination too entails different stylistics of discourse. Often the *cāmiyāṭi* conducts an authoritarian monologue, "in which the people are spoken to, but cannot speak back."[99] Sometimes there is dialogue and occasional contestation. But, though the devotees can contest CM power, eventually it is the word of the *cāmiyāṭi* that prevails upon the folk. It only indicates that the type of relationship that exists between CM and his devotees is rooted not in a *symmetrical* system of orderly, reciprocal mutuality, but is based on one of symbolic interdependence,[100] manifest in and through the ritual mode. It is to be noted that this one-upmanship, when appropriated by a Dalit *cāmiyāṭi,* can be deployed to reverse the equation of power within the caste-hierarchy.

Manifestation of CM/*Cāmiyāṭi's *Sovereign Power through Koœai Rituals

Cāmiyāṭi, by being the patron[101] of the sacrifice offered to the village deity of the village can be regarded as the local-level equivalent of the king[102] and functions as "the representative par excellence of the socio-religious totality of the village."[103] He represents CM who is believed to protect the settlement over which he is "sovereign like the royal goddess (who), in conjunction with the state deity, protects her kingdom."[104] Here, sovereignty is symbolically central in the village goddesses' festivals, albeit in 'reduced version', and the village is ritually represented as a miniature kingdom recreated through sacrifice. The hierarchical solidarity of the village community, Reiniche notes, is constructed at the time of the village goddesses festivals, and "this social order is built around the joint sovereignty of the goddess (village god) and the 'royal' village kingdom, and is itself constitutive of the universal socio-cosmic order."[105]

My field experience reveals that what is said of village goddesses in terms of sovereignty can be said of CM too. The sovereign role of CM and his *cāmiyāṭi* is very clear from the act of *vēṭṭai* undertaken by *cāmiyāṭi* himself as a representative of CM. It is further substantiated by the kinds of expressions verbalized during the discourse of divining. This being the case, the wielding of the role of *cāmiyāṭi* and its ritual power by a Brahmin who was the village headman proves to be very strategic, so that no conflict but unity prevails between his role as the representative sovereign of a miniature kingdom, the village and the ritualized sovereignty vested in the role of the *cāmiyāṭi*. He manages to establish this unity only by the appropriation of the symbolic capital available in the subaltern religious terrain.

Exaltation and Reciprocity Through Koṭai Rituals: A Dialogics of Ritual Power

Cāmiyāṭi, believed to attain the transcendent status of power of CM during *vēṭṭai*, is entitled to a mandatory singularity of the role of 'divination.' As the situational sovereign of the event of *koæai, cāmiyāṭi* is "the guarantor of and regulator of competitive forces of power,"[106] the principle of high order power of CM that "subsumes and subordinates the competitive forces of powers of the world."[107] It is this transcendent singularity of *cāmiyāṭi* that contributes to the display of power in divination. This transcendent power is situational and temporary, because, more often than not, divination takes place in the context of rituals and it is said to last for twenty to thirty minutes.

This situational transcendence is part of a circuit of reciprocity. By grandeur of reception (*kutiaḻaippu*), *pūcai*, blood sacrifice and *paṭaipu*, the deity is believed to be propitiated. In return for reception, propitiation and celebration of various events of *koṭai*, the deity CM becomes bound by a vaguely defined and generalized obligation to respond to the needs of the local community. Further, the circuit is characterized by two distinct ritual modalities embodying different moments in the relationship of reciprocity established through the ceremonies of "ritual hospitality."[108] Ritual hospitality aims at establishing enduring relations of reciprocity through the exchange of gifts consisting predominantly of food. The first modality in the ritual hospitality is that of human's offerings to the deity and highlights human-to-god interaction. It has three ritual moments: (i) vegetarian offering of *poṅkal*, (ii) non-vegetarian offering of cooked meat and (iii) blood sacrifices of animals and/or humans. The second modality describes god's interaction with the humans. It consists of two ritual moments: (i) acceptance of offerings of the folk by *cāmiyāṭi* on behalf of CM, symbolized in *ūṭṭu* (ii) gifting of CM's food to the people. The *cāmiyāṭi* in some instances gifts a portion of *paṭaipu* to the drummers or to other ritual co-functionaries. As noted elsewhere, those people involved in the celebration of *koæai* also share the *paṭaipu*. The goat or pig offered to the deity is cooked and eaten as a festive meal by the villagers. Thus *koṭai* ritual complex remains ambivalent. It consists of both the rituals of propitiation and rituals of *prasātam* (as we noted earlier in the chapter)—which are explicated in the two modalities of ritual hospitality.

Communicative Modalities of Ritual Power

The display of ritual power in the CM cult is characterized by two distinctive communicative modalities of power that establish the reciprocity of relationship between CM and the folk. Communicative modality is a medium of performance through which message is conveyed, a message that is semiotically imprecise, but all the more potent because of its publicity.[109] In the celebration of *koṭai* festival for CM, the first important communicative modality of power is *vēṭṭai*, whereby the cāmiyāṭi, acting on behalf of CM, publicly establishes his control over evil spirits, defines and installs his role as the guardian deity of the village. In these public and performative acts of valiance, the well-being of the ritual community/village community is focused upon. Here, reciprocity is played out between CM and the village as a whole, on the one hand, and CM and the spirits (the dead, and other malevolent gods), on the other. Divination, the most important event of *koṭai* from the folk's viewpoint, is another communicative modality of power, wherein the individual, more than the community, becomes the nodal point of reciprocity. The second communicative modality of ritual power is an individual one-to-one affair, in which the problems and concerns of the individual are brought openly to the attention of the god.[110] Villagers will sometimes set forth complaints against the god himself, bringing to his notice the needs that are going unfulfilled, apart from plainly stating their problems to the *cāmiyāṭi*. He might adjudicate conflicts, pledge assistance and bring hope to the people. Communicating through the voice of the human medium of *cāmiyāṭi(s)* during divination, CM proves to be a person one can know, argue with,[111] and to interact with. Thus these two modalities of display of power climax in the common people's entering into a world of communication with the ontological power.

Ritual Encounter of Powers of 'Fear'

As fear is both a social and a cultural fact, as noted in chapter one, the CM cult can be identified as a cultural scheme that deals with those situations which are identified as 'fear-provoking' in the given cultural matrix. In Tirunelveli region, the environmental hazards that surround the border of the villages[112] did play a vital role in constituting the 'geography of fear.'[113] As the house and the inhabited village can be considered as the physical worlds of safety, the more one moves away from them, the more the "opportunities for ambiguity, uncertainty, strangeness, disorder and danger become greater."[114] The dangers and threats are believed to reach their culmination "where 'civilization' and 'culture' reach the untamed and wild places where the half-human and superhuman dwell, where mysterious and unpredictable events happen, where normal patterns of action and caution are not effective".[115] The CM cult played an environmentally protective function in the geography of fear. It developed a viable means of coping with threats concurrent with patterning fear around some referents.[116] Through *vēṭṭai*, the CM cult breaks down the barriers of fear by venturing into areas considered dangerous. By doing this, CM establishes his 'power' of control by undertaking an *in vivo* approach to their fears, which involves among other things desensitization to the situation feared. *Cāmiyāṭi*, by courting times and places of danger and daring to handle situations and 'creatures' defined as dangerous, overcomes and overpowers 'fears' of the evil powers as labelled by local cultures.[117] To put it differently, since fear arises from "dangerous and threatening circumstances in the human environment,"[118] rituals of *koṭai* such as *vēṭṭai* can be regarded as "actions taken in relation to the object of fear."[119] Further, since fear, as an emotion, has to do with the bio-social nature of human beings,[120] it basically implies a threat to the body of an individual or the society. Hence expulsion of fear, in *vēṭṭai*, also involves fullness of bodily functions.

Koṭai is a ritual moment when the uncontrolled power of CM is displayed and demonstrated, and not restrained. Placating the god through *paṭaipu* (the cooked food offering), in this context, is not so much to control CM but to show gratitude and to gain direct access to his power through divination, and to delimit, to overcome and to overpower other lesser 'powers of control'. The folk in different villages have evolved their own local version of fears of outside 'forces' and have formed anxieties about their powers to harm internally.

Through rituals of *koṭai,* they deal with them with different intensity but almost in the same way. Many folk rituals directly or indirectly acknowledge "times and place of fear. For these are indeed pressure points where different order collide and defects in human endeavours are revealed."[121]

Koṭai : A Ritual for Tripartite Liminality

For the agrarian rural economy, cultivable land is of great importance as it is the source of their economy. And this cultivable land is a liminal space between the village (the inhabited place) and the *kāṭu* (uninhabited land) or wilderness which is an uncultivable space. Now the wilderness itself and the cremation ground it houses is a liminal space for the spirits of the dead who are lurking in it. The cremation ground, for the dead, is a liminal space between this life and the ancestral world. These dead ones are liminal entities (beings) as they belong neither to the world of the living nor to the world of ancestors or heavens. And they are believed to be under the control of CM, who is lord of the cremation ground. As we saw in the origin myth, CM himself is a liminal god; he belongs neither to the world of gods, nor to the world of humans. He is lord of the cremation ground and of the dead. Hence there is a correlation between the tripatriate structure of liminality; liminality of the space, liminality of the beings and liminality of the god. The *liminal space* of cultivable land and its dependents, the village people, are believed to be under the control of the powerful spirits who are *liminal beings* themselves and they, in turn, are under the control of CM, who is himself a *liminal god.*

Now the *kāṭu,* though not part of the people's living space, is very much part of the geography of the village. It is the source of water for irrigation for the fields, and it serves as a natural boundary between one village and another. Thus, on the one hand, the villagers need the wilderness, as they cannot do without it; but, on the other hand, the wilderness is believed to be a constant source of trouble and misfortune for the village and the field as they are open for attack by the troublesome beings and the evil spirits inhabiting the wilderness, the liminal space. This danger of conflicts of interests has to be dealt with and resolved. As people live with the liminal space of the wilderness, they have to get acquainted with it. Now *koṭai* rituals and its performances are meant to put the folk in touch with the fact of liminality and to acclimatize them to it, by making them see the correlation of the tripartite structure of liminality first and deal with the dangers of the wilderness next. Thus, *koṭai* ritual, according to the folk worldview, aims at the acquaintance of correlations between the tripartite liminalities and the resolution of conflicts between them.

It is to be noted that *koṭai* rituals were originally ritual performances by the liminal folk to a liminal deity for control over the space of the cremation ground. The original worshippers of CM, i.e., the robbing Maṟavar(s), as Pate notes, are liminal people, who are neither in the village nor totally in the wilderness. They often stayed at the border of the wilderness to attack the passers-by and the inside village. The subaltern Dalits who worship CM in Nadurvakurichi or elsewhere are the liminal people. They have an ambiguous locus in the purity-impurity pole of Vedic Hinduism. Though they are placed in the impure realm, yet they are continuously in contact with both the pure and the impure realms, because of which they are exposed to the dangers of both sides. Hence the Dalits are also seen as the most appropriate people to deal with the dangers of the wilderness, the impure world. This is perhaps one of the reasons why the Kaḷḷattiāṉ (as CM is called in Naduvakurichi) of Paḷḷar(s) is regarded as a very powerful god by all the other high castes.

Conclusion

This chapter entitled "A Tripartite Scheme in the Operation of Ritual Power" has described the three stages of *koṭai* ritual: the *Pre-ritual stage, Ritual stage* and *Post-ritual stage.* It has identified the important characteristics of each stage. The important characteristic of the pre-ritual stage is *territorialisation of angst,* that of the ritual stage is *archeology of angst,* and that of the post-ritual stage is *de-territorialisation of angst.* These characteristics basically tell us the way the common folk encounter the limit situations of human existence. They endeavour to overcome these limit situations by tapping ritual power, which enables them to establish communication with the posited transcendence and to solve their problems of life. Thus the operations of ritual power in the tripartite scheme deal more prominently with the *function of ritual power.* Nevertheless, the chapter shows that the dynamics of some of the ritual elements such as divination, ritual hunting and trans-dance, etc., can point to the grater potentiality of ritual power. They reveal the trajectory of ritual power that encompasses other realms, systems and their issues (such as caste hierarchy, oppression of the people on the periphery, etc.), which are extrinsic to the religious realm. This role of ritual, as was mentioned in the first chapter, relates to the *performance of ritual power,* which will be further explored and nuanced in the next chapter.

Notes

1. Bryan S. Turner, *Religion and Social Theory*, Sage Publications, London, 1991 (1983), 244.
2. The three stages form one whole, and one stage leads to the other; The pre-ritual stage leads to the ritual stage and the ritual to the post-ritual stage. Hence the activities in one stage cannot be fully comprehended without understanding the other two.
3. My expression 'archeology of angst' is inspired by Foucault who is known for his pet idea of 'archeology of knowledge.'
4. Cf. Blackburn, *Singing of Birth* , 33.
5. Cf. Nabokov, *Religion Against Self.*
6. Cf. Blackburn, *Singing of Birth.*
7. It is a folk theatre performed by the ritual specialists called *Kaṇiyāṉs*.
8. Cf. Nabokov, *Religion Against Self.*
9. Cf., *ibid.*, 4.
10. Cf., *ibid.*, 44.
11. Cf., *ibid.*, 44-7.
12. *Ibid.*, 44.

13. *Ibid.*, 5.
14. In *The Ritual Process. Structure and Anti-Structure*, Cornell University Press, New York, 1969.
15. In *Outline of Theory of a Practice*, trans. R. Nice, Cambridge University Press, Cambridge, 1977, 115.
16. *Ūṭṭu* literally means feeding. Here it refers to the swallowing of plantain immersed in the blood from the stomach of a pig/goat which is pierced.
17. *Vastu* refers to a particular religious system, which predicts the good and bad effects of building a house facing a particular direction.
18. Nabokov, *Religion Against Self*, 5.
19. Cf. Bergin, "Religiosity and Mental Health: A Critical Reevaluation and Meta-analysis," *Professional Psychology: Research and Practice* 14 (1983), 170-184.
20. Daniel N. McIntosh, "Religion-as-schema, with Implications for the Relation Between Religion and Coping," *The International Journal for the Psychology of Religion* 5/1 (1995), 9.
21. Cf., *ibid.*, 8-10.
22. *Ibid.*, 9.
23. As cited in Bergin, 'Religiosity,' 10.
24. *Ibid.*,10-12.
25. Rhonda M. Laurencelle, Steven C. Abell & David J. Schwartz, "The Relation Between Intrinsic Religious Faith and Psychological Well-Being," *The International Journal for the Psychology of Religion* 12/2 (2002), 109.
26. Cf. Victor Turner. *The Forest of Symbols*, Cornell University Press, Ithaca, N.Y., 1969, 50-52 and *The Drums of Affliction: A Study of Religious Processes among the Ndembu of Zambia*, Clarendon Press, Oxford, 1968. 81-82.
27. Brian Morris, *Anthropological Studies of Religion-An Introductory Text*, Cambridge University Press, Cambridge, 1987, 253.
28. As mentioned in the second and fourth chapters, two of the *cāmiyāṭis* are also secular leaders (Village Administrative Officer (VAO) or Panchayat President), and in such a capacity of leadership they exercised great authority over the matters of the village.

29. Cf. Deflem, 'Ritual, Anti-Structure.'

30. In spite of seeing the liminal period and *communitas* as anti-structure, Victor Turner held that the final stage of ritual process is one of incorporation into the existing social order. However, in his later works, he seems to hold, through his idea of 'liminoid', that ritual process has the potential of social critique and power for social transformations.

31. Cf. Marshall Shalins, *Islands of History*, The University of Chicago Press, Chicago, 1985.

32. Nabokov, *Religion Against Self*, 12.

33. Cf. As cited in Nabokov, *ibid.*

34. Nabokov, *Religion Against Self*, 11.

35. As Nabokov notes, this perspective is contrary to Victor Turner's view that the ritual is the place where human beings spontaneously discover and experience a deep awareness of society as a shared human need.

36. Nabokov, *Religion Against Self*, 10.

37. *Ibid.*, 12.

38. Cf. Deflem, 'Ritual, Anti-Structure.' 5-7.

39. Nabokov, *Religion Against Self*, 10-13.

40. Varnashrama dharma, generally speaking, is the moral code that prescribes norms, rules, duties and behaviours to the different caste groups according to the caste status.

41. Cf. Victor Turner, *The Forest of Symbols*, 33-55.

42. *Vallam*, which is made of lead, is an instrument used for hunting.

43. Mark Juergensmeyer, *Terror in the Mind of God*, Oxford University Press, New Delhi, 2000, 123.

44. Cf. J.L. Austin, *How to Do Things with Words*, Clarendon Press, Oxford, 1962, 4.

45. Pierre Bourdieu, *Language and Symbolic Power*, M.A. Harvard University Press, Cambridge, 1991, 117.

46. Fuller, *Camphor Flame*, 73 and Cf., Nabokov, *Religion Against Self*, 9.

47. Cf. Nabokov, *Religion Against Self*,8-9 and Fuller, *Camphor Flame*, 73.

48. Nabokov, *Religion Against Self*, 9.

49. Cf. Lourdu, *A Study of Sudalaimadasamy;* Reiniche, *Les dieux;* Fuller, *Camphor Flame* and Blackburn, *Singing of Birth.*

50. Cf. C.J. Fuller, "Sacrifice (Bali) in the South India Temple", in *Religion and Society in South India*, ed. V. Sudarsen *et al.* B.R. Publishing Corporation, Delhi, 1987, 22-35 and C.J Fuller, *Camphor Flame.*

51. Fuller, 'Sacrifice,' 27.

52. *Ūṭṭu* in *koæai* can be equated to Victor Turner's festal cuisine referring to certain kinds of food and drink reserved for rites dedicated to specific gods. Cf. Victor Turner, *From Ritual to Theatre*, Performing Arts Journal Publication, New York, 1982, 110.

53. Pate observes that *tiraḷai* is done for propitiation of CM who is the haunter of burning-grounds. This meaning is contradicted by the fact that *cāmiyāṭi*s who, acting on behalf of CM are already fed by the blood of kaṇiyāṉ, which Pate himself has recorded. Hence he does not need to be propitiated again. Further, *tiraḷai* is always given by *cāmiyāṭi*, who represents CM to another. It means that it is given by *cāmiyāṭi* (or CM) to an entity other than CM, i.e., other wild spirits. Cf. Pate, *Tinnevelly District*, 118.

54. At present people approach CM for various other reasons such as theft, unemployment. This shows that people believe that CM's power has become sovereign.

55. Bell, *The Ritual Body*, 307.

56. Cf. Nicholas J. Fox, *Postmodernism, Sociology and Health*, Open University Press, Buckingham, 1993.

57. As cited in Juergensmeyer, *Terror*, 132.

58. Cf. Diane P. Mines "Hindu Nationalism, Untouchable Reform, and the Ritual Production of a South Indian Village," *American Ethnologist* 29/1 (February 2002), 58-85.

59. Juergenmeyer, *Terror*, 123.

60. Fuller "Rituals of the Village," in *The Village in India*, ed. V. Madan, Oxford University Press, New Delhi, 2002, 281.

61. Cf. Turner, *From Ritual*, 110.

62. The word "peri-centre" is preferred to "epi-centre" to denote a central activity in a ritual but that takes place at the peripheral

period (end of ritual) at a peripheral time (in the early morning between dawn and midnight) and that takes place due to its connection between the periphery (*kāṭu*, the forest-uncultivable land) and the centre.

63. Fox, *Postmodernism* 25.

64. *Ibid.*, 26.

65. The term invented by Deluze and Guttari to describe a non-anatomical, politicised body inscribed by power. Cf. Fox, *Postmodernism* , 161.

66. *Ibid.*, 24.

67. It is not a safety valve mechanism for : (i) This is not a mere verbal abuse (an expression of suppressed anger, allowed to let go) in the absence of the oppressors. The presence of high caste people in ritual and the respect shown to Dalits by high caste make it a real display of the inversion of power structure at least temporarily (ii) His prescription and proscription meted out to the high castes is binding on the latter not only at one particular occasion but throughout the year.

68. Cf. Fox, *Postmodernism*, 35-36.

69. The folk believe that he can carry a big implement made of lead weighing 120 kgs and can walk over water, etc., because he possesses extraordinary powers like *Siddhars* (yogi).

70. Fox, *Postmodernism* ,24.

71. *Ibid.*

72. As cited by Bell, *The Ritual Body*, 304.

73. Cf. *ibid.*

74. Cf. Fox, *Postmodernism*, 69.

75. *Ibid.*, 7.

76. *Ibid.*, 8.

77. A strikingly similar process is noted by Nicholas Fox in the relation between the patients and health staff in the context of a hospice.

78. Fox, *Postmodernism*, 108.

79. Doubtless this new text would have its own overthrow in the shape of difference and undecidability

80. Fox, *Postmodernism*, 68.

81. Bell, *Ritual Body*, 308.
82. *Ibid.*
83. *Ibid.*
84. Interview held on 27/03/02 with Ramanathan, a Brahmin from Palayamkottai who had gone to attend the koṭai at Naduvakurichi where Dalit Paḷḷar(s) celebrated koṭai for CM.
85. Cf. Ellen Basso, "A Commentrary on Robbin's *Ritual Communication and Linguistic Ideology*," *Current Anthropology* 42/5, 2001, 161.
86. As quoted by Boss, *ibid.*
87. *Ibid.*
88. Cf. Foucault, *Discipline.*
89. Cf. Comaroff , *Body of Power.*
90. Cf. Bell, 'Ritual Body.'
91. As cited in Bell, *ibid.*, 209.
92. *Ibid.*
93. Cf. *ibid.*
94. Cf. *ibid.*, 305.
95. *Ibid.*
96. *Ibid.*, 211.
97. *Ibid.*, 188.
98. *Ibid.*
99. As quoted in Mikael Karlstrom, "On the Aesthetics and Dialogics of Power in the Post Colony," Africa, 73/1, 2003, 59.
100. Rao *et. al*, *Symbols of Substance: Court and State in Nayaka Period Tamilnadu*, Oxford University Press, Delhi, 1992, 19.
101. In villages like Valliyoor and Sirumalanchi, the *Cāmiyāṭi* (s) were/are indeed the both the sponsor of festivals and the village head-man, be it VAO or Panchayat president.
102. Marie-Louise Reiniche in her study of a village at Tirunelveli, Mel Chevel has observed that the Panchayat president who is a modern equivalent to the traditional headman, by being the patron of the sacrifice offered to the village deity of the village, is regarded as the local-level equivalent of the king. Cf. Fuller, 'Rituals of the Village,' 282-285.

103. As quoted in Fuller 'Rituals of the Village,' 283.

104. *Ibid.*, 284.

105. *Ibid.*

106. Karlstrorm, 'Aesthics,' 66.

107. *Ibid.*

108. Ritual hospitality is similar to domestic hospitality, and is organized around food. In both cases it is presumed that every visitor must be invited to share a meal or must be given food in some form or other to eat or to carry with him/her. Like all forms of exchange, hospitality affects a transfer of valuables that establishes social relationship and social obligation. Cf. *ibid.*, 65.

109. Cf. Karlstrom, 'Aesthetics,' 67.

110. It is to be noted that while in the first modality, the well-being or the interest of the village is generally inclusive of the interests of the individuals, in the second modality the well-being of the individual may not have anything to do with that of the ritual community/village community.

111. Nabokov, *Religion Against Self,* 9.

112. Cf. Stuart, *Manual* and Pate, *Tinnevelly District.*

113. Cf. Scruton, *Sociophobics.*

114. *Ibid.*, 102.

115. *Ibid.*

116. Cf., *ibid.*

117. *Ibid.*, 119.

118. *Ibid.*, 75.

119. *Ibid.*

120. Cf., *ibid.*, 2.

121. *Ibid*, 107.

Chapter 6

The Dynamics of Folk Ritual Power in Society

Pericentralisation as Deconstruction of Sanskritisation

Introduction

This chapter inquires whether the Indian anthropologist M.N. Srinivas's concept of 'sanskritisation', namely, "the process by which a low caste or tribe or other group takes over the customs, rituals, beliefs, ideology and style of life of a high and, in particular a 'twice-born' caste,"[1] can be applicable to the phenomenal complexity of the CM cult, as found in Tirunelveli District, which is analysed primarily from the viewpoint of rituals. It attempts to analyse and assess the suitability of this concept in addressing the related issues of social dynamics and social mobility (the main concerns of 'sanskritisation'), linking it to the origin and function of the CM cult. The immediate context of this analysis is two villages, Valliyoor and Naduvakurichi, where the people at the extreme poles in the caste hierarchy, namely, the Brahmins and the Dalits, are associated with the worship of the CM cult.

Though these two groups of people are linked by the CM cult, I consider the Brahmins as belonging primarily to the religious universe of Sanskritic Hinduism[2] and the Dalits to the subaltern religious universe. It raises a question as to 'how' and 'why' I consider the Brahmins who take to the worship of the subaltern deity, CM, as adherents of Sanskritic Hinduism.

I consider this group of Brahmins as forming part of Sanskritic Hinduism because it is this brand of Hinduism they own wholeheartedly, while they take to CM's worship out of compulsions arising from their existence in the particular setting. As for the Dalits, their religious affiliation to the subaltern cult needs no justification, as their habits, customs and belief systems do not come into conflict with the worship of a non-vegetarian minor god like CM.

Now, as discussion on sanskritisation calls for exploration into the social dimension of peoples' religious customs, and in consonance with the anthropologist Clifford Geertz's view that "religious symbols both express the world's climate and shape it."[3] Hence we have to examine the ways in which symbols and rituals associated with the CM cult reflect as well as shape the socio-economic realities of the people. This necessitates an inquiry into the layers of meaning of the rituals and symbols of the religious universes of the people of Valliyoor and Naduvakurichi. This chapter makes an attempt to undertake this inquiry by relating the ritual corpus of the CM cult with the socio-cultural processes of economic initiatives of these two groups so as to contest the viability of the concept of 'sanskritisation' in explaining such phenomena. While engaging in the interpretation of ritual power, this chapter introduces new concepts of 'surplus of ritual power' and '*peri-centralisation*'. Arguments, insights and concepts from the disciplines of sociology, anthropology and philosophy are woven together to evolve a discourse on the concept of '*peri-centralisation.*' The latter part of the chapter that deals with 'Subaltern Temple Honour' involves, as in the words of Saurabh Dube, "a dialogue between history and ethnography," and an "interplay of (the) archival and fieldwork."[4]

Before we set out on our inquiry, let me recall a few details of the two places in question. As we have seen in the ethnography of these places in the third chapter, Valliyoor houses a famous temple, where the high-caste Brahmins worship the 'low caste' god, the CM.[5] And at Naduvakurichi, the performing of *koṭai* rituals is undertaken by the Dalit Pallars at the behest of the local Brahmins[6] who seemed to have come under duress of the deity CM, who in turn, demanded worship from them and made himself their guardian deity.[7] When we inquire into the origin of the temple of CM and the *raison d'être* of *koṭai* in the context of these two groups, it becomes clear that there is a ritual relationship amounting to a ritual exchange between the Dalits and the Brahmins.[8] At Naduvakurichi, we see the Dalits perform *koṭai* rituals on behalf of the Brahmins, and the Brahmins participate in this ritual, albeit *passively*, as a matter of obligation. In contrast, at Valliyoor, the Brahmins themselves perform the *koṭai* rituals, while the Dalits participate but *actively*. It is to be noted that the latter's active participation is considered a must for the Brahmin's celebration of *koṭai*. Besides, the members of the particular Brahmin family that celebrates *koṭai* at Ayyaṉ Kōvil (the name of VAO Brahmin's CM temple) have to be present in the celebration of *koṭai* at the Dalit's temple due to the fact that the head of this Brahmin family had earlier taken away the stone-tub (cf. Note No. 5). This indicates that subaltern *koṭai* ritual brings about a web of ritual relationships between people of different social groups, and this takes us to a discussion on the theme of 'ritual as network in the subaltern religious universe.'

The Meaning of 'Ritual as Network in Subaltern Religious Universe'

A ritual network can be understood as a set of concrete ritual-based relations linking an individual to other individuals who are members of diverse systems of enduring groups and categories. Ritual network creates interdependency and interpersonal relationship between the involved members in a ritual context. Since, as Edmund Leach observes, "ritual makes explicit the social structures... (the structure which is symbolized in ritual), it is the system of socially approved 'proper' relations between individual groups,"[9] the interdependent relations between different caste groups in ritual network are the reflection of interdependency in the social network.

Though such interdependency is also found in the ritual network of Sanskritic Hinduism, what differentiates the subaltern ritual network is the fact that such interdependency is realized and enacted in the site of subaltern religious realm[10] which leads to the lowering of the purity of the Brahmins to the impure ritual terrain of the subalterns.[11] Here the high caste Brahmin has to descend in his hierarchy, alienate himself from the realm of purity, and insert himself into the terrain of impurity and pollution. As in the ritual network of Sanskritic Hinduism, here too, the high caste Brahmin employs the low-caste washermen and the Dalits to perform the so-called polluting jobs. But, in the process, he himself gets polluted, displaying ambivalent behaviour patterns. On the one hand, he has to maintain the purity of his Brahminhood by not directly touching the blood of the sacrificial animals like a goat and cock; on the other, he has to be involved in the pollution rituals. In the process he not only has to gradually get involved in the polluting acts of the lower castes but he also has to publicly demonstrate that he *is* so. For instance, after coming back from *vēṭṭai* he has to show the people that he has taken the bones of the dead, and he has to stick them on the forehead of CM's image as if to prove to others that he had gone to the cremation ground first and performed rituals of a polluting nature there. As the researcher in other places of worship did not observe the sticking of the bone of the dead, this act of the Brahmin can indicate that he is responding to a covert compulsion to demonstrate his authority as a *cāmiyāṭis* in the subaltern religious terrain.

Is a Brahmin permitted by the Hindu law books to perform rituals at the cremation ground? Does he not acquire the impurity of the death of other castes? Different authors answer this question differently. As regards impurity from the death of other castes incurred by the Brahmins, on the one hand early *Dharamasastras* like *Manusmirti* forbid such contacts with the dead. On the other hand, it is also to be noted, as Kane and Orenstein have observed,[12] that later *Dharamasastras* held that the Brahmins are the least affected by the impurity of the death of others lower than them in the caste hierarchy.[13] While the Brahmins are the most insulated by *Dharmasastras* against the impurity of the death of other castes, the Brahmin *cāmiyāṭi's* engagement with the subaltern religious rituals makes him do that which is ordinarily forbidden for him during the rituals for the dead. For instance, Manu forbids the twice-born Brahmin from any offering into dead ashes, the rituals at midnight and the inclusion of service castes during the rituals for the dead.[14] By such acts, a Brahmin defies the above-mentioned concerns of *Dharmasastras,* and he exposes himself to the impurity deriving from all the dead in the village. At Valliyoor, the Brahmin as a village VAO-cum-CM *cāmiyāṭi,* is entitled to collect not only the revenue of all the villagers but also the impurity arising out of their deaths. While the *Dharmasastras* deliberately protect a Brahmin more than others from such defilements, subaltern religious rituals expose him to such predicaments.

In any case, the Brahmin *cāmiyāṭi* has to manifest the subaltern shaman's behaviour such as ecstatic dance and divination, etc. Since such behaviour of shamans is seen in the subaltern worldview as a result of his contact with blood by drinking of blood or *ūṭṭu* etc., one can read the Brahmin's emulation of such subaltern religious behaviour as an implicit acknowledgement of his contact with the realm of pollution through an explicit behaviour of a subaltern kind. Here the Brahmin shaman has to display to the public the resultant behaviour of that which he cannot openly acknowledge. The Brahmin shaman openly acknowledged this ambivalence when he expressed his inner urge to adopt the popular subaltern forms of ritual such as fire walking, drinking of the blood of a goat, which is interpreted by people as the consequence of osmosis with the power of CM.[15]

This ritual repertoire of the Brahmins points to the fact that the Brahmin has not only to contest and transgress the social and religious boundaries of Brahminhood, but must negotiate with the same boundaries[16] of the subaltern worldview to establish and to maintain the authority of his leadership in the subaltern ritual network. Thereby he unconsciously undertakes downward iteration in the caste hierarchy. In all these ritual performances he has to negate and subvert the dominant symbolic order that he himself has set up in history.

Here he engages himself in a self-defeating exercise in order to establish ritual domination over others. Such an engagement lands him in the violation of Hindu dharma in favour of state law. The CM temple in Valliyoor is supposed to be the private property of a Brahmin family. Karnath has earlier noted that, though denying of entry for the Dalits into temples or access to public places were offences punishable by State Law, attempts were made to circumvent the law by making them out to be private property.[17] The field data at Valliyoor reveals that the same strategy is used by dominant Brahmins to safeguard the rituals of the subaltern religious terrain against the intervention and accusation of pollution by Sanskritic Hinduism. Here a private temple becomes not only a public space for circumventing the Hindu dharma prescribed for Brahmins, but also a site of contestation and violation of such laws in favour of untouchable and Sudra rituals.

The above discussion clearly indicates that the phenomenon of the ritual relationship between the Brahmins and the Dalits, and of the Brahmin's association with the subaltern religious terrain goes against the theory of sanskritisation proposed by M. N. Srinivas. Hence the study proposes another concept, "*peri-centralisation,*" to refer to the downward iteration of the high caste (Brahmins) towards the periphery. The definition of *peri-centralisation* will be given a little later.

If the high caste Brahmins appropriate the *koṭai* rituals of the subaltern religious realm, it is because the rituals have more power than what they seem to offer during the celebration of *koṭai*. Hence the potentiality of ritual power needs to be explored, and that takes us to the idea of surplus of ritual power.

The Surplus of Ritual Power

As a subaltern god "grips" a particular person to act on his behalf as "*cāmiyāṭi*" (shaman/ritual persona) he gets enormous ritual power.[18] The ritual power, through the generation of 'privileged contrast' as we have noted in chapter one, becomes a means either to contest and negotiate social power/political power or to maintain and safeguard the newly obtained socio-economic statuses. This potentiality of ritual can be called "surplus of ritual power," which is obtained by the ritual persona, i.e., the *cāmiyāṭi* and his cohorts. It is because of this power that he gets additional social status (social power) and appropriates political power in many instances.[19] But it has to match his personality and moral credibility, because people recall quite a few instances where misbehaving *cāmiyāṭis* have been punished and killed by CM. From the ritual persona of the *cāmiyāṭi*, this surplus of power spreads to his family, as god CM is seen as the god of his/her family. In the next generation, as his family grows, the ritual persona/the social persona of ritual power, in whom the god's power is ingrained, and through whom the god's power is exercised and transmitted, also grows. In the third and fourth generation it extends to the clan, and later it is claimed as the god of a particular caste in the village. Thus surplus of ritual power creates relations of power and networks of power, as noted by Foucault.

The ritual power as well as the surplus of ritual power is concentrated more in the (ritual) centre (the shaman) than in the outer realm. Though ritual power is theoretically available to all (irrespective of caste, sex, age, clan and creed), in reality it is commonly and legitimately tapped and transmitted more by the people in the centre than by others. Subsequently it is logical to hold that the *surplus of ritual power* is appropriated, exercised, and asserted to a greater extent by the centre than by the periphery. This is not to deny the availability of ritual power outside this group. Anyone can claim that he/she is possessed by a god/goddess provided he/she demonstrates the characteristic features of possession. Only a very few would qualify over a period of time by proving to be promising agents of an effective divination.[20] But this occasional appropriation of ritual power may not be recognized by the ritual persona, and subsequently it may not qualify one for divination in a particular temple. This points to the non-availability of *surplus of ritual power* to the occasional appropriators. It is vital to keep in mind that this centre of ritual power created by the folk/

subaltern religious phenomenon is associated more with the people of the periphery of society than of the high castes.

The legitimising power of surplus of ritual power emerges from the "power of fear" towards a god–the untold fear the common folk have picked up in the village tradition of a particular god or goddess. The power of fear plays a vital role in subaltern religiosity. Fear of CM is the biggest source of power, which will be dealt with later in the chapter. Though 'fear' of a folk god is commonly interpreted as baseless or superstitious, what a social anthropologist should not overlook is the alternative legitimising role it plays for subaltern agency, as opposed to the legitimising role played by the Brahminic priesthood in sanskritisation. Besides, fear also played a crucial role in making the Brahmins (the VAO and the Panagkudi Paṇṇaiyār) at Valliyoor adopt the subaltern rituals. This helped them to safeguard their property, to remain economically powerful and administratively or politically dominant, as we see in the case of VAO. This shows the appropriation of the surplus of ritual power (of the subaltern religious terrain) by the Brahmins, which highlights once again the existence of alternative discourses of social mobility to "sanskritisation." Let us now move on to the concepts of verticality and encompassment to nuance ritual power a little more.

Verticality and Encompassment

Verticality and *encompassment* are two key principles for understanding of ritual persona. The *cāmiyāṭi* and his ritual power have both dimensions of verticality and encompassment. Verticality refers to the central and pervasive idea of the *cāmiyāṭi* as someone who is above human beings and human institutions such as families, caste, judiciary, etc.[21] Through the image of encompassment he is seen as transcending ever widening series of circles, beginning with individuals, families, human habitations, fields and village borders.

The perceptions of verticality and encompassment are produced through the ritual practices that legitimize and naturalise his authority at the local level. Ritual persona is "imagined", that is, a constructed entity which is conceptualised and made socially effective through particular imaginative and symbolic devices and rituals. Through images, metaphors, and representative ritual performances such as *vēṭṭai* and *cāmiyāṭṭam* he comes to be understood as a concrete, overarching, and spatially encompassing entity. Through such practices, he represents himself as a reified entity of power with a particular spatial property of encompassment. By doing so, he helps to secure his legitimacy, to naturalise his authority and to represent himself as superior to, and encompassing, other systems of networks and centres of power, such as caste hierarchy, judiciary, etc.

In the vertical topography of power, *cāmiyāṭi* appears as the middle latitude, the zone of contact between the power "up there" and the people caught up in the mire of contingencies of human life "down below". This contact zone is conceived as the domain of power that is tapped by the common folk for solving their problems, as observed in the previous chapter.

Picturing CM's and *cāmiyāṭi's* relation to society through the image of vertical encompassment fuses in a single, powerful image a number of analytically distinct functional propositions: As a guardian of the village he engages in the surveillance of the borders of the village which is enacted and recognized during *vēṭṭai*; as an exorcist he is believed to liberate people from the influence of evil spirits; as a judge he settles interfamily squabbles; as a police officer he identifies the thief and the guilty by punishing them. *Cāmiyāṭi* is thus seen as an encompassing power both as extensive with the territorial boundaries of the village and intensively permeating the geographical and social spaces of that territory.[22]

People seem to recognize that a host of mundane rituals and procedures are required to animate and to naturalize these metaphors if CM *cāmiyāṭi* has to be imagined as both higher than, and encompassing the village. It is realized through the images of vertical encompassment embedded in the routinized practices of rituals and the different myths performed and enacted during the celebration of *koṭai* festival. Verticality and encompassment not only form the basis for the authority of ritual persona and ritual power, but also produce a conceptual ambience for the evolution of surplus of ritual power that gives rise to the social mobility of the ritual persona.

Ritual Power and Social Mobility

Ritual power facilitates social mobility by means of surplus of ritual power, thereby altering and repositioning the social status of the ritual persona. Here, the relationship between ritual power, *peri-centralisation* and social mobility is found to be different and more complex than in M.N. Srinivas's idea of sanskritisation and social mobility.

In the sanskritisation model, the sources of mobility were political and economic systems.[23] The latter is closely associated with "the ecological-demographic system that made it possible for families to move out and bring marginal land under cultivation."[24] According to M.N. Srinivas, in the case of the caste category of the Kshatriyas, the political power wielded by a group is translated into authority by the process of sanskritisation. The ruler and his caste were "potent sources of sanskritisation both in the support and patronage they gave to priestly and learned Brahmins and in providing a particular model of sanskritised life style to those who came under their influence."[25] Both in sanskritisation and in *peri-centralisation*, we see the enhancement of one's social power and status, and both result in social mobility. In the former, political power comes first, and sanskritisation is a means or a process of legitimising power into authority.[26] Here ritual power functions as a mediating category. The *peri-centralisation* process on the other hand is marked by divergent patterns. On the part of the Brahmins at Valliyoor, their political power came first, and the Brahmin's adoption of the CM cult, a downward iteration, was utilised for legitimation of that power. In some instances, ritual power is the starting-point, used as a means for the appropriation of political power and for the legitimisation of such power into authority. In the case of the subalterns, it safeguards the autonomy of their social power obtained by the economic power made available to them as a consequence of education and employment opportunities generated by modernization, urbanization, industrialization and democratisation.[27] As modernisation marked a shift from the old feudalistic caste system, let us move our discourse to the relationship between feudalism and folk/subaltern religions,[28] and to the relevance of folk religions in the modernisation process.

It is to be noted that folk religions had their origins in the feudal system[29] wherein there was neglect of the concerns of the depressed classes, who were a mere workforce for the feudal landlords of the high caste Veḷḷāḷar-Brahmin elites. They were victims of social injustice, judicial nepotism, etc. In such situations, folk religions took care of the concerns of the depressed classes of the people. Though feudalism has gradually become extinct, yet the feudal mindset has survived in the form of caste hierarchy and continues to infect the Indian psyche, with its bad influence on the social fabric till today. Hence, the depressed classes continue to suffer in similar situations of oppression, which explains the popularity and relevance of folk cults today. As the traditional productive system of village economy began to disintegrate and as the productive relationships and the *jajmani* system[30] of reciprocal duties and services were undercut,

> general loosening of social links with the village community set the depressed caste groups free to fend for themselves and to make their economic resources and to look for new patrons or to change their life style ... without the old pressure to conform to norms of village community being enforced by the high castes.[31]

The new patronage of a non-economic nature was provided by the ever-increasing new roles attached to the CM, whose power and popularity is steadily on the increase. Though it is a symbolic patronage, yet it is not totally disjunct from socio-economic systems because, by his vertical and encompassing power, CM is believed by all castes to have dominion over all the aspects of life in the village.

The preceding discussion indicates that the folk cults/ rituals in *koṭai* in particular become the site of assertion of the newly gained autonomy of the depressed classes in this district, as insightfully shown by Diane P. Mines in a recent study.[32] One or two stray incidents of caste clashes that took place during *koṭai* celebrations are to be understood as contestations of such assertions. The ever-growing extravaganza and festivity of *koṭai*, the popularity of folk theatres and folk songs, although being sources of more entertainment, function as an arena for displaying their newly attained socio-economic status, and for the implicit celebration of the autonomy of social identity. In the former feudal system, the social identity of Dalits was linked up with the landlord or patron. A Dalit, for instance, was merely known and labelled as 'servant' (coolie) of such and such a Veḷḷāḷar, Reṭṭiyār, Tēvar or Brahmin, and had no separate identity. In the social register, this was the only entry of address that the Dalits had.

Today, depressed classes have obtained *multiple social identities*,[33] though the old pattern of identity may not have changed dramatically, since some of them continue to work as daily coolies in the fields of Reṭṭiyār(s), Veḷḷāḷar(s) and Tēvar(s). As modernisation has opened up new avenues of educational and job opportunities for the depressed classes, they are also provided with multiple identities. Thus, a particular person is now identified as the father of a teacher, son of a postman, mother of a nurse, secretary of a party, etc. The autonomy of the social identity of the depressed classes has its base in their multiple identities; where one channel fails, other channels of identity provide them opportunity for independence.[34] Folk cults provide occasion for the celebration of such autonomy born out of multiple identities. The spread of the CM cult to new areas must be seen in this light, wherein the worship of CM by a new group is at once a display and assertion of the social status acquired by them over the years.

In Naduvakurichi, the Paḷḷar(s) and Paṟaiyar(s) have established wider social and economic networks beyond their village, due to the spread of education, employment opportunities, industrialisation, urbanisation, and market-economy, as mentioned above.[35] Many have moved out of the village to the nearby city Tirunelveli and established business or found jobs in factories, schools, colleges and government offices. Some of them have flourished almost as successfully as the dominant caste, the Tēvar(s). Hence, the total economic dependency of Dalits on other dominant castes has gradually declined over the years in the twentieth century. The new social and economic networks Dalits have established, like Tēvar(s) and others, has been the source of conflict in this district in the past two decades. While this is the case in most of the other villages, in Naduvakurichi this conflict did not bring about a sharp polarization. It is precisely because of the legitimising power of the CM cult that people hesitate to touch the Dalits and the ritual persona of cāmiyāṭi as we noted elsewhere in the thesis. It both legitimises and safeguards the social ascendancy of the subalterns obtained through different schemes of modernisation. This directs our discussion towards the definition and delineation of different characteristics of *peri-centralisation* in the following pages.

Peri-centralization

Peri-centralisation is a multifaceted process of appropriation of the symbols and rituals of the subaltern religious universe for the purpose of assertion of status, be it economic or social, either by a subaltern or by a non-subaltern. While it implies for the subaltern the appropriation of one's own resources in one's own realm, for the non-subaltern it implies a downward social mobility or iteration towards another realm. Here folk/subaltern religion functions as an epicentre on the periphery and involves a centering activity on the exterior-realm. It is characterized by both centrifugal and centripetal forces. Its centripetal pull is so powerful a gravitational force that it not only creates the concentric circles on the periphery and pulls the interior towards the epicentre of the exterior, but it also tilts the vertical hierarchy towards its centre on the horizontal plane. Likewise, its centrifugal force is very powerful too. It traverses the social fabric of the vertical hierarchy. It is a force of upward encompassment. It vitalizes and revitalizes the subalterns, affirms and confirms their identity, drives them out of the periphery into vertical hierarchy, and thereby enables them to contest their old boundaries, negotiate with newly gained social identity for a place in the hierarchy and reposition their social status.

In the process, it emboldens the subaltern agents to claim and appropriate the habits and customs, rituals and life-styles of the region encompassed (i.e, the cultural universe of the caste hierarchy), and to challenge the monopoly of the twice-born over their symbols and rituals. But the dynamism of the centripetal force brings them every now and then back to its peripheral centre. What is to be noted in this dynamics is that the umbilical chord of the subaltern to his/her centre is not broken. He or she will manifest the symbiotic relationship every now and then in his/her private customs and rituals, acts of worship and in the annual feasts like *koṭai*, etc.

The peri-centralisation process, we have seen, has two sides: the downward mobility of the high castes and the upward mobility of the lower castes. While the centripetal force characterizes the downward mobility of the high castes, centrifugal force is coterminous with the upward social mobility of the depressed subaltern classes.

Peri-Centralisation: A Process of Multi-directional Iteration

While sanskritisation is marked by the uni-directional upward mobility of the lower castes towards the socio-cultural universe of the higher castes, peri-centralisation is characterised by multi-directional iteration or iterative mobility, i.e., mobility that registers fluidity, involving not mere unidirectional process as in the case of upward mobility of sanskritisation, but multi-directional activity. It depicts the occurrence of to-and-fro journeying of the social actors between two or more social/religious/cultural worlds. While on the part of people at the extreme pole (Brahmins/Dalits) it involves iterations either in a downward or in an upward direction, for the people of the middle castes, it opens up possibilities of multi-directional iterations towards the cultural worlds of either the higher castes or the lower castes. The field data reveals that this 'iteration' takes place in search of 'power', be it economic, social or ritual power.

The orbits of these social worlds are basically elliptical, so that the Dalit's/subaltern cultural world is at *perihelion* (closest to the epicentre) and the Brahmin social/cultural world is positioned at *aphelion* (furthest distance from the epicentre). The pull of the peripheral epicentre is felt more at perihelion than at aphelion. These positions, however, do not negate the processual possibility of iterations of these social/cultural worlds towards the epicentre. This multi-directional activity involves adaptation and adoption of rituals, habits and values of another caste, not necessarily of higher castes, wherein people perform acts in violation of caste/clan (*kula*) *dharma* proposed by *Smritis* and *Sastras,* the books of moral code in Sanskritic Hinduism. People from both the high and low castes subvert and transgress the limits set by the strict *varnashrama* dharma ideology.

What happens in the process is that people manifest overt and covert behaviours of different cultural worlds. Though a Brahmin of this category will overtly manifest the religious behaviour of a subaltern (Dalit), yet he will not violate the social customs of Brahminhood i.e., he/she will not touch blood, or eat the offering of cooked meat of the deity during the ritual as subalterns and others do. But covertly in private life, he eats meat, drinks liquor, etc., due to the influences of modernity and urbanization which have made him migrate to the cities, both in India and abroad. It is evident that the urbanized Brahmins find it impractical to keep up the idea of 'purity,' thereby leading a life of ambivalence. Similarly, Dalits/BCs get themselves easily sanskritised to live up to the demands of the new social/economic status provided by modernization. In this upward mobility, they manifest overtly the life-style of 'Sanskritic' culture. But covertly they would continue their original cultural ethos in private life. Thus modernity becomes a key agent in bringing about 'ambivalences' of caste hierarchy in the *pericentralisation* process. The process of iteration mentioned here envelopes all such behaviour of ambivalence involving both overt and covert behaviours.

To sum up, employing Amartya Sen's terminology, while the 'sanskritisation' theory works within the logic of a functioning vector[36] of the dominant hegemony, *pericentralisation* is characterized by the capability set which provides social actors with the alternating functioning vectors, both hegemonic and non-hegemonic, from which one can choose and creatively weave the fabric of one's social life.

Rituals: A Lingua Franca of the Subaltern Agency in Peri-centralisation

Koṭai rituals, as we saw in the case of Dalits in Naduvakurichi, are the lingua franca of the subalterns in the religious realm to demonstrate and display their newly attained social identity. Subaltern rituals/symbols provide the lingua franca through which the subaltern articulation of the newly attained social ascendancy is accomplished.

That pericentralisation is not a unidirectional or one-dimensional process like sanskritisation can be seen in subaltern rituals. It can recruit, integrate and co-opt ritual elements, symbols and insignia from various religious and cultural traditions[37] so as to establish and maintain that ritual performances can redefine old idioms and write a new grammar of dynamics for the subaltern language of culture. Sometimes, subaltern rituals not only exacerbate internal contradictions within the caste-system, but also introduce and institute a set of categories through which such contradictions can be objectified and acted upon.[38] But these categories bear with them the imprint of the feudal system that had given them birth as noted earlier. While caste-coercions still might continue to stifle overt expression of newly gained economic/political power of the subalterns in their everyday life-world, the polysemous metaphors and rituals of the subaltern religious terrain offer a haven for the creative and innovative display of such improved situations. Thus rituals can become social practices that engender privileged contrast as we noted earlier in chapter one.

Protesting Documentation: Countering Sanskritisation

The great traditions, such as the Sanskritic Hinduism, which are regarded as the frames-of-reference in the process of sanskritisation, are known for their written scriptures and various documents that prescribe ritual codes and religious conduct for their adherents. Against this background, sanskritisation puts pressure upon the little traditions to move away from the world of oral tradition to written tradition. But in the CM folk religious phenomenon, like many others, one encounters tremendous resistance to documentation during *koṭai,* which in turn are covert forms of resistance to sanskritisation.[39] The more people are on the subaltern side, the more resistance they show towards documentation of events and rituals during *koṭai.* When asked about the 'why' of this, some said that they were afraid that CM would punish them if they did so, while others maintained that the power of a god would be controlled and would be gradually lost through documentation such as photography and writing.

The underlying reason, though unarticulated, would be that Dalits/illiterate folk lose power and control over what is documented, as this is open to different interpretation. The power of CM is identified, established, maintained and reinforced by the discourse about the power of CM. The power of CM has its locus within the discourse about the very power itself. In other words, it is the discourse about the power of a god, which clarifies, defines, confirms, reinstates and reinforces the grammar and the language of the ritual power of gods in the minds of the folk. The vigour and rigour of a particular god's power is encapsulated in the discourse about the power of gods among the folk. Dalits/folk's refusal to translate, transmit and transfuse their oral traditions and ritual corpus into Sanskrit model emerges from the apprehensions about coding and documenting them. For them, documentation is analogous to losing control over the trajectories of the discourse about a god in the literary domain, which is alien to them. Refusal to document them is asserting the negation of the possibility of manipulation of discourse about their god. It is so, because it is the documented and coded scripture which strangled them and subjugated them for centuries, and to which access was denied to them in the age-old Indian history.

Hence, the subaltern's resistance to documentation in the *peri-centralisation* process can be understood as the articulation of growing consciousness among the subalterns to subvert any attempts by the caste hierarchy to co-opt them into the Sanskritic Hindu fold.

Peri-centralisation: A True Portrayal of Labour Dependency on Low Castes

In Sanskritic Hinduism and in its Vedic ritual complex, there is minimal dependency of the Brahmins on low-caste ritual labour (of service-castes) for ritual efficacy in the first place. Besides, the service castes are paid in kind or in cash, an act that makes low castes economically dependent on the high castes. In the *peri-centralisation* process, the ritual efficacy of the high caste Brahmins is wholly dependent on low-caste ritual labour for which the low castes—Sampāṉ(s) and service castes are not paid by the Brahmins.

In *peri-centralisation* the ritual labour-dependency of Brahmins on lower castes rightly depicts the true picture of economic labour-dependency of high caste Brahmins on the low castes, while the Sanskritic ritual complex belies the economic ground reality. The Sanskritic ritual complex, which inverses the ritual labour dependency equation by making the low caste economically dependent on Brahmins for their ritual labour is in fact a symbolic violence. This is so because it not only contradicts the ground reality of economic labour dependency of Brahmins on non-Brahmins, but it also displaces the symbolic capital of the religious realm from its space and relocates it in the Sanskritic religious universe, a process which in turn perpetuates the exploitative caste hierarchy.[40]

In the downward iteration of *peri-centralisation* process, the Brahmin transgresses his purity realm in search of symbolic capital and finds it elsewhere in the untouchable realm. It is the pursuing of symbolic capital that makes him realize his full dependency on low castes (subaltern) for "ritual labour," which rightly displays his real dependency on the same people for economic labour. However, in the Dalit component of *peri-centralisation* process as in the case of Naduvakurichi, there is no dependency of Dalits on other high castes for ritual labour.

Ritual labour of the lower castes is a paradoxical phenomenon in south Indian villages as M. N. Srinivas, Deliege, Beck and Fuller have noted. Though the Dalits are included in the division of labour (as musicians and sacrificial slaughterers) during the village festivals, they are rarely incorporated as co-equal worshippers of the village deity. As Deliege notes, "This is consistent with the Harijan's (Dalits) ambiguous position in the caste system as a whole, for they are both rejected from it as 'outcastes' and included by it because their economic and ritual services are required to sustain the system."[41] Dalits, as they are associated with evil and wild spirits dwelling in the forest, must also be present in the village temple feasts "as symbolic denizens of the exterior in opposition to which the village is represented as a civilized centre. From the latter's perspective, Harijans are included precisely so that they can be portrayed as excluded, and the ambiguity of their role is intrinsic to the ritualisation of village unity."[42] Thus the unity of the South Indian village is ritually predicated on the Dalit's exclusion. In the downward component of pericentralisation process, the above-mentioned logic of ritualisation of village unity is inverted in the subaltern religious terrain wherein the polluted Dalit, who belongs to the uncultivated exterior and forest regions beyond the village, and the higher caste Brahmin, who inhabits the civilized centre meet, and are included as co-equal worshippers.[43]

Thus, in the downward dimension of *peri-centralisation* process, we see that the so-called unequal Brahmins and the *avarna* (outcastes) are locked in a 'marriage of equals', the former's authority partly vested in the latter's recognition of former's ability to satisfy their (Dalits) god, but not without their involvement in the impure realm of the cremation ground, which is assigned to the latter in *varna* ideology. Such a 'marriage' cannot take place without the ritual co-operation of the subalterns, as we have seen.

This *pericentralisation* process inverts and subverts the traditional *varna* ideology, shaking the system at its very roots. It overturns the ideological system of "purity" on which caste hierarchy is constituted. It compels the 'pure' Brahmin caste to transgress the boundaries of *varna* ideology and to generate overlapping of realms based on the dichotomy of the 'pure' and the 'impure.' The "impure" realm seems to engulf and to encompass the "purity" realm in such a decisive and compelling manner that the Brahmins at Valliyoor have no other option but to engage in the transgression and violation of frontiers every year, as one of the Brahmin informants put it, "perform the ritual and prosper or face the doom."[44] In fact, the power of CM is believed to manifest itself more when the Brahmin's eagerness to appropriate the style, content and values of impure low-caste ritual complex is actualized more.

Reversal of Relations of Power in Pericentralisation: A Strategy of Visibility

As Foucault mentions, "the relation of power (which is) constituted in visibility"[45] forms the very logic of Indian caste-society in its demarcation of segregated spaces, both the first space and the third space, based on the principle of "purity" and "impurity." By recreating and reconstituting new visibility domains, new relations of power can be generated in subtle ways. New "effects of power" can be inscribed upon old sets of power relations. The climax events of *koṭai* rituals, such as *vēṭṭai, cāmiyāṭṭam* and divination are manifestations of such strategy. A *cāmiyāṭi,* be it a Dalit or a Brahmin, as a representative of the folk, both the pure and the impure, establishes contact with the impure world, triumphs over the evil powers latent there, and comes into the realm which is more pure or less impure,[46] thereby puncturing and deflating the purity hyperbole of the caste hierarchy.

The Brahmin *cāmiyāṭi* imposes on himself the polluting activities that lead to the stigmatizing social identities considered integral to Dalits in the caste hierarchy. 'The technologies of self-disclosure'[47] employed by the Brahmin men and women during *cāmiyāṭṭam,* are the unimaginable reversal and defiance of the orthodox 'technology of the self' prescribed to them. As one Dalit villager commented "they are like us: we drink, they drink; they also eat meat; both of us worship CM; we perform *vēṭṭai*; so too they do; we dance *cāmiyāṭṭam*; so also they dance like us."[48]

Similarly, the technology of self-disclosure engaged in by the Dalit *cāmiyāṭi* during *vēṭṭai, cāmiyāṭṭam* and divination is carried out not without its implied social nuances. The impure Dalit, acts as a representative of Brahmins and others, subsumes unto himself the pole of purity, goes into the cremation ground, the impure realm, and establishes his control over evil powers. When he returns, he is regarded as a victor over evil powers, though it is not a victory of the "pure" over the "impure". The *Maiyāṇa pūcai* (the rituals meant for the spirits) at the cremation ground registers emphatically the recognition of the potentialities of power of the impure over the pure and that of "the lowest, most outer sphere that is most dynamic, rich with generative potential, capable of containing other forms and power."[49] What underlies this performance is the recognition of "mutual constitutive power of domains"[50] and a "latent and necessary affinity."[51] In as much as *kāṭu* (uncultivated land) is the source of life for the *vayal* (cultivated land) and for the village, in terms of being a storage space for water and as a border between villages, it is perceived as a source of threat, too, with the dead and evil spirits inhabiting it. As *nāṭu* (village) needs *kāṭu, kāṭu* also needs the people of the village for its maintenance and for the appeasement of its spirits.

The performances of *vēṭṭai, cāmiyāṭṭam* and divination must be seen against the background of interrelatedness of the two domains, the pure and the impure. The fact that the Dalit *cāmiyāṭi* performs these rituals already stands to reveal the capabilities vested in the ritual persona of Dalits, of the impure realm to puncture and to deflate the principle of purity on which the caste hierarchy is based.

The CM Cult: A Point of Convergence Marked by Bi-directional Encompassment

As we have noted in the previous chapter, the CM's temple is located at a point bordering the inner social world (*nāṭu*) and the forest (*kāṭu*). It is a point of convergence between the inner realm and the outer realm, though the characteristics of the deity and of the rituals have to do more with the outer world than the inner space. It functions as an epicentre at the tip of the periphery. Emerging from this epicentre, the *cāmiyāṭi* moves in both directions during *vēṭṭai*. He encompasses both the realms– the inner and the outer. Though *vēṭṭai* was originally seen as a ritual hunting of the borders, yet in its evolution it becomes a ritual movement covering both the outer realm (the uncultivated land) and the inner realm (the inhabited village). Its centrifugal and encompassing activity envelops both the realms, involving both of what Shulman calls, "upward encompassment" and "downward encompassment."[52] Through the ritual enactments, the lowest embraces that which is above, and through the same ritual of *vēṭṭai*, it also envelops all the outer spheres of the periphery of the forest and subsumes everything into it through its power of control. Unlike the Kattavaryan, an ambiguous guardian, who is neither subsumed by the higher beings nor subsumes them,[53] CM is believed to subsume everything unto himself and makes converge within himself all that is above and all that is below.

At Valliyoor, the CM *cāmiyāṭi* receives the honour, and *pūcai* of the higher deities of the major temples, the ritual centre of caste hierarchy. Through this, the CM demonstrates his capability to subsume honours due to him from higher beings. It is the power of its centripetal force that elicits such ritual interaction with the so-called major deities. Its centripetal power is not confined to higher religious beings alone. The CM cult of the periphery in every village attracts the apex castes to the borders, both spatially and socially, whereby it generates new horizons of a third space on the periphery through the agency of subaltern religious domains. This underlines the fact that, unlike in rigid Sanskritic Hinduism, folk/subaltern religious landscapes are governed by a high degree of fluidity and indeterminacy.

Divination : A Moment of Peri-centralisation through Ritualisation of Social Norms

In the subaltern ritual corpus, divination is wielded by *cāmiyāṭi* as a moment of pericentralisation. In this process *cāmiyāṭi* defies the Sanskritic rituals in his attempt to ritualise the social realm. Pollock has noted how Vedic rituals strove to expand the boundaries of the ritual realm to encompass the non-ritual realm through the ritualisation of the social and moral realms.[54] In similar vein, the *cāmiyāṭi* too, through divination, expands his ritual power to assert his moral power over the social realm. In this process, he does not automatically reinforce the dharma of Sanskritic ideology. He makes use of his subaltern agency to establish his dominion over all the others through creative and innovative methods.

Indeed, more often than not, he ostensibly attempts to dislodge the authority of the Vedic dharma and *sastras*. For instance he would utter the command: "Change your house. That is not good for you." The devotee would respond, "*Cāmi* (the Brahmin) said it was a good house according to *vastu*". Then *cāmiyāṭi* would retort in anger, "Who is real *cāmi* (god), me or he? I tell you 'Shift the house'!" In another instance he told a young married girl, "Your husband has illicit connections with another woman. Desert him and all your stomach aches and other bodily ailments will disappear!"[55] This statement of *cāmiyāṭi* blatantly defies the orthodox Hindu thinking that the husband is a god for the wife. Accordingly, the only way for her to attain *moksa* (liberation) or to get a better re-birth in the next life is by faithfully serving him, irrespective of what he is. It parodies the Tamil saying "*Kallāṉālum Kaṇavaṉ Pullāṉālum Purusaṉ*" (whether rock or grass he is your husband).

To another person a *cāmiyāṭi* said, "Why did you come here? You did not believe CM. After going to Civā's temple you have come here. I do not want you here!" To this rebuke, the devotee asked for pardon and forgiveness. What is demonstrated here is the ritualisation of the subaltern agency to defy the authority not only of the orthodox Hindu *dharmas* but also the authority of their all-powerful supreme being, Civā, with whom the subaltern god (CM) is closely associated.

CM: A Deity of the Periphery or Centre

CM, as Pate[56] reports, is the deity who is worshipped before the act of looting and burglary by the people living on the periphery. Besides, it is the deity of the periphery also by the very locus of its temple which is situated on the village borders. In the seventeenth and eighteenth centuries, when the cult spread, one of the historical characteristics of that period was "the encroachment of the 'periphery' over the centre, reversing if only partially and temporarily, the medieval balance between dynamic centres and encompassed peripheries."[57]

During the British times, the process of 'centralization' underwent another mutation, when the centre castes (Brahmins), occupied/encroached the land of the periphery. They had registered vast tracts of lands in the dry and mixed zones, as Ludden[58] has observed. But they could not do it without being encroached upon by the gods of the periphery, as we see in the case of Naduvakurichi and Valliyoor.

While at Valliyoor, Brahmins sustained the worship of the god of the periphery till date, at Naduvakurchi, they handed it over to the 'Dalits'. This process of reversal in the religious realm is concomitant with the actualities of the ground realities, wherein Brahmins and high castes have sold their lands in the last two decades to the people more on the periphery side, i.e., the Maravars and Dalits. Their god CM, who was once at the periphery, has come close to the centre as villages grew, symbolically representing the Dalits, who through modernization, education and employment engage in the 'encroachment of the periphery' over the 'centre' in the social realm.

Ritual Power of CM: An Outside/Alternative Source of Independence for the Subalterns

In caste-ridden Indian society, which is characterized by the relationship of interdependence between different castes and by the accumulation of material, social and cultural resources by the higher castes, subaltern rituals can give a 'power leverage'[59] to the subalterns. Being an excluded and ostracized entity, the Paḷḷar(s) acquire the resources of power not from within the caste-system, the very root of Indian society, but from outside, from gods like CM, thorough rituals. Subalterns place their hope "always on the horizon, on the places beyond the boundaries of territory and values"[60] outside the hegemony of caste hierarchy. Acquiring of power from outside, from non-human agency has significance for the subalterns because the 'non-human' and 'outside' source, a 'power of fear' cannot be easily usurped and arbitrarily manipulated by the high caste. Secondly, it subverts the equation of interdependence. The power structure of the caste hierarchy is operated by the asymmetrical interdependence between high castes and the low castes. But the ritual network of power becomes significant, as it is characterized not by relationship of interdependence, but of dependence of high castes on Dalit *cāmiyāṭi* and the ritual persona, which we discussed earlier in the chapter. This proclaims an emergence of the 'autonomous' for Dalits/ subalterns in the ritual realm.

This emergence of the 'autonomous,' springing forth from an outside source is not a mere illusion born of ritual power. It very well dovetails with the available and accessible sources of social power, outside the traditional caste society. Here, agents from outside caste-society provided the sources of social power or 'bases of power' for the Dalits, such as education, opportunity for different types of employment, etc. Thus the outside source of ritual power of CM for Dalits becomes a symbol of newly acquired social power for the subalterns.

The CM Cult: A Process of 'Twin Redress' of 'Wrongful Actions'

In expounding the dynamics of folk cults, Knipe speaks of a 'twin redress' of 'wrongful action' undertaken in an eclectic way in the context of Virabadhra cult.[61] One is overt, and the other covert. Overt redress refers to the ritual repairing of damage done to the spirits who early in their human lives had faced violent and untimely deaths. In the context of the CM cult, the ritual worship of *pūṭams* (a kind of altar) of the deceased *cāmiyāṭis* who faced such situations squares with the overt dimension of ritual redress.

The second type, i.e., covert redress of wrongful action is manifest in the corpus of subaltern rituals that responds to the Brahmin's exclusion of Sudras and Dalits from their *vaidika* rituals (rituals of Vedic Hinduism) and *sraddha* rituals (one kind of death rituals in Vedic Hinduism).[62] In the process of *'peri-centralisation,'* the ritual activity of Sanskritic Hinduism performed by the subalterns, which characterises the 'upward mobility' of the subalterns can be seen in this light. It is a covert redress of 'wrongful action' of Brahmanical exclusion of Dalits from Vedic/agamic rituals.

This twin redress, when applied to the dynamics of the religious phenomenon of downward iteration, can have different meaning. The Brahmin's adoption of the subaltern god, CM, and their celebration of *koṭai* unfolds the insufficiency of Brahminic/vaidika rituals to redress overtly the wrongful action not only of violent death, but also their wrongful action of excluding the Sudras/Dalits. Brahmins do this not by covertly including them and their rituals in their rituals of CM cult, but by overtly making them ritual co-functionaries and adopting the subaltern rituals almost in toto.

The Role of 'Fear' in Peri-centralisation Process

As we have seen in chapter one, fear and the objects of fear are socially imbibed, induced, constructed and communicated, as the folk of a particular culture or sub-culture share a common life-world and thereby take part in shared symbols.[63] Fear of an object not only functions as a vehicle of interpersonal communication and intra-personal communication, but it can also be appropriated by social actors[64] to generate new systems of meanings by subverting old meaning since, through 'fear,' significant meanings can be transmitted both to the self and to others.[65] Since the objects of fear in a religious universe and its relations of rituals generated and upheld by the society can evoke 'awe' and 'terror' in the minds of people, it can become a source for a different web of social relationships.

Granted that "humans are born with fear potential, just as they are born with anger potential and joy potential,"[66] fear *as a potential*[67] can play a significant role in labelling experience, organizing feelings and channelling the expression of both these for the benefit of oneself and that of others.[68] Fear provides "the capacity to act in accordance with the chain of events and circumstances and, finally, it means the ability to teach this process to others that they also may profit from fearing."[69] This type of understanding of 'fear' and 'fear potential' is appropriated by the folk through religious rituals not only to lead a pragmatic life free of phylogenetic dangers,[70] but also to evolve a new subaltern social discourse of identity assertion. This discourse is rooted in the concept of 'fear' and explicates the subaltern's capability to tap the available resources of the given folk life-world and to innovate new manifestations of socio-religious systems and symbolic universes for the sake of identity assertion.

A 'hierarchy of control' is implicit in folk's understanding of fear and the connotations of fear. Human beings are afraid of the *pēy(s)* (malevolent spirits), and these spirits, in turn, are afraid of small gods; and these gods are afraid of CM, and the hierarchy goes on. Now, it is believed that the evil dead and the evil spirits control human beings, the small/minor gods control evil spirits, and the Major god controls small/minor gods.[71] But, according to the CM myth, CM seems uncontrollable and intractable. This is what makes CM the god of 'power' ('*Tuṭiyāṉa Teyvam*': a common appellation used in this area to refer to the powerful nature of this folk deity). He is an uncontrolled power "which is not contained within a recognised hierarchy but appears, rather, as an immanent force unlocated in time and space and effective in a capricious and rampant manner."[72] Besides, CM belongs to the danger zone in village life, i.e., to the cremation ground. Hence, according to the folk worldview, it is regarded as one of the most difficult things to satisfy this ferocious deity. To perform *vēṭṭai* and other rituals is dangerous for the ones who do it. Hence, the Brahmins of Naduvakurichi handed them over to Dalits - Paḷḷar(s) who took them up because their life is connected with cremation grounds, the danger zone.

This implies that the village society at Naduvakurichi–which is a hierarchical caste society–perceives and acknowledges the Dalits' ability to control the dangerous power of CM, the most "fearsome" god. This social fact gives Dalits an impetus to protest against domination and inequality by engaging in subtle and symbolic forms of rituals. Such acts are not seen by others [Tēvar(s)] to be devoid of social content as subaltern expression of ritual power in society is concomitant with the increasing betterment of social positions of Dalits in the post independence era.[73] This has obviously led to tensions in some instances.[74] But in most of the times, it has not led to caste-violence, because fear of CM's uncontrollable power safeguards their vulnerability, as noted in the case of *cāmiyāṭi* of Naduvakurichi.[75]

At Valliyoor where Brahmins defied the Dalits' CM by snatching away the stone-tub of his temple, CM displayed dominion and power over them by punishing them and making them give due respect to the Dalits in the cult. Here the Brahmin's violation of Brahmanical purity is engaged in not so much out of love for CM, as out of fear of him. Here, fear functions as a cause for the violation of religious rules of Brahminic Hinduism in one's individual life in the first place. Besides, this 'fear' plays the role of including the 'impure' Dalits in Brahminic temple worship, making them co-pilgrims and co-*pūcāri(s)* -priests, and it is fear which puts both Brahmins and Dalits on parity as devotees of CM within the same temple precincts. An outcaste in the classical temple becomes an equal partner in the folk temple, as we have noted elsewhere. What undergirds this social inversion is the "fear" of the power of the god. This status of 'equality' of Dalits with Brahmins at Valliyoor took place in the pre-independence era much before the state began to consider all castes equal.[76]

Here 'equality' between two different socially unequal groups is obtained not through legislation of state law but through the divine compulsion propelled by "fear". What the state legislation managed to enact at least in letter with regard to Temple entry,[77] if not in reality in all cases, the subaltern religious realm achieved both in letter and in reality a hundred and fifty years ago. The Hindu feudal society began to experience the simmering glimpses of equality in the folk religious terrain, at a time when the feudal economic system began to change into 'market' economy,[78] and the formation of a non-partisan 'state' gradually began taking shape under the British Raj.

Further, CM is also a transcendent force through his power of encompassment, as we have noted in chapter four. Through his power, he is believed to transcend space and time and demonstrate his power of protection by playing havoc with the evil forces. It is this power of protection that makes him as *kāval teyvam* (guardian deity) and this is believed to provide a sense of security and identity, especially when the social actors find themselves caught up in the mire of insecurity and loss of identity[79] caused by urbanisation, modernisation and globalisation.

In this context, it is to be noted that the symbolic universe structures and is structured by the social universe. Caste hierarchy can be viewed here as a system of 'hierarchy of control' as discussed above. In the peri-centralisation process, what a subaltern is empowered to do subverts, reverses and inverts the 'hierarchy of control' of the caste system by tapping the resources of symbolic systems. While relying on the 'hierarchy of control' of CM, he draws his 'symbolic capital' from the system of 'hierarchy of control' implicit in the connotations of the 'fear of CM', invents a new social script and articulates a new discourse of 'hierarchy of control' in the social realm. In other words, pericentralisation makes it possible for the subalterns to avail themselves of the symbolic resources, percolating from the 'fear of CM' to draft a new and different hierarchy of social control, as we have noted elsewhere in the book.

In the CM cult, a subaltern discovers a potential weapon of authority to wield a 'new hierarchy of control'. He affirms, confirms, enforces and reinforces not only a new structure of 'hierarchy of control' but also a mechanism of such control by which he inscribes a new *spatiality or spatialization* of bodily movements for high castes and Brahmins. In the age-old Sanskritic Hinduism, the 'caste hierarchy of control' defined and determined the spatialisation of the bodily movements of the subalterns by its demarcation of the pure and the impure spaces and the people, and by restricting the bodily movements of the impure *avarnas* and Sudras from entering the lived space of the twice-born. But in the peri-centralisation process, by making use of the implications of the 'fear of CM', the subalterns invent a new mechanism 'to bend and to break in practice'[80] the old rules of 'hierarchy of control'. They create new forms of 'spatialisation' not only for the high castes and Brahmins, by making them visit the lived spaces of the subalterns, but also for themselves by establishing new forms of third spaces by the same acts.

Through the subaltern ritual realm, Dalits can pose two kinds of threats for the twice born: one, fear of loss of internal authority in the caste hierarchy, and the other, fear of loss of identity.[81] This shows that the surplus of ritual power based on the fear of CM, as we noted earlier in this chapter, can generate 'threats' and 'fears' in the social arena.

In displaying the newly acquired social power the subalterns employ the traditional mechanism of rituals, which better serve against traditional enemies, wherein the reputation of fear of CM is used as a powerful force for caution against attacks on their social ascendancy.

The Role of 'Temple Honour' in Subaltern Religious Universe in Peri-centralisation Process

Subaltern Counter Politics of Temple Honour

In classical/major temples, 'honours' were given, ordered and dispensed first to the ruler (the king), then to the topmost authority of power in the traditional village administration (i.e., village headmen, *nāṭṭāmai*) and then to others according to one's position in the caste hierarchy. In particular, as Nicholas Dirks has shown, these village headmen were representatives of kings.[82] These honours had their material basis in the gift of land or other endowments to the temple as Dirks, Appadurai,[83] and Ludden[84] have shown through their studies in the Tamil region.

At the decline and suppression of these 'little kingdoms' by the British when bureaucratic rationalization of temple management and appointment of new mirasidars/trustees came into vogue, there arose, as a consequence, conflicts with regard to honours. "Honours were explicitly given a price"[85] and subsequently there was a bureaucratic construction of separation of honour into two kinds: "those granted to the government officers and those granted to the heads of traditional kinship groups."[86] New temple honours were created and old ones were changed by the royal power. By making use of the royal power, wealth and social status, a human agent could usurp temple honours. It was not the deity, but these factors that determined the relationship between the deity and a human agent in a particular temple. But in the subaltern temple, the relationship between the deity and the human agent in question is not usurped or cannot be usurped, but is endowed by the deity. Often it is intimately related to one's role as a source of origination of a temple and subsequently one acquires honour (*mariyātai*) gratuitously, regardless of one's social status and economic power.

Historically, the structure of honour underwent change in the major temples in relation to the change in political power and change in temple administration, often leading to conflicts, the developments of which have been described by Appadurai and Dirks.[87] But the structure of 'honour' in a subaltern folk temple does not undergo major change, but rather remains constant, safeguarding them in their social vulnerability against any possible intrusion of hegemonic hierarchy into the spaces of honour. It does accord new 'honour' to those in power, but that in no way alters the first honour (*mutal mariyātai*) neither does it substitute other honours which have been customarily followed, nor does it fix them at an appointed time, superseding the old honours.

In non-subaltern folk temples,[88] there are evidences of disputes over 'honour' held by the non-subalterns. There, the disputes are not between two dominant lineage groups/ families as seen in major temples, but between the lower group and the dominant group which arise from the former's audacity to defy and de-recognise the honour and privilege held by the dominant groups. Here, a close scrutiny of such episodes reveals that disputes arise not over claiming equality of honour, but over the primacy of honour usurped by a patron, as in major temples, through his social status, economic wealth and political power by someone (a subaltern) who is accorded an inferior rank of honour in spite of the fact that he/she (a subaltern) is so central and his service so essential to the ritual complex. Here, however, the dispute is over an issue that is very crucial to the very structure of the ritual complex, raised by someone without whom its structure cannot be sustained. By doing this, the subaltern displays his power to divest the ritual of its vitality that can result in the 'zombification'[89] of the ritual complex.[90] Thus, a subaltern obtains an occasion of power to negotiate terms at the level of honour with the dominant groups in the arena of non-subaltern folk religiosity. But the audacity to negotiate terms with the dominant group does not occur in a situation of economic dependence, but it is concomitant with the change in economic structures, fluidity of the caste-system and the political organization of subaltern consciousness.

Appadurai observes that, not only "organizational and cultural complexity,"[91] but also the enormous amount of jewellery and wealth vested in temples required that there was a need for someone, a supreme power, a ruler in the country (king) to 'oversee' it. While that applies to the major temples, minor gods need no protection. They themselves are considered as kings. A folk/minor god can protect himself and his people. The fact that the temple of subaltern gods had no roofs, no enclosures and no doors confirmed both the facts that they needed no protection from kings, on the one hand, and, conversely, kings/rulers had little/less control over them, on the other. This privilege of 'autonomy' or 'non-privilege' of royal protection is given not by the fact that folk/subaltern gods have no wealth endowed with them[92] and no honours endowed by them, but it is produced by the 'active agency' of folk deity[93] in contrast to the 'passive benevolence' of major gods and by the social function of 'terror'/'fear' unleashed by the ritual power of a folk deity. As Dirks and others have shown, major temples have required "protection and occasional intervention of kings" because "temple honours create a great deal of conflict over issues of rank and authority."[94] But, folk deities are perceived to be capable of arbitrating or adjudicating conflict about honour, either through direct intervention by the mechanics of divine possession on someone who makes 'claims' to honour or through the divination of a *cāmiyāṭi* in possession.

Both at Naduvakurichi and at Kayatar, one observes resistance and unwillingness of the people towards the government takeover of the temple. The prevailing fear is that the government will deprive them of their monetary and symbolic capital in the future and impose the religious hegemony of the major religions on them. Such an imposition is recorded as early as the beginning of the twentieth century in Pudukottai district[95] and the Tamilnadu government had carried out such an unwarranted legal imposition–a 'ban on animal sacrifices,'[96] in the recent past.

Dynamics of 'Temple Honour' in the Downward Iteration of Pericentralisation Process

In the Tirunelveli region, during the late sixteenth and early seventeenth centuries, the Pāḷaiyakāraṉ(s) or Poligars steadily grew[97] under Nayaka rule.[98] The new Marava or other chiefs developed a relationship with an imperial king who endowed them with the gifts of emblems, titles and land. The chiefs became little kings when they emulated the actions of kingly overlords by giving gifts to temples and Brahmins:

> These gifts linked individuals and corporate groups symbolically, morally and politically with the sovereignty of the king, great or little. They created a moral unity and a political hierarchy. ... These gifts, of "real" and "symbolic" resources, were neither token nor signs of political weakness. In many of the smaller states in eighteenth century Tamilnadu, between sixty and eighty percent of all cultivable land was given away to military chiefs, retainers, temples, Brahmans[99], village officers, priests, servants and artisans.[100]

When the British Raj took over the administration, many of the *iṉām* (tax-free) lands were scrapped, their privileges were stripped, and the village officers, mostly Brahmins and

Veḷḷāḷars, who functioned as the intermediaries between the locals and the government, became very rich landowners, as we have seen in the second chapter. The village *Munsiff* (headman) was appointed to keep the village accounts of the land revenue and maintain law and order.[101] Village officers turned out to be "the key store of the arch" of the Madras administration,[102] and village headmen "remained resourceful peasant leaders endowed with symbols of authority, superior economic assets and powerful local allies."[103]

In Valliyoor, the Brahmins who worship CM belong to the family of village officers (VAOs) These Brahmin VAO's appropriation/worship of CM must be seen as a strategy of escalating one's command over the symbolic and material capital of one's rule,[104] which the little kings or Pāḷaiyakāraṉ(s) had followed. On the one hand they realised the fame of CM as a god of 'power' that protects the things of wealth, cattle and fields, and rightly recognized that its worship is closely associated with symbolic and material capital. On the other hand, they realized that, to have a command over people, the ruler/administrator has to have command over their symbolic and material capital. This is what led the VAO's family to pursue the worship of CM in the mixed zone, the strategy they seemingly learned from the Pāḷaiyakāraṉ(s) in the dry zone.

Dirks, Ludden and others have shown how Pāḷaiyakāraṉ(s) grew to the status of 'little kings' by obtaining symbolic capital through 'gift-relationship' not only with the Nayaka overlords but also with temples, Brahmins, servants, artisans and members of royal castes.[105] But Brahmins at Valliyoor differed in their strategy of appropriation of material capital. The neighbouring Pāḷaiyakāraṉ(s) made use of 'plunder', rather than the revenue system or bureaucratic rule, as a political modality to engage in 'expansive and incorporative activity' of material capital.[106] But the Brahmins made use of their authority as VAOs given by 'revenue systems' and vested in bureaucratic rule to plunder land and wealth, by registering vast tracts of land in their own name, as Ludden has noted.[107] While, for the Pāḷaiyakāraṉ (s), 'plunder' was a suitable alternative of political modality to revenue system, for the VAOs, the revenue system became an enabling antecedent to 'plunder' of a different kind. However, just as CM worship was originally associated with the event of 'plunder' as noted earlier in the second chapter, so also it came to be associated with the Brahmins at Valliyoor.

Besides, it had been the case down the history in Tamil Society, that the ideology of the sovereignty of the king was constituted by the sovereignty of the major deity, Civā or Visnu. The king was indeed regarded as the *avatara* of the god himself. Many local chiefs received honour in the temple by participating in the granting of royal gifts. In doing so, they established a relationship with the "king predicated on the sharing of king's sovereignty."[108] This meant that the chief was a minor sovereign, having his power and control over a territory. As we have just seen, studies of peasant history done in this area reveal that village officers came to enjoy a kind of sovereignty at the time of the British administration. In Valliyoor, where Brahmins became village headmen, they sought their sovereignty over land not only through administrative powers, but through ritual powers too. In classical Temples, where the Maṟavar kings (*Aivarājākkaḷ)* were given honour, they were neglected. It meant their newly acquired and growing sovereignty was unrecognised. Hence, they appropriated the subaltern religious realm to ratify their sovereignty. Subaltern temple honours and titles constituted, governed, consolidated and reinforced a kind of minuscule administrative power of governance for Brahmins.

The type of sovereignty acquired and manifested in the subaltern temple in the person of *cāmiyāṭi* is different from that of the classical temple. Unlike as in the classical temple where the concept of "*cāmiyāṭi*" is absent, mere wealth cannot acquire such honours in a subaltern temple. The honour of a *cāmiyāṭi* is the gratuitous gift of a god. Anyone is entitled to such an honour both in theory and in practice. Secondly, sovereignty is given concrete expression in physical terms in subaltern temples. *Vēṭṭai* demonstrates his control over physical territories and lands. His verbal expressions during divination show that he embodies a power that has control over the lives of people, both of which are absent in the strategies of 'honour' in major temples. In major temples, the acts of honour do not constitute the content of sovereignty, while the very act of acquiring of honour and its strategies of display through rituals like *vēṭṭai* constitute, manifest and reinforce the idea of sovereignty in the subaltern religious universe.

In Valliyoor, in the case of the Brahmins, it can be shown that the *cāmiyāṭis*' acquiring of honour corresponds to the ground reality that manifests his sovereignty. As a village officer, he was in control of the "territory" and also in the case of Sirumalanchi where a low caste *cāmiyāṭi* is the panchayat president. But in most of the cases, the sovereignty of a *cāmiyāṭi* does not correspond to human administrative powers over territories, but stands for the trans-human power over the territory. It is to be recalled that the lands of the Brahmins did not enjoy the patronage of the Nayaka rule[109] any more after their fall, and they did not have enough of protection. Even though the Brahmins were landlords, who were *Kāṇiyāṭcikkāraṉ(s)-*(overseers), as we have seen in chapter two, they were never involved with the land. They were not at home with its possession. Hence they were psychologically vulnerable to be attacked by both the non-human (evil spirits of the uncultivable land) and human forces (the dacoits), the Kallars. In such a predicament, they had to find their own means of protection of land from Maṟavar(s). Brahmin landlords at Valliyoor obtained protection of their land by appropriating the god of the periphery, CM. Accumulation of land brought them wealth but not real security. They sought protection and safety by worshipping CM who is a *kāvalkāraṉ* (guardian) par excellence, whom everybody was afraid of. No one would ever dare to approach the temple at night, as recalled by the elders in the village. By implanting such a god in their backyard, they protected their harvest and cattle.

Autonomy of Subaltern Religious Universe in Pericentralisation Process

It is generally a popular notion, espoused also by some scholars,[110] that the subaltern religious universe is a preparatory process towards Brahminic Hinduism, an initial phase which progresses towards the better phase of major religious tradition. It implies an assumption that the subaltern religious universe as it evolves gets purified and sanskritised, revealing thereby its increasing dependency on Sanskritic Hinduism. Such a process implies a diminution of folk/ subaltern religious elements.

Though the CM cult is not an exception to this development, what emerges strongly is the continuation of the core of subaltern folk rituals and maintenance of their subaltern nature. This is not to deny the 'sanskritising' tendency of the cult, which is evident in the ceremony of sanctification (*Pratishta*) that is held once in twelve years or more for CM temple, and in the saying of Sanskritic mantras by the Brahmin *pūcāri(s)* as witnessed in Vijaynarayanam. The growth of the CM cult is not merely one of Sanskritic nature but predominantly one of development of the ritual corpus of the subaltern religious universe. As the CM cult spreads from one place to the other, what is continued and maintained primarily are the non-Sanskritic subaltern/folk rituals. Even as the pomp and the extravaganza of the *koṭai* of a particular CM temple grow, the occurrences of non-Sanskritic rituals only increase and do not diminish. The 'must'-continuation of these core rituals of non-Sanskritic nature in the CM cult, which are based more on the logic of 'fear,' is one of the key factors that has continued to maintain its autonomy as a subaltern religious phenomenon, in spite of attempts of sanskritisation by the upstart caste groups such Maṟavar(s) and Illatu Piḷḷaimār(s) as we saw in the ethnography of the cult. Another dimension that helped the continuation of its autonomy is the matrix of divination, which attracts people from various walks of life.

Even when the social actors belonging to the highest echelons of Indian society, the Brahmins, the protagonists of Sanskritic Hinduism began worshipping CM, they could not do away with non-Sanskritic subaltern rituals. To ensure their devotion to CM and to maintain their newly acquired economic status, they had to maintain the autonomy of the non-Sanskritic ritual repertoire of the CM cult.

Peri-centralisation: An Assessment

A Process Different from De-Sanskritisation and Sanskritisation

The process of peri-centralisation is not to be equated with the de-sanskritisation mentioned by M.N. Srinivas[111] In his view, de-sanskritisation refers to the fact of non-dominant (intermediary) castes being influenced by the culture of the non-sanskritised dominant castes, which he terms as risk. What is perhaps implicit in his remark is his fear that such imitated behaviour patterns of the dominant caste will not merit social status. But the field experience of the present research has revealed that the intermediary Reṭṭiyār(s) and Veḷḷāḷar(s) have appropriated the rituals of CM (rituals of a caste lower than theirs) that is closer to the bottom than to the top in the hierarchy. This is so, precisely because it gave them social security, and it legitimised their ritual power into social authority. Here *peri-centralisation* functions as a process by which the higher caste adopts the rituals/life styles of lower castes, the process by which the higher caste transforms their ritual power into social authority and social status. It clearly indicates that in this case Brahminic ideology is not the source of legitimisation for these middle castes. Moreover, some Brahmins of this district themselves seek the legitimacy of the subaltern rituals.

In the Brahminic *peri-centralisation*, the non-priestly Brahmins do not need the priestly Brahmin for performing their rituals as in Sanskritic Hinduism, since that function is fulfilled by the 'ritual persona'. Generally speaking, among Brahmins, priestly Brahmins in Sanskritic Hinduism have low social status because they are paid by their patrons like other dependent castes,[112] while in *peri-centralisation* discourse the Brahmin *cāmiyāṭi* at Valliyoor is a landlord, who is certainly more respected than his priestly counterpart in Sanskritic Hinduism.[113] Similarly the priestly shaman of the lower castes commands more respect from his own community than his Brahminic counterpart in Sanskritic Hinduism does from his community. Even outside their community the Dalit shaman gets more respect than other Dalits, while a priestly Brahmin gets less respect than other Brahmins. Furthermore in Sanskritic Hinduism, Brahmin families who specialize in the performance of funeral rituals are considered to be inferior to other Brahmins[114] because of their ritual association with the dead. But on the contrary, the Brahmin shaman, despite his ritual association with the dead at the cremation ground, seems to enjoy greater social privilege. This clearly reveals the asymmetry of ritual power between sanskritisation and *peri-centralisation* in the first place and, secondly, it also indicates how the subaltern religious realm and *peri-centralisation* discourse contradicts the logic of Sanskritic Hinduism.

In the sanskritisation process, social scientists have noted that the names indicative of caste are being given up in favour of Sanskritic names while naming the children.[115] In the *peri-centralisation* process, the name of the subaltern god CM are preserved by the Dalits and are increasingly adopted by the intermediary castes for whatever reason. In Naduvakurchi the name 'Kaḷḷattiāṉ' is a popular name among Maṟavar(s) and Reṭṭiyārs.

According to M.N. Srinivas, sanskritisation presupposes for the lower castes a "higher group self-consciousness" which results from the contact with a source of the "Great Tradition" of Hinduism.[116] But *peri-centralisation* presupposes the lower group's religious consciousness resulting from the contact of the ritual corpus of Little Traditions. Furthermore, sanskritisation leads to a heightened sensitivity to the ideas of purity and pollution.[117] This implies that in the process of sanskritisation the low caste constantly takes the initiative to be pure, alienates itself from its age-old customs, rituals, habits that could be seen as impure and polluting by the high castes. However, in the *peri-centralisation* process, the Brahmins have to imitate and emulate the rites and rituals of the lower castes, which involve blood sacrifices and other rituals that establish contact with the bones of the dead in the cremation ground. The whole repertoire of such rituals is definitely impure and defiling. It is demeaning and dehumanising for the Brahmins who are supposed to be custodians of purity in Sanskritic Hinduism.

Seen from the angle of the subaltern people, sanskritisation is a process of alienation. It disassociates the lower castes from their customs, habits and rituals. It uproots them from their socio-eco-cultural context and estranges them from their moorings of the subaltern worldview. But *peri-centralisation* gives their local sub-cultures a pride of place. It affirms and confirms their age-old rituals, habits and customs. It reinstates them in their cultural roots. It proclaims and propagates their ritual power to other dominant groups, not by distancing themselves from their original native sub-culture, but by reinstating their religious legacy in the minds and hearts of others.

Further, in Sanskritic Hinduism, the high castes were prohibited from accepting cooked food and drinking water from the lower castes, and the latter were prohibited from coming into physical proximity with the former or entering the inner portions of the houses of the upper castes. While the urbanization process makes this segregation discourse increasingly redundant, *peri-centralisation* takes the contestation of segregation back to its original site of village settings. First, in the ritual context of CM Cult, the Brahmins at Valliyoor have to closely associate with the washermen and Dalits (*sampāṉ*), where there is close physical contact between them. In *paṭaippu* , the Brahmin has to pretend to eat the food cooked by Dalits on behalf of CM. Dalits and others are also allowed to go into the Brahmins' house to visit the source tree of CM as we saw in the ethnography of the CM cult at Valliyoor. All these activities help explode the myth of segregation but subtly in the village setting.

Similarly, at Naduvakurichi, the subaltern CM cult and ritual power brings the Brahmins/Maṟavar(s)/Reṭṭiyār(s) and other more or less dominant castes to the Dalit-CM's unclean and polluted space. His hamlet is no more a segregated region. Ritual power incorporates, integrates and transforms the polluted outer space into the social space. The polluted outer space is no more a confinement, no more an unencompassed and unencompassable social space. As the ritual power becomes all encompassing, it transforms the 'unencompassed space' into the 'encompassed', 'inaccessible' into 'accessible', 'non-negotiable' social space into a 'negotiable' one, and symbolically makes the unencompassable social space all encompassing. The traversing of the Dalit locality by the dominant castes is not a mere one-time annual activity during *koṭai* but a regular occurrence that takes place every Tuesday and Friday when people go to CM temple and to the house of shaman to tap CM's ritual power. Thus *peri-centralisation* underlies a process of integration and incorporation for the subalterns.

A Process Different from Asprashyeekaran

The process of *peri-centralisation* needs to be distinguished from *Asprashyeekaran* (Encompassing Untouchability) described by Shyamlal.[118] According to the author, "*Asprashyeekaran* is the process by which a high or low caste person or a tribal accepts membership of an untouchable caste and thereby lowers his social as well as ritualistic position. He loses his previous caste identity over a period of time, say, in a generation or two. The process of Asprashyeekaran also involves imbibing the customs and beliefs and adopting the ways of life of a lower or an untouchable caste."[119] It is a process of de-sanskritisation and conversion,[120] effecting a change of identity of upper castes such as Rajputs, Brahmins, Jats and Charans of Rajashthan into lower untouchable castes such as Bhangis, Chamars, Bhambhis, Jatavas etc.

While *Asprashyeekaran* speaks about the change of identity and embracing of untouchability for various reasons, the process of *peri-centralisation*, like that of Sanskritisation, focuses not on conversion of a social group but on the adoption and imitation of the culturo-religious behaviour of one social group by another for the purpose of legitimisation or usurpation of social power or socio-economic status. Further, while *Asprashyeekaran* is characterised by the process of downward *mobility*, '*peri-centralisation*', strictly speaking, is characterised by downward *iteration*. While the former is qualified by the permanent change of caste identity which results in the lowering of the social status of a high caste caused by the adoption of the culture of low castes, the latter is typified by its temporary fluidity, ambivalence of identities. It is characterised by oscillation between multiple caste identities caused by the periodically repeated emulation of culturo-religious activity of either high castes by the low castes or those of low castes by the high castes or of both by the intermediary castes. Besides, the motivational factors of *Asprashyeekaran* are distinctily different from those of *peri-centralisation*. As Shyamlal enlists in his book, the reasons for the change of the high castes into low castes were either excommunication, or defeat or an escape from new foreign rule.[121] But the reasons for *peri-centralisation* are none of the above. As mentioned many a time in the book, it occurs often for the purpose of sanctioning of one's newly acquired status or as an act of tapping of ritual power to overcome the negative predicaments of human living.

A Process Different from Universalisation and Parochialisation

Through his ethnographic study of Kishan Gari village and in his attempt to explain the fluidity of the caste system in place of the unified theory of sanskritisation, McKim Marriott proposed two alternative concepts: 'universalisation' and 'parochialisation'. Universalisation refers to the process of the great tradition's carrying forward of materials which are already present in the little traditions which it encompasses. Such a great tradition has authority in so far as it constitutes a more articulate and refined restatement or systematisation of what is already there.[122] On the other hand, parochialisation refers to the fact of the unlearned and non-literate little tradition obstructing the direct transmission or spread of elements downward from the great to the little. Downward spread, like universalisation, is likely to be characterized by transformations.[123] In both these concepts, the little and folk traditions are explained only *relationally*, in terms of their relationship to the great tradition and from the viewpoint of the spread of the great tradition. Thus the discourse does not consider folk religion *per se*. Hence the subaltern agencies' role in the little tradition in contesting and negotiating the social boundaries is overlooked. Moreover, universalisation does not clarify the question, "universalisation of what?" Is it of the great tradition, or the little tradition? Though Marriott begins his discourse on universalisation with reference to the great tradition, later on he moves on to the universalising feature of little local traditions. Naturally one wonders if and how the definition/description of universalisation meant to explain the proselytising character of the great tradition can adequately describe and capture the dynamics of the spread of folk cults.

In contrast, the *'peri-centralisation'* process takes the phenomenon of the subaltern religious universe per se and tries to locate it in the social context from where it emerges and in which it is rooted. Primarily, it takes the subaltern religious universe as an autonomous entity by itself and does not attach 'great' significance to its relationship to the 'great tradition'. In relating it to the social contexts, it unfolds its relationship with different social actors and unearths the submerged meanings of the social dynamics that lie hidden behind the ritual power. In this engagement, it attempts to theorize on the social processes in relation to the different *social actors* of various religious universes (great/little tradition), but not in relation to mere interaction between these universes. In other words, the theoretical concerns are raised and analytical tools are evolved from the viewpoint of subaltern social actors, not from the viewpoint of the institutions of the great traditions.

Conclusion

To sum up the discussion in this chapter, the comparison of the interpretation of CM's *koṭai* rituals at Valliyoor with Naduvakurichi reveals how "each ritual complex constructs a social body befitting the specific historical circumstances in which these rituals operate, each addressing different concerns and ritualising different contrasts."[124] As Comaroff notes of the *Tshidi* of South Africa, our study also indicates that ritual can afford the orchestered expression–and therein the symbolic display–of key experiences of contradiction between the assumptions of the old cultural order[125] of the *varnashrama dharma* and the new conditions of emerging socio-economic orders. In the case of Valliyoor, the ritual takes us back to the historical moment wherein Brahmins displayed a contradiction between the expectations of Brahminic Hinduism and their adoption of subaltern religious behaviour paaterns necessitated by the change in their socio-economic status as VAO's and landlords. In the case of Paḷḷar(s) at Naduvakurichi, the ritualised body brings to the fore the contradiction between the social practices ascribed to the subalterns by the caste hierarchy and their new modes of spatialities triggered off by the dynamics of economic orders and developmental projects in the modernisation process.

While the former's ritualised body self-referentially highlights the ambivalences of the topmost order within the caste hierarchy, the symbolic schemes of the subaltern's ritualised body could mean that the assumptions of caste hierarchy can be questioned by someone who was always regarded as an outsider or outcaste (Dalit). And this new position of power vested in the subaltern's ritualised body with schemes to repair an aberrant social order is recognised by everyone within and without the caste hierarchy and cannot be questioned. Thus, as Foucault and Comaroff observe, ritual practices become "those social practices that localise power relations within social body, creating an economy or hierarchy of power relations inscribed as a whole within each other."[126] In the case of the subalterns, the ritualised body becomes more subversive, as it contrives to appropriate and control key symbols of power, and thereby aims at altering and reinscribing the old systems of meaning schemes.

To conclude, this last chapter has endeavoured to engage in a dialogue with the concept of 'sanskritisation' from a twin perspective: from the perspective of the performance of 'ritual power' and from the subaltern perspective. These perspectives, based on the findings and analyses of the phenomenon of the CM cult in the Tirunelveli district, have, in the process, themselves been deepened and enriched, on the one hand; and they have facilitated the critique of 'sanskritisation' in this new context, and given birth to another concept, *'peri-centralisation'* on the other. It is to be noted that *peri-centralisation* is a process, not a product. Hence, its dynamism is likely to generate more and more new horizons, which call for more such explorations in other contexts, as undertaken in this chapter.

Notes

1. In *The Cohesive Role of Sanskritization and Other Essays*, Oxford University Press, Delhi, 1989, 56.
2. In understanding the concept of Sanskritic Hinduism, I adopt the meaning initially given by M.N. Srinivas, and used by other contemporary theoreticians like Romila Thapar.
3. Clifford Geertz, *The Interpretation of Cultures: Selected Essays*, Basic Books, New York, 1973, 95.
4. Dube, 2.
5. According to the myth recounted in the village tradition of the low caste people, when a rich Brahmin VAO (village administrative officer) family shifted a stone-tub from the Dalit's CM temple premises to his house, CM came along with it and demanded worship from them.
6. A Dalit lady, Aavudaiachi, brought a fish from the river and was about to cut the fish when it spoke up: "I've come to bring good fortune, don't kill me!" Then the frightened lady left the fish in the Brahmin house. From then on, the Brahmin family had difficult times for two years and when they approached the soothsayer, they were told that Cuṭalaimāṭaṉ had come home and that, if he were to be worshipped, all misfortunes would vanish. Thus, the concerned Brahmin family put up an altar in front of their house under Kaḷḷatti tree (hence the deity, CM is called Kaḷḷattiāṉ), and gave *koṭai.* The deity did not accept it because the offerings were only vegetarian items. Then by lots they decided to ask the Pallars to give *koṭai* to CM on their behalf and gave for this purpose the children's burial ground. There the Dalits put up an altar for Kaḷḷattiāṉ and began worshipping CM.
7. One of the factors that has provided the Brahmin families the liberty to take to Dalit's rituals is the fact that caste panchayats have become legally redundant after independence resulting in the loss of their hold over its members as regards social intercourse, the customs of the caste regarding feasts and other ceremonies. (cf. M.N. Srinivas, ed. *Caste: Its Twentieth Century Avatar*, Viking, New Delhi, 1996. 89).

8. It is in place to remember that both in Valliyoor and Naduvakurichi, the Dalits find an important place in the origin-myths of CM-worship among the Brahmins.

9. Cited in Morris, *Anthropolical Studies*, 220.

10. As context opens up different layers of meanings of the text in hermeneutics, so too the locus of a social event is a site of interpretation for the social anthropologist providing a gamut of wealth of social meaning.

11. In Valliyoor where the Brahmins have numerical strength and economic power (dominant caste), they have appropriated the surplus of ritual power to safeguard their power, whereas in Naduvakurchi where they have no numerical strength and economic power, they have given up ritual leadership which they have appropriated to the Dalits.

12. As cited in Diane Paul Mines, "Hindu Periods of Death 'Impurity'", *Contributions to Indian Sociology*, 23/1 (1989), 103-130.

13. It is regarded as a later development by Dumont, Tambiah and Marglin as they note that "shortened period of impurity may reflect the Brahman author's self-interested desire to minimize the 'austerities' imposed upon themselves as survivors." (*ibid.* 104) They derive this conclusion, as Kane observes that Manu (5.84) and other lawgivers raise their voices against lengthy-periods of incapacity as escapes from Brahmin's more urgent duties such as the Vedic study and maintaining everyday "purity". They propose to minimize the definition and duration of death-caused incapacity as ways of controlling "laziness." Cf. Mines, ibid. This can very well point to the prevailing rule of longer period of 'impurity' for the Brahmins at the time of Manu, as it is commonsense that the whiter the cloth is, the more the possibility of getting stronger stains.

14. Cf. *The Laws of Manu*, trans. W. Doniger, Penguin Books, New Delhi, 1991, 58-73.

15. Mr. Anadaraman, the *cāmiyāṭi*, a retired VAO, could not implement his inner urge because of opposition from his family as he himself acknowledged in the interview with the researcher.

16. Fiana Bowie, *The Anthropology of Religion*, Blackwell Publishers, Oxford, 2000, 70-89

17. Karanath, "Caste in Contemporary Rural India", in *Caste*, ed. Srinivas, 100.

18. The exercise of ritual power is not merely temporary, since ritual activities take place throughout the year. People go to the temples on Tuesdays and Fridays for divination. Hence it is not a mere safety valve phenomenon where the suppressed anger of the subalterns towards the dominant caste is given an outlet once a year.

19. The *cāmiyāṭi* of Sirumalanchi is recently elected as the Panchayat president as an independent candidate.

20. While in Maṟavar (BC) village of state temple the *cāmiyāṭi(s)* belong to different castes, both in the Brahmin temple and in the Dalit temple other castes were not allowed to get possessed. This might indicate the unwillingness of the people at the extremes of caste hierarchy to share their opportunities of ritual power with others. It is so, because compared to the middle castes they have only a few opportunities for social mobility. This again shows the determination of these people to monopolize the surplus of ritual power that percolated outside the religious realm.

21. The type of problems that are brought and solutions given by him in divination clearly indicates that he is above everyone and encompasses all.

22. The above-mentioned roles of *cāmiyāṭi* are observed in the rituals of divination and *vēṭṭai.*

23. Cf. Srinivas, *The Cohesive Role,* 62.

24. *Ibid.,* 63.

25. *Ibid.*

26. *Ibid.,* 55-67.

27. Karanath, 'Caste,' 88.

28. Cf. G. Patrick, "An Inquiry into Ayya Vali: A Subaltern Religious Phenomenon in South Tiruvitankur," A Ph.D Thesis of the University of Madras, 2001, 23.

29. The vestiges of feudal system are seen in the dress code and implements of the *cāmiyāṭi,* and in the idioms of the people.

30. *Jajamani* system refers to the Indian feudal system of patronage that existed between the landlord and the farmers. Karanth notes that the decline of *jajamani* relationships has accelerated the process of dissociation of castes and traditional occupations, forcing the specialists castes to look to avenues for earning a

livelihood. Such disassociation was further accelerated by other factors such industrialization, the spread of education, urbanization and the emergence of new occupations. Karanath, 'Caste,' 90.

31. Cf. Forster, "The Depressed Classes and Conversion to Christianity" in *Religion in South Asia*, ed. Oddie, Manohar, New Delhi, 1991, 71.

32. Cf. Diane P. Mines in "Hindu Nationalism." Here the author has shown how the people of Yanaimangalam in Tirunelveli district drew on regional and national movements as they contested the social and spatial contours of their local lives and their villages through ritual action.

33. Steven M. Parish, *Hierarchy and Its Discontents*, Calcutta, Oxford University Press, 1997, 113.

34. People make use of one of these identities, both to benefit from government schemes and to liberate themselves from the clutches of oppression. For this purpose, they fall back upon one of the multiple identities as and when it proves to be useful. For instance, if they cannot get something done by making use of the identity of caste, they will make use of their religious identity. At times, one identity prevails over others and gets clearly polarized in a particular area. For example, during caste clashes different multiple identities might fuse into one identity, namely, caste. What is to be noted here is that the possibilities of multiple identities did not exist for the oppressed groups during the time of the feudal order.

35. Here I differ from Karanth in his view that the former "untouchables", find it extremely difficult to move away from their traditional duties inside and outside the network of *jajamani* relations. My field data does not support this view. I find that the degree of occupational mobility of Dalits is as good as that of Thevars.

36. According to him, functioning vector refers to the person's actual realization, while capability set refers to alternative combination of functioning vectors from which a person can choose. Cf. Amartya Sen, *Development as Freedom*, Oxford University Press, New Delhi, 2000, 79.

37. A native Tamil scholar told me that the shape of the alter at Kayatar and the symbol of half-moon on it is the result of influence of Islam on folk Hinduism. Similarly Vaikundasami

integrated Saivism and Vaishnavism at his religious experience at Tiruchendur.

38. This will be discussed later under the heading 'Peri-centralisation: A True Portrayal of Labour Dependency on Low Castes.'

39. This has hampered and foiled the researcher's initiative to record the field-data through conventional methods such as camera and tape recorder, during *koṭai.*

40. Note that the space component of folk religiosity such as the place of worship (field), and non-agamic temple construction can be well contrasted with 'space' component of Sanskritic Hinduism. Cf. Elmore, Whitehead and Sarah Caldwell. While the former is closely associated with the elements of day-to-day economic activity of the people, the latter is alienated from it. One wonders if the process of alienation of symbolic capital is one of the contributing factors that put the Dalits in a subordinated position within the caste hierarchy.

41. Robert Deliege, *Paraiyars du Tamil Nadu,* 1988, 117 as quoted in *The Village in India,* ed. Madan, 281.

42. C.J. Fuller "Rituals of the Village," 282.

43. *Ibid.*

44. As shared by a Brahmin, named Narayanan, in an interview on 20-07-02.

45. Cf. Fox, *Postmodernism.*

46. Cf. Reinche, *Les dieux,* 219-338.

47. Cf. Fox, *Postmodernism.*

48. As shared by a Samban, named Vativelu.

49. David Dean Shulman, "Outcastes, Guardian, and Trickster: Notes on the Myth of Kattavarayan" in *Criminal Gods,* ed., Hiltebeitel, 60.

50. Cf. Rao, *Symbols of Substance,* 313.

51. Cf. Shulman, "Outcastes."

52. *Ibid.,* 58-63.

53. *Ibid.,* 35-63.

54. Cf. Sheldon Pollock, "From Discourse of Ritual to Discourse of Power in Sanskrit Culture," *Journal of Ritual Studies* 2/2 (Summer 1990), 315-345.

55. The words of divination of a *cāmiyāṭi* recorded at Naduvakurichi during *koṭai* festival there.
56. Cf. *Gazetteers of India, Tirunelveli District,* Vol. II.
57. Dirks, *Hollow Crown,* 27.
58. Ludden, *Peseant History.*
59. For a further understanding of the 'Traditional Indian Concept of Power," cf. Jai B P Sinha, *The Cultural Context of Leadership and Power,* Sage Publications, New Delhi, 1995, 140-148.
60. Scruton, *Sociophobics,* 112.
61. David M. Knipe, "Night of the Growing Dead: A Cult of Virabhadra in Coastal Andhra", in *Criminal Gods,* ed., Hiltebeitel, 123-157.
62. Cf., *ibid.*
63. Cf., Scruton, *Sociophobics,* 37.
64. Cf., *ibid.*
65. *Ibid.,* 46-47.
66. *Ibid.,* 39.
67. As we noted in chapter one, according to socio-phobics, fear potential is an inborn capacity to learn fear. Cf., ibid, 39-40.
68. Cf., *ibid.,* 40.
69. *Ibid.*
70. According to the folk worldview, 'dangers' to the well-being of 'human life' come from various sources such as evil spirits, sicknesses, epidemics, etc..
71. Cf. Wadley, *Shakti.*
72. Scruton, *Sociophobics,* 40.
73. Cf. S.V. Rajadurai, *Dalitiyamum Ulaha Muthalaithuvamum,* Vitiyal Pathippagam, 2001, 33-35.
74. Cf. Mines, "Hindu Nationalism."
75. One of the Dalit *cāmiyāṭi*'s son had recently eloped with a Thevar girl during the time of research.
76. Cf. S.V. Rajadurai, *Dalitiyamum,* 33-35.
77. Cf., *ibid.,* 33.
78. Cf. Ludden, *Peseant History.*

79. Such a sense of insecurity and need for the protection is felt not only by the poor, illiterate dalit-bahujans but also by the educated and well qualified Brahmins as in the case of Valliyoor Brahmins.

80. Nick Crossley, "The Phenomenological Habitus and its Construction," *Theory and Society* 30/1 (February 2001), 83.

81. Scruton, *Sociophobics*, 110.

82. Cf. Dirks, *Hollow Crown*.

83. Cf., *ibid.* and Arjun Appadurai, *Worship and Conflict under Colonial Rule: A South Indian* Case, Cambridge University Press, Cambridge, 1981.

84. Cf. Ludden, *Peseant History*.

85. *Ibid.*, 365.

86. *Ibid.*

87. Cf. Appadurai *Worship and Conflict* and Dirks, *Hollow Crown* .

88. Non-subaltern folk temples refer to those temples that belong to the middle castes such as Maravars, Reddiars and Konars who are economically better off and socially considered higher than Dalits. In such temples of CM one observes some initial signs of Sanskritisation.

89. It refers to the process of making something inert.

90. Such a situation was witnessed in Palamadai two years ago where a Dalit *cāmiyāṭi* refused to get blessing from a Maravar before *koṭai* and garland him after *vēṭṭai.* At that time, there was some communal tension that was diffused by an amicable settlement. Cf. Dirks, *Hollow Crown*, 374-377.

91. Appadurai, *Worship and Conflict*, 50.

92. My field data reveals that some acres of land are attached to the *ottapaṉai* Cuṭalai at Vijayanarayanam and the Dalit temple at Naduvakurichi is regarded as very lucrative.

93. One instance of 'active agency' of a subaltern deity is the punishment given by CM at Kayatar to a little king called Vettuperumal because of disrespectful behaviour shown towards him.

94. Dirks, *Hollow Crown*, 287.

95. *Ibid.*, 360.

96. In 2003, the Tamilnadu Government unwarrantedly promulgated a legislation banning the killing of animals in places of worship, which was later revoked towards the end of the year 2004.

97. By providing protection to local communities, often from their own predatory raids, and by consolidating their local authority through the network of their own sub-caste dominance, and wielding ritual and military mechanism they forged new forms of political relationship and replaced the Veḷḷāḷarr chiefs.

98. Dirks, *Hollow Crown*, 52.

99. Gifts to Temples and to Brahmins were primarily given by Pāḷaiyakāraṉ(s) to attain kingly status.

100. Dirks, *Hollow Crown*, 53.

101. *Tirunelvelli District Gazetteer*, Vol. I, 2002, 232.

102. *Ibid.*, 234.

103. *Ibid.*

104. Dirks, *Hollow Crown*, 48.

105. *Ibid.*, 152-154.

106. *Ibid.*

107. Cf. Ludden, *Peasant History*.

108. Dirks, *Hollow Crow*, 29.

109. Cf. Roa, *Symbols of Substance*, 218-219.

110. Scholars who hold this view more implicitly or less explicitly include M.N. Srinivas, Madeleine Biardeau and Reiniche.

111. Cf. M.N. Srinivas, *Cohesive Role*, 66.

112. Ibid., 4.

113. This is true irrespective of the presence of lower caste habits such as meat eating and consumption of liquor among the Valliyoor Brahmin shaman family. This is not to deny the presence of such values in other Brahmins (who have not adopted this cult), which is described as 'dual culture', the result of urban exposure, education and the loss of caste's traditional authority over its member (Cf. Srinivas and Karanth in *Caste*). The same reasons can very well be attributed to the shaman family at Valliyoor. But the striking thing about Valliyoor Bramins is that Dalits openly talk about the presence of such

values and habits among Brahmins, thereby creating a discourse on the adherence of subaltern culture by the Brahmins.

114. Srinivas, *Cohesive Role* 4.
115. Karanth, 'Caste,' 93.
116. *Ibid.*, 77.
117. *Ibid.*, 84.
118. Cf. Shyamlal, *From Higher Caste to Lower Caste: The Process of Sanskritization*, Rawat Publication, New Delhi, 1997.
119. *Ibid*, 51.
120. *Ibid.*, 28.
121. *Ibid.*, 56-66.
122. Cf. McKim Marriott, ed., *Village India*, University of Chicago Press, Chicago, 1955, 197.
123. Ibid.,199.
124. Bell, *The Ritual Body*, 307.
125. *Ibid.*, 308.
126. *Ibid.*, 309.

CHAPTER 7

CONCLUSION

While commenting on the development of the sociological and anthropological studies of religion in India, Rowena Robinson observes that the early structural-functionalist approach as well as the folk-civilization continuum model (for example, the works of Marriott, Radcliff-Brown, Singer and Srinivas)[1] linked the village to the 'great Sanskritic tradition,'[2] and combined the empirical field-based data with the textual tradition. They accorded centrality to the upper caste essentialized version of Hinduism and treated it as synonymous with India.[3] Although the work of Dumont introduced subjective meaning into the study of the field, yet it regarded *text* as the source of indigenous categories of meaning. It was not so much religious practices, but the ideas of *karma/dharma* as known to the villagers–the concerns of textual categories – that became the subject of study. Even the subsequent studies based on the Dumontian structuralist approach such as Veena Das's *Structure and Cognition*, R.K. Jain's *Text and Context*, Khare's *Hindu Hearth and Home*, Madan's *Non-Renunciation*, Heesterman's *The Inner Conflict of Tradition*, Pocock's *Study of Religious Beliefs and Practices in a Gujarat Village*, Parry's *Death in Banaras*, Diana Eck's work on the Hindu cosmos, Susan Wadely's *Sakti*, etc., focused more on the cosmic thought and structure in the sociology and anthropology of religion. Such an approach privileged the text and cognitive models derived from it, thus centering on the upper-caste and essentialised versions of Hinduism, treating them synonymous with Hinduism as such.

Based on these observations, Rowena Robinson voices her concern for new studies that would historicise religion and ground it in regional, spatial and temporal realities rather than on textual traditions.[4] Along these lines, the present study shows, that if one looks at the religious practices of the agrarian Indian village, not from the view-point of *textual* cognitive models, but from the viewpoint of their embeddedness in social, material and political contexts, one can arrive not at the upper-caste essentialised textual version of Hinduism, but at a non-essentialised, non-textual but contextual and *performative* version of alternative models to Sanskritic Hinduism. In other words, treating religious practices not so much as performative fulfillment of textual categories, but as a special kind of social practice that brings about privileged contrast, will invert the fundamental assumptions the of upper-caste Sanskritic Hinduism, as we have seen in the present study. Thus, such non-essentialist context-privileging approaches to the religious practices like rituals of a folk cult (like CM cult) can lead to findings and conclusions that might have the potential to challenge some of the dominant models of sociological and anthropological studies of religion which are premised on the assumptions of privilege of text over context, thought over action, and hegemonic models (upper-caste version of Hinduism) over non-hegemonic models (lower-caste and outcaste versions of Hinduism).

Accordingly, the present work has taken up for its study and analysis the folk *ritual corpus* of the cult of CM. It endeavours to explore its ritual power, making use of Luhmann's distinction between 'function' and 'performance'. At the level of 'function', the work shows how enactment of rituals can be instances of 'human transcendence', more in an anthropological sense. Through the yearly celebration of *koṭai* rituals, people seek new possibilities of overcoming limit-situations. To the common folk who face the ongoing struggle of human existence, the function of ritual enactments helps resist the 'domination of fear', arising from various human and trans-human agencies.

As regards the 'performance' of ritual power, my book has demonstrated how the ritual power of the folk religious cult of CM has created new religious sites where different social segments of the caste hierarchy have found a confluence. The privileged social group of the Brahmins and the underprivileged social group of the Dalits converge in the religious site to tap its ritual power for their different purposes. For both, it has served to display and safeguard the newly gained social status and economic identities. For the former, it performed a manipulative role, and for the latter it served as a subaltern agency to affirm their economic ascendancy and to voice their social emancipation. Thus ritual power in the folk religious terrain seems to offer space for competing roles.

In similar vein, the book has inquired into how 'ritual power' of the subaltern religious universe can generate multifaceted articulations and strategies for different social actors within the caste hierarchy—not only for the subalterns who construct innovative and creative strategies of resistance to caste hierarchy, but also for the topmost in the hierarchy, the Brahmins and others. By such strategies, the high castes too strike a chord of discontent not only with the cultural schemes of Brahminic Hinduism, but with the other Brahmins and the other twice-borns within the caste hierarchy. The work shows that this has drastically altered the portrait of religious consciousness of the *beau monde* of Indian society, the Brahmins at Valliyoor.

While attempting to unravel the meaning and relevance of the rituals within the socio-economic-historical background of the respective ritual functionaries, the book has proposed a new concept: *'peri-centralisation,'* and has shown how folk religion can become a site display of social process by exploring how it can function as "an inherently historical set of signifying beliefs and practices whose meaningful constructions–and active refiguring of perceptions–of the social world are at once tied to the process of domination and to strategies of resistance to authority,"[5] as Dube explains.

The work has also demonstrated the power of ritual performances like *cāmiyāṭṭam, vēṭṭai* and *aruḷvākku* in the production of contradictions and subversion of roles in the caste hierarchy. In Indian society where the social structures are based on ideological foundations (like the caste system), changes take place not by the overthrow of old systems/ ideological apparatuses in a sudden way, but by gradual production of new contradictions in the existing ideological realms, that accompany the new socio-economic developments. These new contradictions may not rapidly accentuate the disintegration of old ideological systems, but by puncturing and deflating the hyperbole of the hierarchical caste system, they bring about greater fluidity for the emergence of new socio-economic situations. Hence introduction of new contradictions in the old systems can well be deemed as an effective subaltern strategy of bringing about transformation in the Indian society.

In the Indian scenario, since the socio-economic structures are more often than not religiously created, sanctioned and sustained, production of such contradictions in the religious realm could be a key factor for social transformation.[6] The resources for the production of such contradictions can be found in the very ritual persona of a subaltern *cāmiyāṭi*, and in his/her ritual performances like *aruḷvākku, cāmiyāṭṭam,* and *vēṭṭai.* These resources can be organized by charismatic individuals who emerge as leaders (ritual or otherwise) to address questions of social discrimination or oppression. It is pertinent at this point to remember as examples the ways in which some socio-religious reformers like Vallalar, Narayanaguru and Vaikuntamcami integrated the ritual and symbolic resources.

Further, the findings of the present study take issue with Weber's view on Hinduism and economic development.[7] While the Weberian theory holds that Hinduism obstructs economic growth,[8] the study, based on the field data of CM's cult origin and growth in different villages in the district of Tirunelveli, tries to find new answers to this old question. The study treats neither the region of Tirunelveli as static nor the folk cults such as CM as 'stagnant' with the mechanical routinisation of its rituals. It does not see the play of power as unalterable and the dynamics of change immaterial to the land of Tirunelveli and to the folk cult of CM. While in the second chapter the book has demonstrated changes in the economic equations of the district of Tirunelveli, in the subsequent chapters it argues that new forms of folk religion accompany changes in the socio-economic realties of the place. Thus the book calls into question one of the commonly held notions of folk religions as pre-modern or mere remnants of the old feudal system by indicating how old cultural forms can obtain new schemes of socio-economic meanings in the course of history, as we will see in a moment..

Another area that the study draws our attention to is the question of continuity and change. The studies done by Rowena Robinson[9] and Susan Bayly[10] are very stimulating. However, they have discussed this question of continuity only within a *sub-system* of religious symbols or ritual practices and seen how people in a particular cultural setting have continued or discontinued the symbols and practices of the overarching *system*, namely, *culture* in relation to *the advent of a new sub-system*, i.e., various religions such as Christianity, Islam, etc.

The present study, though, does not deal with the question of continuity as a research problem *per se*, yet it has implications for the study of 'continuity and change.' It explores the dynamics of 'continuity and change' not in relation to religious systems of the major religions, as the above-mentioned authors have done, but in relation to a 'folk religion' and its ritual power. These areas have not received as much attention and academic treatment as they deserve, given the ubiquitous extent of the phenomenon in the cultural landscape of India. The study does this by inquiring into the changes (in the origin and growth of a folk religious phenomenon) that occurred in the symbolic meaning schemes of the folk religious arena of the CM cult in relation to the *advent of a new socio-economic system*, namely, *modernity*.

In the second chapter, the book has delved into the dynamics of change that followed the initial phase of modernization inaugurated by the British. The policy decisions regarding administration, education, employment, market, etc., made by the colonial state brought about transformation not only in the socio-economic systems, but subsequently, they became a collateral factor for the emergence of different folk religious forms. It was not a mere change that took place in the past and was pertinent only to a particular point of time in history. It was not experienced as a residual phenomenon that passed away along with the death of the colonial state. The changes brought about by the colonial state were carried out by the independent Indian state which has carried over the impact of modernity to the present. Modernization has undoubtedly acquired new accents and varied emphases through different economic systems such as capitalism, liberalisation and globalisation, but it has also yielded different benefits to different sections within the caste hierarchy. The different agents of change have provided an impetus to different actors by bringing in alternative economic systems and schemes at different times, and, through them, new opportunities for the liberation of the subalterns from the old economic system of caste hierarchy. Thus, it has effected a change in society over a period of time. All these phenomena have brought about not only fluidity within the socio-economic systems but also transformations in the religious systems.

The present work shows that, by making use of temple honours and the nuances of ritual power, social actors can articulate the newly acquired symbolic power. This has been appropriated by different social actors across the spectrum of the caste hierarchy at different times in different intensities. The changes experienced by the people by their appropriation of new systems have shown up in the symbolic universe. New cohorts of castes and families have appropriated the subaltern religious terrain and generated new forms of socio-symbolic discourse in the district of Tirunelveli. They have not drastically altered the folk forms of worship, but have infused new social meanings into the old symbolic systems. Thus they have altered the old cultural conceptual schemes and meaning systems in the ever-growing new contexts, be it the colonial state, independent India, or the global world. Here, modernity, through various agents such as the colonial state, the independent state and the global world order, has provided new socio-economic constructs to social actors within the caste hierarchy. They, in turn, have apprehended and appropriated the benefits and the privileges of such contexts on the one hand, and, in the process of social transformations, have constructed, constituted, adduced, disseminated and explored new systems of meanings to old religious forms, and have created new socio-symbolic cultural discourses, on the other.

My book has thus unfolded the interplay between culture and modernity in the domain of folk religious cults, in the process of demonstrating how the symbolic can mirror - and can be mirrored by - the subtle transformations in culture and society. It shows that, through the medium of a subaltern religious universe, folk culture can provide new cultural schemes to the subalterns to display new forms of power acquired by the appropriation of the benefits of modernity and industrialisation. Thus modernity has its insidious effects on the delicate balance of power relations within the caste hierarchy, and can become a partner with religion and culture to generate new texts of discourses of symbolic power. It is to be noted that, as modernity can add colours to religion, so, too, culture and religion can add new shades of meaning to the thesis of modernity.

Subsequently, the study offers scope for theorizing on the relationship between subaltern religion and history. Novetzke, reflecting on this topic in one of his recent articles, notes that in the Subaltern Studies there was antagonistic dialectic of modern historiography between religion and history.[11] He notes religion still remained as a private affair and observes: "Religion, as a sphere of experience or of subjectivity, makes no references to politics, economics, culture, or society to explain its activities, and this poses a challenge to the modern historical practice of explaining the past."[12] The present work can be seen an attempt to overcome this limitation by showing how subaltern religious realm can become a site for the construction of collective subjectivity of subaltern agents in history at various times as we have seen above. The book has shown that the subaltern, by having recourse to the 'religio-ritual systems' or 'supernatural elements' of folk cults, have engaged in the appropriation and the display of the new socio-economic statuses in history. Thus the work has highlighted the role of supernatural agency in human history and has demonstrated how the numinous can be historically understood as a site of agency,[13] thereby indicating how the Subaltern Studies Collective has the potential to bring back the forgotten dimension of Hegel's idea of the Spirit in the invocation of the supernatural (certainly the superhuman) in explaining history, as Chakrabarty and Novetzke have proposed.[14] By such attempts, the historiography of the Subaltern Studies Collective, may not produce a discourse within the field of modern historical study. But it calls for the recognition of another way of construing and constructing history by the subalterns in their own way, often in relation to religion and its constituents such as ritual, memory and beliefs, thus interrogating the opposition between history and religion brought about by modern historiography.[15]

Notes

1. Cf. McKim Marriott, ed., *Village India,* Chicago University Press, Chicago, 1955; A.R. Radcliff Brown, *The Andaman Islanders,* The Free Press, Glencoe IL, 1964 (1922); Milton. Singer, *When a Great Tradition Modernizes,* Praeger, New York, 1972; M.N. Srinivas, *Religion and Society among the Coorgs of South India,* Clarendon Press, Oxford University Press, 1952.
2. Cf. Rowena Robinson, ed., *Sociology of Religion in India,* Sage Publications, New Delhi, 2004, 20-21.
3. Cf. *ibid.,* 21.
4. *Ibid.,* 22.
5. Dube, 6.
6. It is so, because they effectively can break the age-old dichotomies such as purity and impurity, high castes and low castes. The study has shown such things taking place in the folk religious terrain through the rituals of *koṭai*.

7. It is to be noted that for Weber the emergence of capitalism is a key indicator for economic development.

8. Cf. Max Weber, *The Religion of India,* trans. H. Gerth & D. Martindale, Free Press, New York, 1958. The studies that analysed these questions further are: Kapp, *Hindu Culture, Economic Development and Economic Planning in India,* Asia Publishing House, Bombay, 1963 and Mishra, *Hinduism and Economic Growth,* Oxford University Press, Bombay, 1962.

9. Cf. Rowena Robinson, *Conversion, Continuity and Change,* Sage Publications, New Delhi, 1998.

10. Cf. Susan Bayly, *Saints, Goddesses & Kings,* Cambridge University Press, Cambridge, 1989.

11. Christian Lee Novetzke, "The Subaltern Numen: Making History in the Name of God," *History of Religions,* 46(2), 2006, 99-126.

12. *Ibid.,* 102.

13. *Ibid.*

14. *Ibid.* 118-121.

15. The reading of the above mentioned article by Novetzke will help the readers to understand this point in perspective.

Bibliography

Abbot, J. (1932), *The Keys of Power*. Methuen & Co., London.

Alexander, Bobby C. (1991), "Correcting Misinterpretations of Turner's Theory: An African-American Pentecostal Illustration." *Journal of Scientific Study of Religion* 30/1, 26-44.

Aloysius, G. (1998), *Religion as Emancipatory Identity*. New Age International Publishers, New Delhi.

Appadurai, Arjun (1981), *Worship and Conflict under Colonial Rule: a South Indian Case*, Cambridge University Press, Cambridge.

Athereya, A.B. (2001), *Gangai Kondan 1916-1984 Working paper No. 56*, MIDS, Chennai.

Austin, J.L. (1962), *How to Do Things with Words*. Clarendon Press, Oxford.

Bailey, Susan (1992), *Saints, Goddesses and Kings*. Cambridge University Press, New Delhi.

Banerjee, Sumantha (2002), *Logic in a Popular Form*. Seagull Books, Calcutta.

Basso, Ellen (2001), "A Commentary on Robbin's *Ritual Communication and Linguistic Ideology*." *Current Anthropology*, 42/5 (December), 600-603.

Beck, Brenda E. F. (1981), "The Goddess and the Demon. A Local South Indian Festival and its Wider Context." In *Autour de la Deesse Hindoue*. Edited by Madeleine Biardeau. *Purusartha*, 5, 83-136.

Bell, Catherine (1990), "The Ritual Body and the Dynamics of Ritual Power." *Journal of Ritual Studies* 4/2, 299-313.

———(1992), *Ritual Theory, Ritual Practice*. Oxford University Press, New York.

Bergin, G. (1983), "Religiosity and Mental Health: A Critical Reevaluation and Meta-analysis." *Professional Psychology: Research and Practice,* 14 , 170-184.

Beyer, Peter (1997), *Religion and Globalisation.* Sage Publications, London.

Biardeau, Madeleine (1989), "Brahmans and Meat-Eating Gods." In *Criminal Gods and Demon Devotees.* Edited by Alf Hiltebeitel. State University of New York Press, Albany, 19-34.

Bigenho, Michelle (2000), "Sensing Locality in Yura: Rituals of Carnival and of the Bolivian State." *American Ethnologist,* 26/4, 957-980.

Bjorck, Jeffrey P. (1995), "A Self-Centered Perspective on McIntosh's Religious Schema." *The International Journal for the Psychology of Religion,* 5/1, 23-29.

Blackburn, Stuart (1988), *Singing of Birth and Death.* University of Pennsylvania Press, Philadelphia.

Blackburne, Stuart H., and A. K. Ramanujan (1986), *Another Harmony: New Essays on the Folklore of India.* Oxford University Press, Delhi.

Bloch, Maurice (1989), "Symbols, Song, Dance, and Features of Articulation: Is Religion and Extreme Form of Traditional Authority?" In *Ritual, History and Power: Selected Papers in Anthropology.* Edited by idem. The Athlone Press, Atlantic Highlands, New Jersey.

——— (1992), *Prey into Hunter. The Politics of Religious Experience.* Cambridge University Press, Cambridge.

Boag (1922), *Madras Report.* Part I, Vol. XIII, Census of India, 1921, Government Press.

Bourdieu, Pierre. *Outline of Theory of a Practice.* Translated by R. Nice. Cambridge University Press, Cambridge, 1977.

——— (1991), *Language and Symbolic Power.* Polity Press, Cambridge.

Bowie, Fiana (2000), *The Anthropology of Religion.* Blackwell Publishers, Oxford.

Caldwell, Sarah (1999), *Oh Terrifying Mother.* Oxford University Press, New Delhi.

Capps, L., and E. Ochs (1995), *Constructing Panic: The Discourse of Agoraophobia.* Cambridge University Press, Cambridge.

Carrasco, David (1998), *Religions of Mesoamerica.* Waveland Press, Inc., Illinois.

Carrette, Jeremy R. (2000), *Foucault and Religion*. Routledge Taylor & Francis Group, London and New York.

Census of India 2001, Provisional Population Totals, Paper-3, Tamil Nadu, Series 34. Complied by Dr. C. Chandramouli. Government Press, Chennai, 2003.

Census of India, 1931, vol XIV Madras, Part II, Imperial and Provincial Tables. Government Press, Madras, 1932.

Cervone, Emma (1998), "Festival Time, Long Live the Festival: Ethical Conflict and Ritual in the Andes." *Anthopos* 93, 101-113.

Comaroff, Jean (1985), *Body of Power, Spirit of Resistance*. University of Chicago Press, Chicago.

Crossley, Nick (2001), "The Phenomenological Habitus and its Construction." *Theory and Society* 30/1 (February), 45-72.

Csordas, Thomas J. (1999), "Ritual Healing and the Politics of Identity in Contemporary Navajoa Society." *American Ethnologist*, 26/1, 3-23.

Dalfovo, Albert Titus (1997), "The Lugbara Ancestors." *Anthropos*, 92, 485-500.

De Coppet, Daniel, ed. (1992), *Understanding Rituals*. Routledge, London and New York.

Deflem, Mathieu (1991), "Ritual, Anti-Structure, and Religion: A Discussion of Victor Turner's Symbolic Analysis." *Journal of Scientific Study of Religion*, 30/1, 1-25.

Del Negro, Giovanna P. and Harris M. Berger (2001), "Character Divination and Kinetic Sculpture in the Central Italian *Passeggiata* (Ritual Promenade): Interpretative Frameworks and Expressive Practices from a Body-Centred Perspective." *Journal of American Folklore* 114/451, 5-19.

Deliege, R. (1988), *Les Paraiyars du Tamil Nadu*. Sreyler Verlag Wort und Werk, Nettal.

Denzin, Norman K. (1978), *The Research Act*. McGraw-Hill Book Company, New York.

Denzin, Norman K. and Yvonna S. Lincoln, eds. (1998), *Collecting and Interpreting Qualitative Material*. Thousand Oaks, Sage Publications.

Dirks, Nicholas B. (2002), *Castes of Mind: Colonialism and the Making of Modern India*. Permanent Black, Delhi and Princeton University Press, New Jersey.

———(1989), *The Hollow Crown: Ethnography of an Indian Kingdom.* Orient Longman Limited, Bombay.

District Census Handbook, Part XII-A, Tirunelveli Kattobomman District, Village and Town Directory, Census of India, 1991.

Dreyfus, Hubert L. and Paul Rainbow (1982), *Michael Foucault: Beyond Structuralism and Hermeneutics.* University of Chicago Press, Chicago.

Driver, Tom F. (1991), *The Magic of Ritual: Our Need for Liberating Rites that Transform Our Lives and Our Communities.* HarperCollins Publishers, New York.

Dube, Saurabh, ed. (2004), *Postcolonial Passages.* Oxford University Press, New Delhi.

———(1998), *Untouchable Pasts–Religion, Identity and Power among a Central Indian Community 1780-1950.* State University of New York Press, Albany.

Elmore, W.T. (1984), *Dravidian Gods in Modern Hinduism.* Asian Educational Services, Delhi.

Embirbayer, Mustafa and Jeff Goodwin (1994), "Network Analysis, Culture and the Problem of Agency." *American Journal of Sociology* 99/6, 1411-1454.

Fact Finding Survey Report on Tirunelveli District 1972, conducted by Indian Overseas Bank, Madras, TNA.

Fardon, Richard, ed. (1983), *Power and Knowledge: Anthropological and Sociological Approaches.* Proceedings of a Conference held at the University of St. Andrews in December 1982. Scottish Academic Press, Edinburgh.

Fausto, Carlos (2000), "Of Enemies and Pets: Warfare and Shamanism in Amazonia." *American Ethnologist* 26/4, 933-956.

Fetterman, D. (1989), *Ethnography Step by Step.* Sage Publications, California.

Forster, Duncan B. (1991), "The Depressed Classes and Conversion to Christianity." In *Religion in South Asia.* Edited by Geoffrey A. Oddie. Manohar, New Delhi.

Foucault, Michael (1995), *Discipline and Punish: The Birth of the Prison.* Translated by Alan Sheridan. Vintage Books, New York.

———(1980), *Power/Knowledge: Selected Interviews and Other Writings–1972-1977.* Edited by Colin Gordon. Pantheon Books, New York.

Fox, Nicholas J. (1993), *Postmodernism, Sociology and Health.* Open University Press, Buckingham.

Fuller, C.J. (2002), "Rituals of the Village." In *The Village in India.* Edited by Vandana Madan. Oxford University Press, New Delhi.

———(1987), "Sacrifice (*Bali*) in the South India Temple." In *Religion and Society in South India.* Edited by V. Sudarsen, G. Prakash Reddy, and M. Suryanarayana. B.R. Publishing Corporation, Delhi, 22-35.

———(1992), *The Camphor Flame. Popular Hinduism and Society in India.* Princeton University Press, Princeton, New Jersey.

Gazetteers of India, Tamil Nadu State, Tirunelveli District, Vol. I. Edited by Velmani. Chennai, 2002.

Gazetteers of India, Tamil Nadu State, Tirunelveli District, vol. II. Edited by Velmani. Chennai, 2002.

Geertz, Clifford (1973), *The Interpretation of Cultures: Selected Essays.* Basic Books, New York.

Gluck, S.B. and D. Patai, eds. (1991), *Women's Words: The Feminist Practice of Oral History.* Routledge & Kegan Paul, New York.

Gnanasekaran (1992), *Nāṭṭārcamayam.* Queri Publications, Coimbatore.

Gottlieb, Alma (2002), "Afterword." *Ethnology,* 21/4, 381-390.

Hanssen, Kristin (2002), "Ingesting Menstrual Blood: Notions of Health and Bodily Fluids in Bengal." *Ethnology,* 21/4, 365-379.

Hiltebeitel, Alf, ed. (1989), *Criminal Gods and Demon Devotees.* State University of New York Press, Albany.

Holdrege, Barbara A. (1990), "Introduction: Towards a Phenomenology of Power." *Journal of Ritual Studies,* 4/2, 5-37.

Holmberg, David (2000), "Derision, Exorcism, and the Ritual Production of Power." *American Ethnologist,* 27/4, 927-949.

Jain, Ravindra K. (1970), *South Indians on the Plantation Frontier in Malaysia.* New Haven.

Jayarathnam, R. (1967), "Indian Emigration to Ceylon." *Indian Economic and Social History Review,* 4/4, 320-59.

Josephides, Lisette (1999), "Disengagement and Desire: the Tactics of Everyday Life." *American Ethnologist,* 26/1, 139-159.

Josselen, R. (1987), *Finding Herself: Pathways to Identity of Women.* Jessey-Boss, San Francisco.

Juergensmeyer, Mark (2000), *Terror in the Mind of God.* Oxford University Press, New Delhi.

Kane, Pandurang Vaman (1953), *History of Dharmasastra, Vol. IV.* Bhandarkar Oriental Research Institute, Poona.

Kaplan, Martha, and John D. Kelly (2000), "On Discourse and Power: "Cults" and "Orientals" in Fiji." *American Ethnologist* 26/4, 843-886.

Kapp (1963), *Hindu Culture, Economic Development and Economic Planning in India.* Asia Publishing House, Bombay.

Kjaerholm, Lars (1986), "Myth, Pilgrimage and Fascination in the Aiyappa Cult: A View From Fieldwork in Taminlnadu." In *South Asian Religion and Society* Edited by Asko Parpola. D.K. Agencies Ltd., New Delhi, 121-161, 126.

Karlstrom, Mikael (2003), "On the Aesthetics and Dialogics of Power in the Post Colony." *Africa* 73/1, 57-76.

Kendall, Gavin, and Gary Wickham (1999), *Using Foucault's Methods.* Sage Publications, London.

Knipe, David M. (1989), "Night of the Growing Dead: A Cult of Virabhadra in Coastal Andhra." In *Criminal Gods and Demon Devotees.* Edited by Alf Hiltebeitel. State University of New York Press, Albany, 123-156.

Koenig, Harold G. (1995), "Religion as Cognitive Schema." *The International Journal for the Psychology of Religion,* 5/1, 31-37.

Kritzman, ed. (1990), *Michael Foucault.* Routledge, New York.

Kumar, Dharma. (1965), *Land and Caste in South India.* Cambridge University Press, Cambridge.

Langford, Jean M. (1999), "Medical Mimesis: Healing Signs of A Cosmopolitan 'Quack'." *American Ethnologist,* 26/1, 24-26.

Laurencelle, Rhonda M., Steven C. Abell, and David J. Schwartz (2002), "The Relation Between Intrinsic Religious Faith and Psychological Well-Being." *The International Journal for the Psychology of Religion* 12/2, 109-123.

Layton, Robert (1997), *An Introduction to Theory in Anthropology.* Cambridge University Press, Cambridge.

Levi, Jerome M. (1999), "Hidden Transcripts Among the Raramuri: Culture, Resistance, and Interethnic Relations in Northern Mexico." *American Ethnologist,* 26/1, 90-111.

Lewis, Gilbert (1988), *Day of Shining Red: An Essay on Understanding Ritual*. Cambridge University Press, Cambridge.

Lieblich, Amia (1998), Rivka Tuval-Mashiach, and Tamar Zilber. *Narrative Research*. Sage Publications, New Delhi.

Lourdu, D. (2000), *A Study of Sudalaimadasamy Cult in the Tirunelveli District of Tamilnadu: A Minor Project Report submitted to UGC*. St. Xavier's College, Palayamkottai.

Ludden, David (1989), *Peasant History in South India*. Oxford University Press, Delhi.

Lushington, S.R. (1858), *Report of Collector of Tinnevelly to the Board of Revenue*, T.N.A. Chennai.

Madan, Vandana, ed. (2002), *The Village in India*. Oxford University Press, New Delhi.

Manu (1991), *The Laws of Manu*. Translated by Wendy Doniger. Penguin Books, New Delhi.

Marglin, Frederique Apffel (1977), "Power, Purity and Pollution: Aspects of the Caste System Reconsisered." *Contributions to Indian Sociology*, 2/2, 245-270.

Marriott, McKim, ed. (1955), *Village India*. University of Chicago Press, Chicago.

Mather, Charles (2003), "Shrines and the Domestication of Landscape." *Journal of Anthropological Research*, 59, 23-45.

Mathew, George (1982), "Politicisation of Religion: Conversion to Islam in Tamil Nadu." *Economic and Political Weekly* 17/25, 1027-1034.

McIntosh, Daniel N. (1995), "Religion-as-Schema, With Implications for the Relation Between Religion and Coping." *The International Journal for the Psychology of Religion*, 5/1, 1-16.

Mencher, Joan P. (2002), "A Tamil Village: Changing Socio-economic Structure in Madras State." In *Village in India*. Edited by Vandana Madan. Oxford University Press, New Delhi, 165-181.

Merquier, J.G. (1985), *Foucault*. Fontana Press, London.

Meyer, Eveline (1986), *Ankalaparamecuvari Cul*. Steiner Verlag Wiesbaden Gmbh, Stuttgart.

Mines, Diane Paul (2002), "Hindu Nationalism, Untouchable Reform, and the Ritual Production of a South Indian Village." *American Ethnologist* 29/1 (February), 58-85.

——— (1989), "Hindu Periods of Death 'Impurity'." *Contributions to Indian Sociology* 23/1, 103-130.

Mishra, N. (1962), *Hinduism and Economic Growth*. Oxford University Press, Bombay.

Moore, Henrietta L., ed. (2000), *Anthropological Theory Today*. Polity Press, Cambridge.

Morris, Brian (1987), *Anthropological Studies of Religion*. Cambridge University Press, Cambridge.

Mukerjee, Nilmani (1962), *The Ryotwari System in Madras, 1792-1882*. Calcutta.

Nabokov, Isabelle. *Religion Against Self: An Ethnography of Tamil Rituals*, Oxford University Press, Oxford and New York, 2000.

Nelson, K. (1989), *Narratives from the Crib*. Harvard University Press, Cambridge.

Novetzke, Christian Lee (2006), "The Subaltern Numen: Making History in the Name of God." *History of Religions*, 46/2, 99-126.

Oppert, Gustav (1983), *On the Original Inhabitants of Bharatavarsa or India*. Westminster/Leipzig, Harrassowitz.

Orenstein, Henry (1970), "Death and Kinship in Hinduism: Structural and Functional Interpretations." *American Anthropologist*, 72, 1357-1377.

Paloutzian, Raymond F. and Brenda S. Smith (1995), "The Utility of the Religion-as-Schema Model." *The International Journal for the Psychology of Religion*, 5/1, 17-22.

Pandian, J. (2001), "Symbolic Inversions: An Interpretation of Contrary Behaviour." *Anthopos*, 96, 557-562.

Pandian, Jacob (1991), *Culture, Religion, and the Sacred Self: A Critical Introduction to the Anthropological Study of Religion*. Prentice-Hall, Inc., New Jersey.

Parish, Steven M. (1997), *Hierarchy and Its Discontents*, Calcutta, Oxford University Press

Pate, *Tinnevelly District Gazetteer*, Manonmaniam Sundararanar University, Tirunelveli, 1993 (1961).

Patrick, G. (2001), *An Inquiry into Ayya Vali: A Subaltern Religious Phenomenon in south Tiruvitankur*. A Ph. D. thesis of the University of Madras.

——— (2003), *Religion and Subaltern Agency*, Department of Christian Studies, University of Madras, Chennai.

Petridis, Constantine (2001), "Chokwe Masks and Franciscan Missionaries in Sandoa, Belgian Congo, ca.1948." *Anthropos*, 96, 3-28.

Radcliff Brown, A. R. (1964), *The Andaman Islanders*. The Free Press, Glencoe IL, (1922).

Raheja, Goodwin Gloria (1950), *The Poison In The Gift*. The University of Chicago and London.

Rajadurai, S. V. and V. Geetha (1993), "Dalits and Non-Brahmin Consciousness in Colonial Tamil Nadu." *Economic and Political Weekly*, 28/39, 2091-2098.

Rajadurai, S.V. (2001), *Dalitiyamum Ulaha Muthalaithuvamum*, Vitiyal Pathippagam.

Ramasamy, Thulasi (1985), *Nellaimāvaṭṭa Nāṭṭupura Teyvaṅkaḷ*, World Tamil Research Centre, Chennai.

Rao, Velcheru Narayana, David Shulman, and Sanjay Subrahmanyam (1992), *Symbols of Substance: Court and State in Nâyaka Period Tamilnadu*. Oxford University Press, Delhi.

Rappaport, Roy A. (1999), *Ritual and Religion in the Making of Humanity*. Cambridge University Press, Cambridge.

Reiniche, Marie-Louise (1979), *Les dieux et les hommes: étude des cultes d'un village du Tirunelveli, Inde du Sud*. Mouton, Paris.

Robbins, Joel (2001), "Ritual Communication and Linguistic Ideology: A Reading and Partial Reformulation of Rappaports's Theory of Ritual." *Current Anthropology*, 42/5 (December), 591-614.

Robinson, Rowena, ed. (2004), *Sociology of Religion in India*. Sage Publications, New Delhi.

———(1998), *Conversion, Continuity and Change*. Sage Publications, New Delhi.

Runyan, W.M.C. (1984), *Life Histories and Psychobiography: Explorations in Theory and Method*. Oxford University Press, New York.

Russell, Bernard (1995), *Research Methods in Anthropology*. Altamira Press, New Delhi.

Sanmugasundaram (1997), *Sudalaimadan Vazhipadu*. Kavya, Bangalore.

Sappington, A.A. and Julie Baker (1995), "Refining Religious Belief—Behavior Relations." *The International Journal for the Psychology of Religion*, 5/1, 39-48.

Schwandt, Thomas A. (1997), *Qualitative Inquiry*. Sage Publications, Thousand Oaks.

Scott John (1991), *Social Network Analysis*. Sage Publications, London, Newbury Park. New Delhi.

Scruton, David L. (1986), *Sociophobics: The Anthropology of Fear*. Westview Press, Inc., Boulder & London.

Sen, Amartya (2000), *Development as Freedom*. Oxford University Press, New Delhi.

Sethukumaran, N., ed. (1973), *Mukkudal Pallu*, Vanathi Press, Madras.

Settlement Registers Complied for Tinnevelly District, TNA, 1870.

Shaffir, W.B. and R.A. Stebbins, eds. (1991), *Experiencing Fieldwork: An Inside View of Qualitative Research*. Sage Publications, Thousand Oaks, CA.

Shalins, Marshall (1985), *Islands of History*. The University of Chicago Press, Chicago.

Shulman, David Dean (1989), "Outcastes, Guardian, and Trickster: Notes on the Myth of Kattāvarāyaṉ." In *Criminal Gods and Demon Devotees*. Edited by Alf Hiltebeitel. State University of New York Press, Albany, 36-67.

——— (1980), *Tamil Temple Myths*. Princeton University Press, Princeton, New Jersey.

Shyamlal (1997), *From Higher Caste to Lower Caste: The Process of Sanskritization*. Rawat Publication, New Delhi.

Sing, Vijai P., and Harikesh N. Misra, eds. (1975), *Research Methodology*, Rawat Publications, Jaipur and New Delhi.

Singer, Milton (1972), *When a Great Tradition Modernizes*. Praeger, New York.

Sinha, Jai B. P. (1995), *The Cultural Context of Leadership and Power*. Sage Publications, New Delhi.

Srinivas, M. N. (1952), *Religion and Society Among the Coorgs of South India*. Asia Publishing House, Bombay.

———(1989), *The Cohesive Role of Sanskritization and Other Essays*. Oxford University Press, Delhi.

——— (1987), *The Dominant Caste and Other Essays*. Oxford University Press, Delhi.

——— (1996), ed. *Caste: Its Twentieth Century Avatar*. Viking, New Delhi.

Stephen, Michele (2000), "Witchcraft, Grief, and the Ambivalence of Emotions." *American Ethnologist*, 26/3, 711-773.

Stewart, Pamela J. and Andrew Strathern (2002), "Power and Placement in Blood Practices." *Ethnology*, 21/4, 349-363.

Stuart, A. J. (1876), *Manual of Tinnevelly District*, Madras.

Subramanian V. S. (compiler) (1986), *Temple Inscriptions of Tirunelveli District*. Vol. Xiii, TNA, Chennai.

Sudarsen, V., G. Prakash Reddy and M. Suryanarayana, eds. (1987), *Religion and Society in South India*. B.R. Publishing Corporation, Delhi.

Susan Bailey (1992), *Saints. Goddesses & Kings*. Cambridge University Press, New Delhi, (1989).

Turnbull, Thomas, "Geographical and Statistical Memoirs of Tirnnelvelli and its Zamindaries." (C. 1823) *Revenue Department Sundries*, No. 38, TNA, Chennai.

Turner, Bryan S. (1991), *Religion and Social Theory*. 2d ed. Sage Publications, London.

Turner, Victor W. (1968), *The Drums of Affliction: A Study of Religious Processes among the Ndembu of Zambia*. Clarendon Press, Oxford.

———(1974), *Dramas, Fields, and Metaphors*. Cornell University Press, Ithaca and London.

———(1982), *From Ritual to Theatre*, Performing Arts Journal Publications, New York.

——— (1979), *Process, Performance and Pilgrimage*. Concept Publishing Company, New Delhi.

——— (1969), *The Ritual Process*. Routledge & Kegan Paul, London.

——— (1969), *The Forest of Symbols*. Cornell University Press, Ithaca, N.Y.

Van Gennep, Arnold (1960), *The Rites of Passage*. The University of Chicago Press, Chicago.

Wadley, Susan S. (1985), *Shakti: Power in the Conceptual Structure of Karimpur Religion*. Munshiram Manoharlal Publishers, New Delhi.

———(1991), ed. *Powers of Tamil Women*. Manohar Publications, New Delhi.

Waghone, Joanne Punzo (1989), "From Robber Baron to Royal Servant of God? Gaining a Divine Body in South India." In *Criminal Gods and Demon Devotees*. Edited by Alf Hiltebeitel. State University of New York Press, Albany, 405-426.

Weber, Max (1958), *The Religion of India*. Translated by H. Gerth and D. Martindale. Free Press, New York.

Whitehead, Henry (1976), *The Village Gods of South India*. Summit Publications, Delhi.

Wilfred, Felix (2005), *The Sling of Utopia*. ISPCK, Delhi.

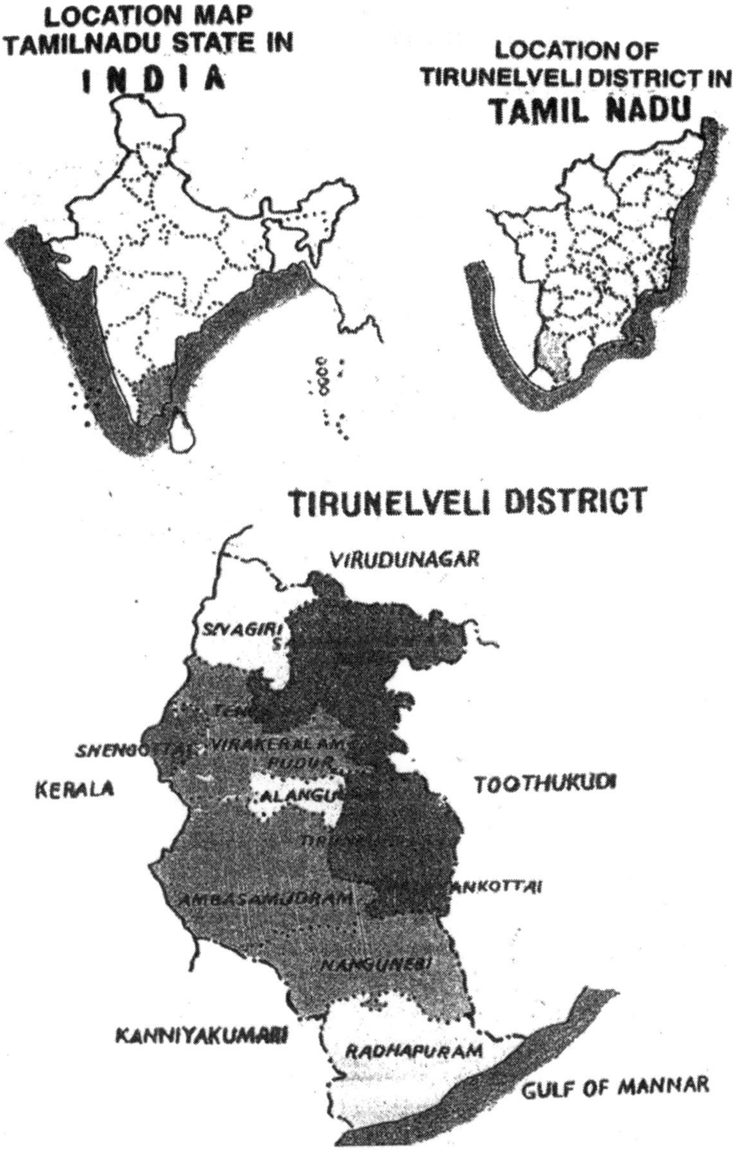

A Map taken from Gazetters of India, Tamil Nadu State, Tiruneiveli District, Vol. 1, 2002, ed. Dr. K. S. K. Velmani

INDEX